WITHDRAWN
University of
Illinois Library
at Urbana-Champaign

ARCHAEOLOGICAL SURVEY AND SETTLEMENT PATTERN MODELS IN CENTRAL ILLINOIS

by

Donna C. Roper

ILLINOIS STATE MUSEUM
Scientific Papers, Vol. XVI

MIDCONTINENTAL JOURNAL OF ARCHAEOLOGY
Special Papers, No. 2

Published by The Kent State University Press, Kent, Ohio 44242, for the Illinois State Museum, Springfield, Illinois 62706.
Copyright 1979 by The Illinois State Museum. All rights reserved. No part of this publication may be reprinted in any form or by any means without prior permission from the copyright holder.
Library of Congress Cataloging in Publication Data
Roper, Donna C
   Archaeological survey and settlement pattern models in central Illinois.
   (MCJA special paper; no. 2) (Illinois State Museum, Scientific Papers, Vol. XVI)
   A revision of the author's thesis, University of Missouri–Columbia, 1975.
   Bibliography: p.
   1. Indians of North America—Illinois—Sangamon Valley—Antiquities. 2. Sangamon Valley, Ill.—Antiquities. 3. Illinois—Antiquities. 4. Land settlement patterns, Prehistoric—Illinois. I. Title.
II. Series.
E78.I3R66 1979   977.3'55   79-4539
ISBN 0-87338-230-7
ISSN 0445-3395
Library of Congress Catalog Card Number 79-4539

Manufactured in the United States of America
Printed by the authority of the State of Illinois, P.O. 11570—M—6-79

Contents

Preface	8
I. Introduction	9
II. Theory and Method	10
Theory	10
Method	17
III. The Sangamon River Survey	19
The Survey	19
Artifact Analysis	23
Phase Criteria and a Sangamon River Woodland Chronology	25
Phase Criteria	25
The Woodland Period in the Sangamon River Valley	35
Site Types	40
IV. The Biophysical Environment	42
The Prairie Peninsula	42
Climate	44
Rainfall	44
Temperature	47
Plant Communities	47
Analysis of Land Survey Data	51
Floodplain Forest	54
Upland Forest	55
Undergrowth	58
Prairie	60
Summary of Vegetation	61
Physiography	61
Drainage	65
Fauna	68
Mammals	71
Amphibians and Reptiles	72
Birds	72
Fish and Mussels	73
Seasonal Variability	74
Plants	74
Hydrology	74
V. Analysis	77
The Environmental Variables	77
Analysis of Middle Woodland Sites	82
Cluster Analysis	82
Multidimensional Scaling	87
Analysis of Late Woodland Sites	99
Cluster Analysis	99

	Multidimensional Scaling	101
	Summary	114
VI.	Models of Woodland Settlement Patterns in the Sangamon River Valley	114
	Middle Woodland	114
	Ceramic Type I Sites	115
	Ceramic Type II Sites	120
	Projectile Point Sites	123
	Late Woodland	131
VII.	Summary and Conclusions	141
	Acknowledgments	144
	References	146

List of Plates

Plate	Page
1. Early and Middle Woodland Pottery	27
2. Middle Woodland Pottery	28
3. Middle Woodland Pottery	29
4. Middle Woodland Pottery	30
5. Hopewell and Weaver Pottery	31
6. Late Woodland Pottery	33
7. Early and Middle Woodland Projectile Points	34
8. Middle and Late Woodland Projectile Points	41

List of Figures

Figure		Page
1.	Refuging System Zones	13
2.	Sangamon River Area	20
3.	Illinois Woodland Chronology	26
4.	Middle Woodland Site Distribution	36
5.	Late Woodland Site Distribution	39
6.	Prairie Peninsula	44
7.	Monthly Precipitation at Springfield and Cairo	45
8.	Difference of Mean Precipitation	46
9.	Average Springfield Monthly Temperatures, 1880–1946	48
10.	Varimax Rotated Factor Loadings as Histograms	52
11.	Forest and Prairie Distribution in Sangamon Valley	57
12.	Soil Associations in the Sangamon River Drainage	64
13.	Soil Texture and Vegetation Zones	66
14.	Drainage Ranks of Major Streams	67
15.	Availability of Plant Foods	75
16.	Natural Divisions of Illinois	83
17.	Dendrogram of Cluster Analysis, Middle Woodland	85
18.	Stress and Correlations for Multidimensional Scaling, Middle Woodland	90
19a.	Plot of Dimensions I and II, Middle Woodland	91
19b.	Plot of Dimensions I and III, Middle Woodland	92
19c.	Plot of Dimensions II and III, Middle Woodland	93
20.	Dendrogram of Cluster Analysis, Late Woodland	100
21.	Stress and Correlations for Multidimensional Scaling, Late Woodland	103
22a.	Plot of Dimensions I and II, Late Woodland	104
22b.	Plot of Dimensions I and III, Late Woodland	105
22c.	Plot of Dimensions II and III, Late Woodland	106
23.	Late Woodland Sites	109
24.	Three-Dimensional Contrast of Situations and Ideal Site	116
25a.	Idealized Cross-Section of Lower Sangamon with Idealized Middle Woodland Sites	124
25b.	Site Catchment of Selected Middle Woodland Site (I,5a)	125
25c.	Site Catchment of Selected Middle Woodland Site (II, 5a)	126
26a.	Idealized Cross-Section of Middle Sangamon with Idealized Middle Woodland Sites	128
26b.	Site Catchment of Selected Middle Woodland Site (I, 4b)	129
26c.	Site Catchment of Selected Middle Woodland Site (Projectile Point, 4b)	130
27a.	Idealized Cross-Section of Lower Sangamon with Idealized Late Woodland Sites	133

27b. Site Catchment of Selected Late Woodland Site (I) — 134
27c. Site Catchment of Selected Late Woodland Site (II) — 135
28a. Idealized Cross-Section of Middle Sangamon with Idealized Late Woodland Sites — 136
28b. Site Catchment of Selected Late Woodland Site (I) — 137
28c. Site Catchment of Selected Late Woodland Site (II) — 138

List of Tables

Table	Page
1. Ground Cover and Rainfall	22
2. Material Evidence Types	43
3. Average and Extreme Dates of Frosts	47
4. Frequencies of Selected Species	53
5. Varimax Rotated Factor Loadings	54
6. Varimax Rotated Factor Scores	54
7. Undergrowth Species	59
8. Potentially Available Animal Species and Habitats	68
9. Seasonal Flood Probabilities	78
10. Cophenetic Correlations, Middle Woodland	84
11. Three-Way Contingency Table, Middle Woodland Sites	86
12. Varimax Rotated Multidimensional Scaling, Middle Woodland	88
13. Correlations of Original and Canonical Variables, Middle Woodland	89
14. Cophenetic Correlations, Late Woodland	99
15. Three-Way Contingency Table, Late Woodland Sites	101
16. Varimax Rotated Multidimensional Scaling, Late Woodland	107
17. Correlations of Original and Canonical Variables, Late Woodland	108
18. Eilers Site Faunal Remains	120

PREFACE

This monograph is a condensed, slightly revised version of a doctoral dissertation presented to the Department of Anthropology at the University of Missouri-Columbia. Appendixes but only small sections of text have been deleted. A small amount of new material has been added to better organize the study. Deletion of appendixes removes the basic data as well as the ceramic analysis, which has been published elsewhere (Roper 1977). The reader who needs the original data and documentation is referred to the original study (Roper 1975).

The bulk of the manuscript was written between October 1974 and March 1975. Since then, I have continued to work on settlement pattern analysis similar to that reported here. Although it would now be possible for me to revise considerably the theory section of the second chapter in particular, the present discussion is in no way contradictory to my present thinking; moreover, it *is* the basis for my present study. I have therefore allowed it to stand, with minor editing, as finally phrased in early 1975. I have, however, inserted an explicit discussion of settlement patterns, settlement systems, and methods as I have recently clarified them, and occasionally rephrased other passages to be consistent with this discussion. I emphasize that the net contribution of these additions to this paper has been to enhance its latent structure and in no way contradicts the intent of the original study.

October 3, 1978

I. INTRODUCTION

A major purpose of this study is to formulate preliminary models of Woodland settlement patterns in the Sangamon River drainage of central Illinois. The research begins with observations of the distribution of prehistoric sites, and proceeds by synthesis of these observations into a model of settlement patterns. An important factor in site distribution and in the form of a settlement pattern is the structure of the features of the biophysical environment, particularly topography, drainage, soil, flora, and fauna. It follows that the most relevant observations for model building will be those concerning the distribution of archaeological remains in relation to such features.

Present site location and settlement pattern study procedures in the Midwest tend to focus on the immediate location of a site. Locational decisions are not merely a response to a particular place, however, but to a broader setting. For example, a site may not be located merely in a forest, but in a broad forest, or near an upland edge where the inhabitants have access to upland resources, or in proximity to bottomland resources. It is argued that this *situation* is just as important as, or perhaps even more important than, the characteristics of the site itself.

It is imperative that analytic techniques be developed to account for the broader setting of a site and do so in a rigorous, replicable manner. The present study employs site catchment analysis to examine the resource potential of the territory surrounding a site. However, instead of an intuitive assessment of the resource potential of a single site (or at most a few sites), as is frequent in site catchment studies, the present analysis uses multivariate statistical techniques to evaluate a number of variables for 193 sites. The analysis of the relation of a site to those resources readily available to its inhabitants is used to generate models of Woodland settlement patterns. Inferences, however, are based upon an explicit theory of environmental utilization (Chapter II).

A potential problem is the degree to which confidence may be placed in the derived model when, as in the present study, the sites were recorded using traditional survey techniques. There is some evidence that traditional survey techniques are biased (e.g., Mueller 1974), although quite credible and supported models have been built on the basis of traditional survey information (e.g., Fitting 1969; Struever 1968b,c). However, in such situations there is no way to evaluate the bias, and therefore no way to evaluate derived models.

Use of traditional survey data in the study of settlement patterns provides the seeds of its own test, however. Quantitative researchers are aware of a "sampling paradox," i.e., the most efficient sample is a stratified sample, yet to intelligently stratify a universe prior knowledge of its characteristics is necessary; but this is the reason for sampling in the first place. The researcher therefore seems to have to either guess at sampling strata, or use a less efficient sampling design. Traditional survey data are useful at this point. Analyzing these data using the same general categories of variables that would be employed in a stratified sampling design, and employing an inductive multivariate statistical research strategy, can lead to intelligent sampling decisions, i.e., to hypotheses concerning the most relevant factors of, in this case, site location (see Benfer 1975 for an essay and worked example of this type of research strategy). In this case, traditional survey data are regarded as a non-probability sample of the population of sites, and are used as an alternative to guessing about the most effective sampling strategy.

Constructing settlement pattern models for Illinois Woodland is not new. Struever (1968b,c) has worked primarily with Early and Middle Woodland settlements in the Illinois River Valley. He has been followed most notably by Farnsworth (1973), studying Middle Woodland settlement patterns in the Macoupin Creek Valley, a tributary of the Illinois River. The present study is concerned with Middle and Late Woodland settlement patterns in the Sangamon River Valley, a major tributary of the Illinois River system. The Sangamon River is an east-to-west flowing stream, in contrast to the north-south course of the Illinois. At the lower end of the Sangamon, the structure of the environment is quite similar to that of the Illinois Valley. Moving upstream, however, the biophysical environment gradually takes on characteristics peculiar to the Sangamon and other smaller valleys draining central Illinois. Thus, the valley provides an ideal situation to test some of the limits of Middle Woodland settlement pattern models hypothesized in the more uniform environment of the Illinois Valley (see Roper 1974 for a preliminary account).

The Late Woodland period has been largely ignored in studies of settlement patterns in central Illinois. The presence of a large amount of Late Woodland material in the Sangamon Valley thus provides the opportunity to expand greatly the available information on Late Woodland settlement patterns in Illinois.

II. THEORY AND METHOD

Theory

In considering the process of human interaction with the biophysical environment, it is apparent that several general propositions may be employed to structure observations of settlement phenomena.

1. *The biophysical environment is not uniform, either spatially or seasonally.* This fact should be obvious to anyone: fish are only available in the water, nuts only come from forests in the fall. This fact is of great importance in determining how a group of people must move to interact with their natural environment.

2. *Man is a refuging animal.* A "refuging animal" is one that shows a rhythmic dispersal from and return to a fixed point in space (Hamilton and Watt, 1970: p. 263). This point and its implications are examined below.

3. *Human beings are organized into communities.* The community is the basic unit of anthropological settlement pattern studies. Arensberg and Kimball

(1965) have presented one of the most comprehensive and usable definitions of community. They define it in terms of five criteria: (1) it is a population aggregate; (2) it has as constituents two sexes and at least three generations; (3) it has a temporal dimension, i.e., it lasts longer than its individual members; (4) it shows rhythmic dispersal of its members alternating with their aggregation (i.e., refuging behavior); and (5) it is the basic unit of cultural transmission. In other words, "the community is a basic minimal unit of population sufficiently organized and differentiated to insure both biological and cultural continuity" (Clifton, 1968: p. 17). It also exploits a specific territory to provide itself with food, clothing, warmth, and other perceived necessities.

4. *The community will not use all resources available to it.* For one thing, certain resources are outside the needs or technological capacity of the community to exploit. For another, even the most superficially stingy environment generally contains abundant potential foods. Humans seem to be selective eaters even in extreme situations (see, e.g., Lee 1968). Most resources are not entirely specific to a single microenvironmental zone but rather tend to crosscut several of them. Flannery (1968: p. 75) has argued it is these selected resources rather than microenvironments to which people adapt. If so, the seasonal and spatial distribution of the resources comprising the total nexus of desired resources is a critical determinant of the manner in which a community occupies and exploits its territory.

5. *Communities will tend to act in a rational manner in exploiting their natural environment.* This is a statement of the Principle of Least Effort, a principle basic to economic geography (e.g., Garner 1967), town planning (e.g., Doxiadis 1970), and any other discipline concerned with human settlement. It holds that events reach their goal by the shortest possible route (Garner, 1967: p. 304). In other words, it postulates a minimization of movement, with consequent maximization of return. Several archaeologists propose it as a basic principle in the manner in which prehistoric peoples exploited their natural environment (e.g., Plog and Hill 1971; Green 1973).

6. *The archaeological record is reflective, at least in part, of the structure of the behavior operative in its deposition.* Without this assumption, study of the archaeological record would revert to study of forms of artifacts with no regard for behavior.

7. *Settlement—the process of establishing settlements over the landscape—is an adaptation to two sets of conditions, "site," and "situation."* These two terms are borrowed from geography. Site characteristics have been defined as "the features of the local environment on which settlements are established and over which they grow" (Eschman and Marcus, 1972: p. 28). It is this set of conditions which is most frequently used in study of settlement patterns. A number of examples could be cited from the Midwestern literature alone, but, to take one example, McGregor (1957) studied the distribution of prehistoric sites in the Illinois River Valley. The major characteristic he employed was the landform on which the site was located: floodplain, terrace,

etc. Site characteristics are undoubtedly important in settlement location, but the situation is probably as important. Geographers (in the case of this definition, working with urban phenomena) have defined situation as referring "both to the physical conditions relative to site that extend over a wider area than the actual settlement occupies and to man's cultural characteristics within and around the city" (Eschman and Marcus, 1972: p. 28). Unfortunately, in archaeological context, opportunity for study of cultural situation is limited although it undoubtedly could be done more often than heretofore. Study of the biophysical situation is not, however, so impractical.

To understand why situation as well as site is important, let us see how a refuging animal uses its natural environment. In the formulation by Hamilton and Watt (1970: pp. 264–65) refuging behavior leads to the establishment of a series of concentric and broadly overlapping zones (Fig. 1). First is the *core,* i.e., the central place. Second is the *trampling zone,* arising from traffic to and from the core. Third is the *biodeterioration zone,* that may result from overexploitation by individuals using the core. Finally is the *arena,* the main resource-acquisition zone surrounding the central place.

For the moment then, let us imagine a community, established at some point on the landscape, dispersing to and from that point and interacting with its natural environment. An arena or field (cf. Haggett, 1965: p. 41), used over and over again for resource acquisition is thus created. To use this concept analytically, it is useful to consider what the characteristics of the arena might be.

Under the Principle of Least Effort, it is to be expected that resources closest to the site would be taken first. Thus, at any given point in time, resource acquisition could be expected to decrease as a function of distance: $E_p = f(d)$ where E_p = energy procured and d = distance. Further, depletion of desired resources should occur over the short run. It would thus be necessary to disperse farther and farther afield to procure the necessary quantities of resources. Therefore, the amount of energy expended in relation to that procured would increase. This situation is tolerable only up to a limit, however. At the outside, that limit is the point at which energy expended equals energy procured, but in actuality the limit is reached much sooner. In any event, the limit of exploitation should show a drop-off at a fairly readily delimited point. Thus, the first characteristic of the arena: *its size is finite.*

The second important characteristic is the shape of the arena. The most efficient shape is, of course, the circle. With an arena of this shape, all points on the periphery are (theoretically) equally accessible (see Haggett, 1965: 48–49 for a demonstration of this point). Of course, circumstances of uneven terrain, presence of water barriers, proximity to other places, etc. will act to distort this to the extent that, empirically, an arena will probably never be truly circular. Thus, the second characteristic of a site's arena: *it is roughly circular.*

To return to the hypothetical population: it is clear that, as noted, depletion will soon occur, and energy expenditure must rise. Thus, a hypothetical cost curve of energy expenditure relative to energy procurement may be expected to

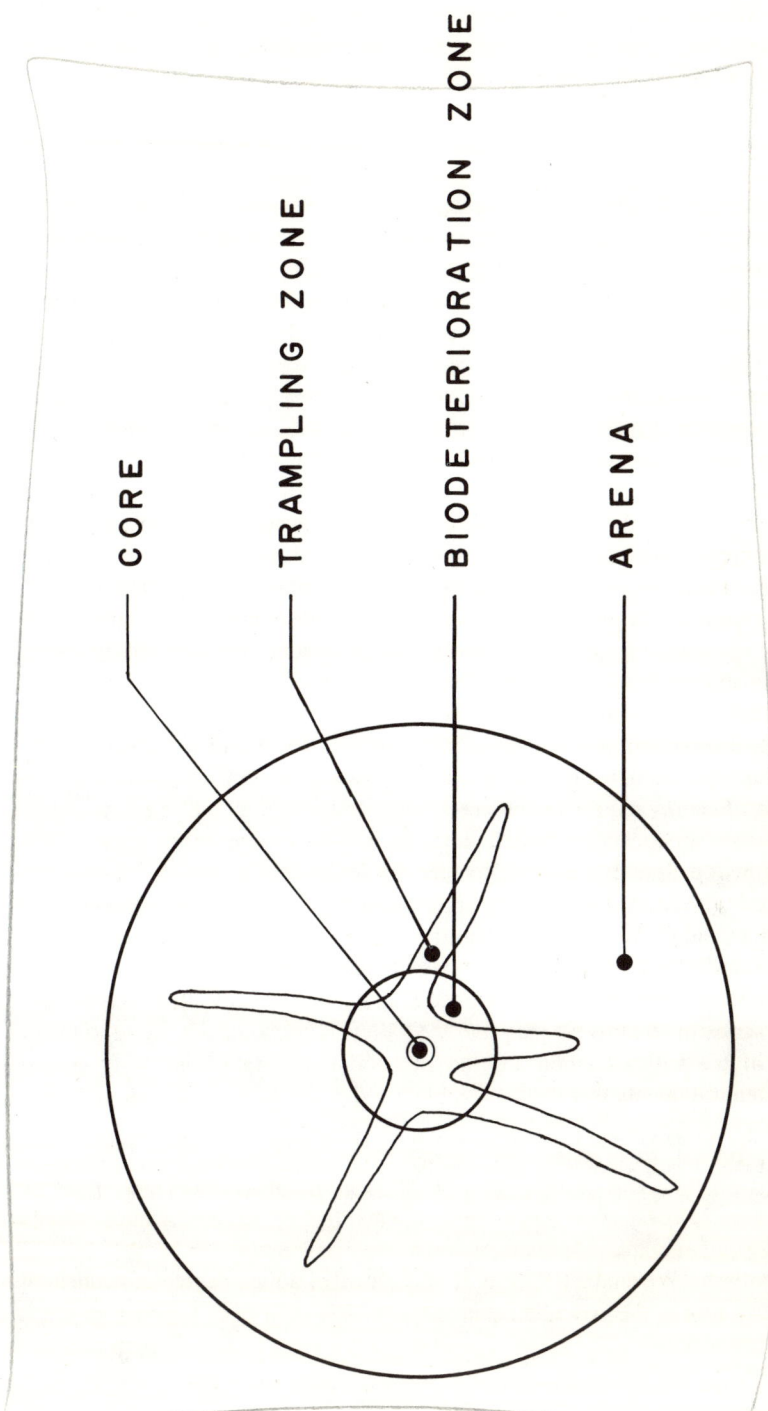

Fig. 1. Zones of a Refuging System (after Hamilton and Watt, 1970: p. 264).

rise as some function of duration of use of the central place. It might be presumed, at the point where it is no longer profitable to exploit a resource from a given point, that the group must move, a situation documented by Lee (1968), for example. The effect of such a movement is, of course, to set energy expenditure back to a minimum. In effect, then, the settlement pattern of such a group is a series of camps, spread over the landscape with a spacing of at least 2r, where r = the radius of the arena.

Such a model is, however, far too simple. The ability of the environment to "recharge," to replenish the supply of foods and other resources, is neglected. That is, because people generally do not make use of the total range of resources available to them, it is possible to use less desirable resources near the site if procuring primary resources become unproductive. Furthermore, even the simplest ecosystems show some seasonal differentiation and exhibit a variability through the year in the kinds and amounts of available foods. Reduction in energy expenditure could therefore be achieved through the natural rhythm of the environment. But the cyclicity and spacing of desired or key resources is very important in the settlement system. A subsistence strategy must be played out to procure sufficient quantities of needed resources, with minimum expenditure of energy. Part of this strategy is the location of settlements or focal points from which procurement takes place, and deciding whether or not such locations should be permanent. Wide spacing of zones requires different sorts of adjustments than are permitted by closely spaced zones. This is an obvious corollary of the need to minimize energy expenditure. A narrow spacing of a diversified series of environmental zones permits a degree of sedentism in that a location optimal in relation to all zones is possible. In such a position, minimization of energy required to procure resources throughout the year is possible. Movement of a camp, after all, does require an investment of energy. The settlement pattern of a relatively sedentary group is thus one of a base camp, perhaps with a series of smaller camps for special functions. Two ethnographic examples might be cited to exemplify such a situation.

Steward (1938) documented the settlement pattern of the Owens Valley Paiute in the Great Basin of the United States. The Owens Valley is intersected by a series of streams flowing into the valley. The mountains rising to either side of the valley contain a series of parallel and rather narrowly spaced microenvironments that made possible a sedentary settlement pattern:

> This extraordinarily varied environment afforded all essential food resources within 20 miles of the villages, which were situated on the various streams. Although people sometimes remained away from home several days, it was usually possible to return within a day or two (Steward, 1938: p.50).

Similarly, Watanabe (1968: p.72) documented a high degree of residential stability among the Ainu of Japan:

> One of the fundamental factors relevant to the high stability of residence among the Ainu may have been the distribution of the ecological zones within narrow river valleys they

inhabited. Zones 1–3 were exploited from a single center, namely the permanent settlement which is usually situated on the edge of the river terrace. The outermost zones 4 and 5 were hunting areas, each exploited from a different hunting hut.

The permanent houses in the settlement were occupied by the entire family for nine to ten months of the year and by housewives and their children nearly all the year.

A similar distribution pattern of ecological zones and a high stability of residence are found among the Northern Paiute in Owens Valley (Steward 1938). In both Hokkaido and Owens Valley, it is presence of narrow valleys that permitted the maintenance of year-round residence.

In broadly spaced microenvironments, however, different settlement arrangements are necessary since it is not possible to stay in the same place all year without inordinate and probably uneconomical expenditures of energy. That is, while the site's arena may contain abundant resources it might not contain the seasonal diversity to be found in arenas with closely spaced microenvironments. Thus, movement might be necessary in order to both minimize energy expenditure and to satisfy biological requirements.

Also possible in such a situation is the establishment of villages throughout all habitats, none of which is self-sufficient, and all of which engage in exchange of products, a kind of situation which Sanders (1956) has called "symbiosis." This situation is ethnographically documented among the Pomo of California (Vayda 1967), who shared an unequally spaced abundance of resources by means of trade feasts.

Other than broadly spaced microenvironments where optimal location in relation to all necessary resources is impossible, another type of situation exists in which it is necessary to be constantly mobile. This is the situation in which the group emphasizes hunting of large game. A classic example is the Plains bison hunters of North America who earned their livelihood primarily by chasing the buffalo. Thus, an elderly Crow recalled: "The great herds of buffalo were constantly moving, and of course, we moved when they did" (Linderman, 1932: p. 27).

The model is still too simple, however. The discussion so far has more or less assumed that food will be immediately consumed, in which case movement and locational decisions are constantly being made. This is not always realistic, however, for many groups can delay consumption of gathered resources. In this way, they take advantage of a superabundance of certain resources at certain times of the year and, by the expenditure of perhaps slightly greater amounts of energy at those times, acquire the means to minimize energy expenditure at other times. Storage and/or other techniques of preservation may thus be part of the strategy of reducing energy expenditure relative to procurement costs. It was storage that enabled the Northwest Coast groups to remain sedentary throughout much of the year:

> . . . the habitat has been presented as a constant source of plenty. But as I have said elsewhere, it was not constant. It did not provide an ever-reliable abundance of natural resources simply

there for the taking. Abundance there consisted only of certain things at certain times and always with some possibility of failure (Suttles, 1968: p. 58).

The techniques for preserving food are certainly as important as those for getting food. Thousands of salmon swimming upstream in September would not make winter a time of ceremonial activity if people lacked the means of preserving them, nor would several tons of blubber on the beach. No doubt some people would not have survived some winters without storage methods (Suttles, 1968: p. 63).

Environmental spacing, seasonal availability of desired resources, trade, storage methods, and social and political organization are thus all important in determining the form of a community's settlement pattern. In the present study, the emphasis is on the first two of these variables, i.e., environmental spacing and seasonal availability of resources. Given the foregoing discussion, it is proposed that a community's settlement system is a solution to the problem of locating sites so as to minimize the amount of energy that must be expended to procure necessary resources, be this by judicious choice of location of a single site, the location of several sites at different times in different situations, development of storage and/or preservation techniques, or a combination strategy.

The need to select optimal situations is balanced to an extent by the need to locate on desirable sites. Requirements might be for a place that is dry, warm, sheltered, perhaps elevated above flood level of the nearest stream, has a good lookout for game, and so forth.

The construction of an optimal solution to settlement demands might mean that the settlement pattern does not resemble one of the purely sedentary or mobile patterns discussed above. Many variations on these extremes are possible. Several such have already been suggested. For example, a portion of the Ainu population live for a part of the year in hunting camps away from the permanent villages and in a different environmental situation to make exploitation of these zones economical (Watanabe 1968). Beardsley, et al. (1956), Chang (1962), and Watanabe (1968) have all proposed typologies of settlement patterns that take into account residential shifts. The former considers not only hunter-gatherers but also agriculturalists of all kinds. Chang and Watanabe's schemes are devised solely to deal with hunter-gatherers. In any event, the most typical settlement pattern involves differential use of the environment from different points, i.e., location in different places at different times of the year, for purposes of procuring different sets of resources. This leads to a series of functionally different sites in different situations. Under the Principle of Least Effort minimization of energy expenditure is expected, and sites with different subsistence roles could be expected in different situations in order to most efficiently carry out those roles. The converse of this has important implications for the archaeological study of settlement patterns. Differently located sites could be expected to have differential access to resources, and possibly to occupy different positions in the settlement pattern.

A further confounding variable is the realization that the structure of the environment may show a gradual change over space. Given structural variation, it might be suspected that settlement patterns will show a gradation over space also. For example, preliminary study of some of the Middle Woodland data from the Sangamon River Valley demonstrated that the choice of closest watersource for site location was highly correlated with the structure of the topography in the Sangamon Valley over space (Roper, 1974: p. 7). Examining the hypothesis of spatial variability in relation to settlement variability helped to explain what at first seemed to be an anomaly in Middle Woodland settlement patterns in central Illinois. It would thus seem reasonable that in attempting to examine the relations of a group of sites to the natural environment the investigator should not merely examine the idea of functional differences, but also contingency-bound differences related to the continuum of structural change throughout the drainage.

This is an important consideration in the present study. Little comparative literature is available concerning Late Woodland settlement patterns in central Illinois, although literature is abundant for Middle Woodland. The problem with existing Middle Woodland studies is that many of them have been carried out in a rather uniform environmental context, leaving no basis for examining continuous change over space, or for looking for the limits of the derived models. The advantages of studying Woodland settlement patterns in the Sangamon River Valley are thus obvious. The river is an east-to-west flowing stream, i.e., its course is perpendicular (roughly) to that of the Illinois River. The Sangamon flows away from the "Grand Prairie"—a frequently glaciated, flat, nearly treeless (prehistorically) area with shallowly entrenched drainage—toward the Illinois Valley—a less frequently glaciated, rather more dissected, thickly forested, deeply incised valley. The Sangamon therefore has a great range of environmental diversity, at least within Illinois. It is thus an ideal situation in which to look for spatially changing configurations of Woodland settlement patterns.

Method

The present study understands the concepts of settlement *pattern* and settlement *system* to be as defined by Howard Winters (1969: p. 110): "By the former is meant the geographic and physiographic relationships of a contemporaneous group of sites within a single culture. The latter term refers to the functional relationships among the sites contained within the settlement pattern." Analysis of settlement patterns and settlement systems are perceived to proceed in somewhat different fashions.

Settlement patterns—geographic and physiographic relationships—are first examined. For present purposes, geographic relationships are understood to refer to those among sites— what are sometimes called "man-man" relationships—while physiographic relationships are taken to refer to those between sites and features of the biophysical environment, such as streams, landforms, vegetation zones, and soils—the so-called "man-land" relationships. Locational theories tend to emphasize one or the other and, accordingly, most settlement pattern studies emphasize one or the other, depending upon the theoretical bias of the investigator and the nature of the problem. Whatever that bias, the subset of locational theory directed toward the specific body of data comprises the method used to examine the phenomena of interest (cf. Dunnell, 1971: p. 34). Implications of the method determine the data collected and the techniques used to analyze them. Note then that a variety of patterns could be observed in the same set of phenomena, depending upon the theory and method of the investigator, since recognition of a pattern is dependent upon the techniques used in its definition (cf. Hudson and Fowler 1972). In this sense, a settlement pattern is a construct of the archaeologist and is not a behavioral unit.

The settlement system is, however, taken to be a behavioral unit in that it refers to the functional relationships among a set of sites or inhabited loci. Knowledge of a prehistoric settlement system requires analysis of site contents, activity sets, assemblages, etc. (cf. Struever 1968c: p. 287) plus a set of laws relating behavior to material objects and their relations (i.e., correlates [Schiffer 1976: p. 13]). There is only one "correct" reconstruction of such a system, making it independent of the methods used in its reconstruction.

In the present study, therefore, it is the settlement system that is of interest, but it is the settlement pattern that will be examined. There is value, however, in such an approach. The study of settlement patterns has always implied the spatial dimension, while present developments in the study of settlement systems are largely along the formal dimension. It is clear, however, that the settlement system does have a spatial dimension. The present study therefore could be taken to be concerned ultimately with the spatial dimension of Illinois Woodland settlement systems, i.e., the articulation of system components with the biophysical environment, and how and why the system segments itself as it does. This study of settlement patterns uses a theoretical framework that accounts for how and why a system segments itself. The method used will be one that models the implications of the preceding theory statement. The way in which the derived settlement patterns may translate into the Middle and Late Woodland settlement system is then postulated.

Given this understanding of settlement patterns and settlement systems, as well as the articulation of theory and method, it is appropriate to briefly discuss the method to be used to articulate the theory described in this chapter with the phenomena in the Sangamon River Valley.

Man-land analysis, or the analysis of physiographic relationships in settlement pattern analysis, has been largely concerned with the description of the *site* of sites—the landform and soil a site is on, the vegetation zone it is in, its nearest watersource, and other similar variables are examined. The theoretical basis of the present study, however, requires the examination of sites in relation to a broader segment of their environment—that segment surrounding the site, its *situation*. It is precisely for such evaluations that site catchment analysis was developed. The development of this method and how and why it has been used is the subject of a separate manuscript to be published elsewhere (Roper n.d.). The reader is referred to that paper for details of site catchment analysis and a critique of the directions it has taken.

In general, site catchment analysis assumes the notion of human beings as refuging animals (Hamilton and Watt 1970), dispersing from and returning to a central place, and provisioning themselves by interacting with that segment of the biophysical environment immediately surrounding the central place (the arena). It therefore proceeds by first demarcating what has been called an *analytical arena* (Roper 1975: p. 27) or, more standardly, a *territory* (Higgs et al. 1975: p. ix) or *exploitation territory* (Vita-Finzi and Higgs 1970: p. 7). Several techniques for demarcating such a territory have been used, including walking for a specified amount of time from a site (time contours), drawing circles of specified radius or radii around a site (distance contours), or using Thiessen polygons or linear spacings to estimate the actual territory allotted to each site. The area of each resource zone within each site's territory is then measured and comparisons made. Techniques for comparisons may include figures, graphs, and/or, as in this study, statistical analysis of the data for each site. (A review of technique and variations at each step is given in Roper n.d.)

This study is therefore organized as follows. Chapter III describes the survey in the Sangamon River Valley and presents the Woodland chronology of that valley. The biophysical environment, highly important to this analysis, is described at some length in Chapter IV. Chapter V contains the heart of the study: the description of data generation and the analysis of those data for the Sangamon River Valley Woodland sites. This chapter is lengthy and includes a detailed discussion of the results of the statistical analysis. Some readers of the original study (Roper 1975) have objected that the discussion is highly technical. But, although numerical results are given, the discussion is presented in terms of Euclidean geometry and can be visualized as simply as our familiar three-dimensional world. The text explains in detail exactly how groups of sites differ from one another. Chapter VI translates this discussion into the perhaps more comfortable prose of archaeology and synthesizes the analytical results into an interpretation of Woodland settlement patterns in the Sangamon River Valley. From this interpretation, hypothetical models of Woodland settlement systems are generated. Chapter VII summarizes the work by answering the research questions posed at the beginning of the analysis.

III. THE SANGAMON RIVER SURVEY

The Survey

The Sangamon River study area is an artifical research area, arbitrarily demarcated by the Illinois State Museum in 1971. It encompasses about 7385 square kilometers (2885 square miles) and includes roughly the lower two-thirds of the

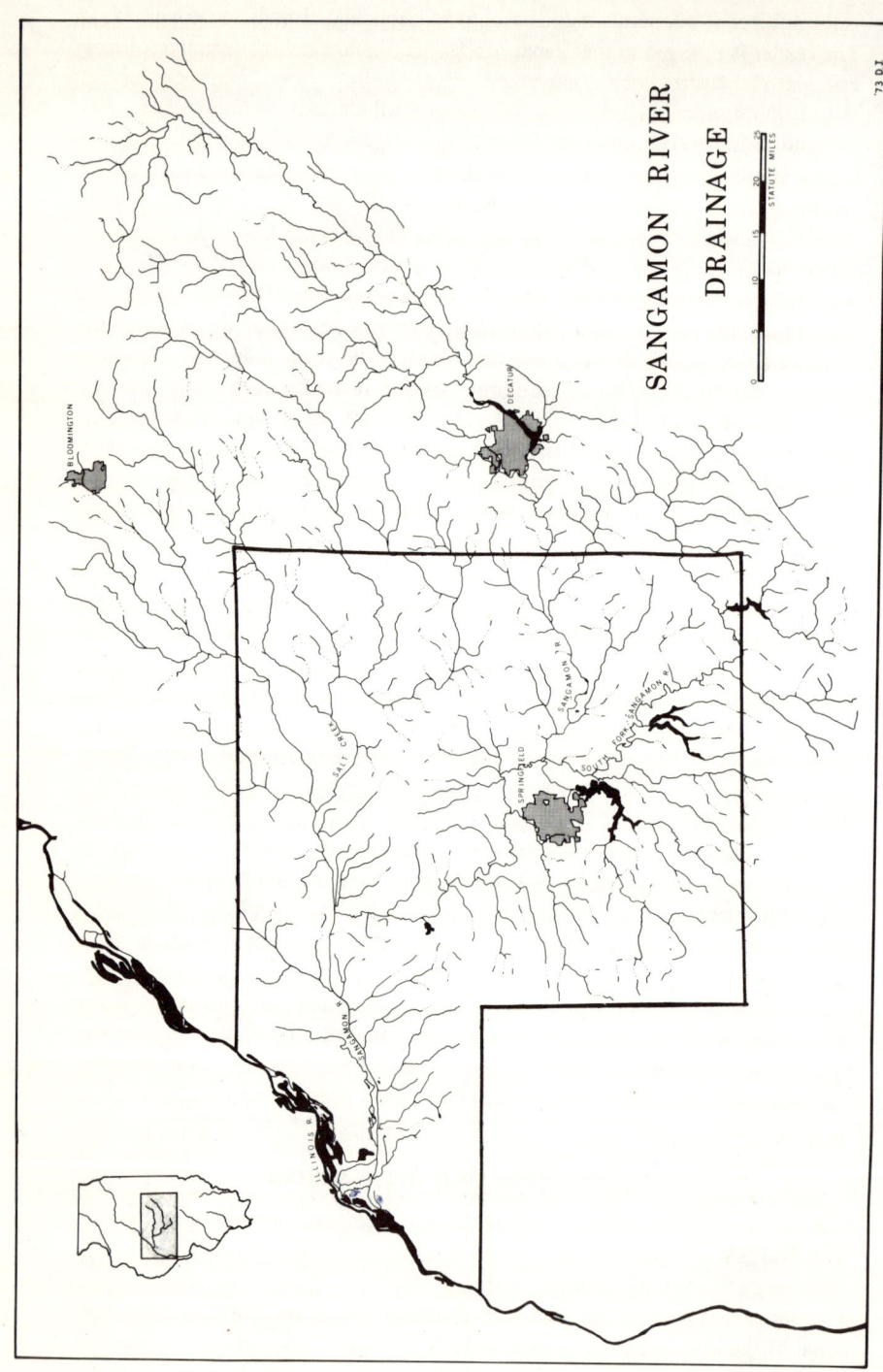

Fig. 2. The Sangamon River Drainage and the Study Area

Sangamon River Valley and its major tributaries, the Salt Creek and the South Fork of the Sangamon River, along with the attendant tributaries of all three streams (Fig. 2). All or part of Cass, Christian, Logan, Mason, Menard, and Sangamon counties are included within the study area.

The Sangamon River study area has been a focus of archaeological activity since March 1971. Activities (as of 1974) included annual survey programs, limited testing of several sites, and salvage operations on several others. Most of the survey has been carried out in a traditional manner, although one project of the program attempted to control for the vegetation variable in a small part of the drainage (Claflin 1975). Support for the Sangamon River archaeology program has been through the Illinois State Museum Society, the Historic Sites Survey program, and for one year (1 July 1971 to 30 June 1972) a National Science Foundation grant (GS–28986) to Walter E. Klippel.

Central Illinois is a predominantly agrarian area. Springfield (pop. approx. 100,000) is the only sizeable city within the study area. Most of the land is given over to small farms, engaged primarily in cash-grain farming and livestock raising. A large percentage of the land is in cultivated fields potentially providing nearly optimal survey conditions for the archaeologist. Since landowners have seldom refused permission to carry out survey activities on their property, a large portion of the drainage potentially provides optimal survey conditions and is accessible to survey activities.

Because agricultural practices are seasonal by nature, attention must be given to scheduling an archaeological survey. Gregory D. Johnson evaluated the effects of agricultural practices on survey activities in the Sangamon River Valley in the spring of 1971. He found that prior to last frost in mid-April, survey was extremely good (1971: p. 7). From mid-April, fields were spring-plowed and planted, thus beginning to impair survey activities. By May 20, survey was impossible in fields in wheat or oats (1971: pp. 11–12). Survey in corn and soybeans was good through May and June, but increasing height of these crops began to limit a surveyor's peripheral vision and to obscure a greater percent of the ground. However, hoeing of these crops during this time greatly impaired survey activities. Survey in corn and soybeans was virtually impossible by mid- to late-June due to high ground cover (1971:p. 13). The personal experience of this writer suggests, however, that during most years survey even in corn and beans became difficult by the middle of June. Precipitation generally decreases at about the time these crops are hoed and the ground does not receive sufficient rainfall for good visibility before the crops become too high (see precipitation graph—Chapter IV).

Fall plowing is common practice in Illinois, however. Given normal precipitation, the fields are barren of ground cover, have been plowed, and probably sufficiently washed to make survey conditions excellent from about mid-November through April (G. D. Johnson, 1971: p. 16). Survey activities in the Sangamon River drainage since the fall of 1971 have been scheduled to take advantage of these conditions.

Some data are available to evaluate partially the actual impact ground cover and rainfall conditions had on site recording. Of the 193 sites considered in this study, data were available on the ground cover and rainfall conditions encountered during survey of 116 sites. Each site was scored for the ground cover and rainfall variable as: 0-50% or 50-100% ground cover, and light or heavy rainfall. Table 1 summarizes the frequencies of sites recovered under these different conditions. The results tend to suggest that (1) either fields with light rainfall were avoided, or (2) sites are not highly visible under such conditions, or both; but (3) even with heavy ground cover it is possible to find sites.

TABLE 1

Ground Cover and Rainfall Condition on Surveyed Sites

Ground Cover	Rainfall		
	Light	Heavy	Total
0–50%	4	75	79
50–100%	4	33	37
Total	8	108	116

A case for the first conclusion could possibly be made in that little survey was done between July and February, thus avoiding the low rainfall conditions that prevail immediately after fall plowing. On the other hand, hoeing of crops and spring plowing occur during the period of active survey work and set the rainfall variable back to zero. It has been this writer's experience to step onto known sites with insufficient rainfall and find no traces of prehistoric material. Perhaps because of such experiences, insufficiently rained-on fields were indeed avoided, and well-washed fields were sought instead.

At the initiation of the survey, the files of the Illinois Archaeological Survey at the Illinois State Museum were checked for sites previously reported in the survey area. Few sites were reported, and some of these had inadequate information. An attempt was made to revisit and relocate the previously known sites, and to obtain surface collections. Success was varied. Some sites were readily located, others were not. Several had been destroyed.

Assistance from local collectors was solicited. This is a potentially valuable and time-saving technique (see Farnsworth [1973] for an example of the utility of this technique), although it is biased toward larger sites. Similarly, conversation with landowners was sometimes helpful in locating sites on their property, and sites were sometimes discovered when landowners or other interested persons brought artifacts to the museum for identification.

Ultimately, however, the most valuable site location technique was foot reconnaissance. Fields were systematically walked at intervals of about 15 meters. Upon locating prehistoric material, the interval between transects was narrowed to about 3 meters, and all visible cultural debris collected. Limits of scatter were determined, the area was measured (usually by pacing), and a sketch map drawn, relating the site to prominent, permanent features. When reconnaissance was completed, the site was assigned a temporary field number and located on a U.S. Geological Survey topographic map (normally of the 15' series).

Sites were recorded on a standard survey form. Two different site survey forms were used at different times during the course of the survey. From March to September 1971, the Illinois Archaeological Survey form was used. The information requested on this form is minimal and pertains mainly to legal location of the site, general environmental information, and material collected, both the latter items depending upon free recall by the surveyor. In the fall of 1971, a more detailed form was developed for the Lower Sangamon Survey, using a checklist type of recording. Although this form still incorporates some subjective bias, it standardizes many categories from site to site and surveyor to surveyor. Of the 193 sites included in this study, 140 were recorded on the new Sangamon Survey form.

In the laboratory, site locations were transferred to office copies of the U.S.G.S. 15' quadrangles, and were plotted on county soil maps and vegetation maps (J. Johnson 1972). At that time, they were assigned a permanent number and recorded on Illinois Archaeological Survey forms for transmittal to that agency.

Artifact Analysis

A prerequisite to the type of locational analysis reported in this study is a means of chronological control over the sites to be analyzed. The better the control, the more meaningful the locational analysis. In the absence of extensive internal chronological data, the sequence in adjoining areas may be used to construct a working chronology for the area of interest.

In most parts of North America, the most chronologically-sensitive artifacts are ceramics and projectile points. To use these artifact classes for chronological control, the study of the Sangamon River material required: (1) specification of criteria for identification of ceramics and projectile points, (2) identification of traditional types of ceramics and projectile points represented in the survey collections, (3) specification of criteria for assignment of components to cultural phases, and (4) assignment of sites using these criteria.

Criteria for identification of ceramics were incorporated in a key generated for identification of all central Illinois Woodland ceramics. An explanation of why and how the key was designed, and the key itself, have been published elsewhere (Roper 1977). Using the key, it was possible to identify the Sangamon River ceramics.

All sherds of less than 1.5 cm in maximum dimension, i.e., those somewhat smaller than a dime, were eliminated. The remaining sherds were then sorted into rim and/or decorated sherds and undecorated body sherds. The latter were then sorted into twelve temper-external surface treatment categories, and each category was counted.

The rim and/or decorated sherds were examined individually and scored for a number of observations: temper, external surface treatment, decorative type, appendages, lip angle, lip treatment, lip decoration, and lip surface treatment. In addition to decorative type, a number of these attributes have been found to have temporal significance in other parts of Illinois (see Bluhm 1951; Fowler 1955; Struever 1965, 1968b).

A total of 11223 sherds were examined using these procedures. This total comprises 9529 undecorated body sherds and 1694 rim and/or decorated sherds.

A potentially serious bias is introduced when Woodland sites are identified solely on the basis of presence-absence of ceramics. Woodland peoples did not deposit pottery at all places they inhabited, nor, particularly on small sites or sites with poor survey conditions, are ceramics necessarily exposed on the surface. Behaviorally, non-use and therefore non-deposition of ceramics may be a characteristic of ephemeral, male-oriented hunting camps. Such loci will never be recognized within the Woodland settlement system if ceramics are the only criterion for identification of a Woodland site. The problem is a dual one: (1) what indicators can we use to differentiate a non-ceramic Woodland site from an aceramic, by definition, Archaic site, and (2) once a non-ceramic Woodland site is recognized, how do we assign it within Woodland? At this juncture in our research, the only possible criterion is projectile point morphology, an admittedly much less satisfactory criterion than ceramic design. However, projectile points do in many instances serve as "type fossils" and work by White (1965, 1968) and others in Illinois has demonstrated a temporal correlation of certain ceramic types with certain point types. It was thus with the goal of attempting to place temporally as many sites as possible, and to identify as much of the range of Woodland site types as possible, that projectile point typology was employed.

Whereas traditional ceramic type definitions in Illinois are monothetic, projectile point definitions are polythetic, i.e., no feature or set of features is necessary and sufficient for class inclusion. Construction of a key on the basis of the literature alone therefore is not possible. Because only attribute summaries are given (e.g., means, range, etc.) in most descriptive reports, it would be necessary to acquire large quantities of already identified specimens for study. Such a procedure was impractical. An alternative exists in the form of completely redoing the typology using numerical taxonomic techniques. This is equally impractical, however. If merely the Sangamon specimens were classified using such techniques, there would be no way to relate the derived groups to already established types, and the chronological objectives of examining the points would not be met. To start anew to classify rigorously points from Illinois (as was done for Nevada by Thomas [1970]) would require reexamination of points from all over Illinois and is equally as impractical at this point. Therefore, it was necessary to employ the less satisfactory method of intuitive assessment of projectile point types.

All specimens from pottery-bearing sites were laid out on a table and with the use of major references, as well as consultation with colleagues facing similar problems, were grouped into categories corresponding to the named types: Kramer, Snyders, Dickson, Steuben, Madison, and the general category Late Woodland. Questionable cases (e.g., badly broken specimens) were excluded. Several other named types were recognized but excluded since their chronological placement is ambiguous. The material from non-ceramic sites was then searched for recognizable Woodland points. Again, nothing that could not be identified with reasonable confidence was included. As a check on intuitive judgment, the aggregate of points was sorted twice, with an interval of about two months between the first and second sortings. The agreement, while not formally measured, was very high. (Further discussion of Woodland projectile points in the Sangamon River Valley is given in Roper [1975: pp. 313-23].)

Phase Criteria and a Sangamon River Woodland Chronology

The most logical sequence with which to compare the Sangamon River material is that established for the Illinois River Valley, particularly its central portion. Not only is the Sangamon a tributary of the central Illinois, but the Woodland sequence of the central and lower portions of the Illinois River Valley is possibly the best understood prehistoric sequence in the Midwest.

Two chronological frameworks for the central and lower Illinois River Valleys are currently used (Fig. 3). The most comprehensive is that presented by Griffin (Griffin, Flanders, and Titterington, 1970: pp. 1-10) for the whole of the Illinois River Valley. The other is that of Struever (1968b) for the lower portion of the Illinois Valley only. The two are generally similar, but differ in a few details.

For the most part, the areally more inclusive Griffin sequence is employed here. Griffin distinguishes separate phase sequences in the lower, central, and upper Illinois Valleys. Only the central and lower valley sequences are shown in Fig. 3. The sequence in the upper valley is not as well known and was of no utility in construction of the Sangamon River chronology. Ceramic criteria for identification of a component to a phase are also shown in Fig. 3.

Phase Criteria

The Red Ochre phase has long been recognized in central Illinois (Cole and Deuel 1937) but is defined primarily from mortuary context. There have been some speculations that Marion, represented by Marion Thick pottery, is the habitation counterpart of Red Ochre (Munson 1966), a point of view not rejected, but viewed with caution by Linder (1974: p. 157). Certainly, Marion Thick pottery does occur, albeit in small quantities, in the central Illinois Valley (e.g., Munson 1966).

Black Sand was also recognized by Cole and Deuel (1937) in the central

Illinois Valley. Griffin notes that: "The term Black Sand was applied to the non-Hopewellian material found in the village under Mound F⁰77 at the Liverpool site and in the village numbered F^v88" (1970: p. 1, 5). The ceramics were later named Black Sand Incised by Griffin (1952: p. 98). This type is characterized by decoration consisting of the incised lines, in geometrical

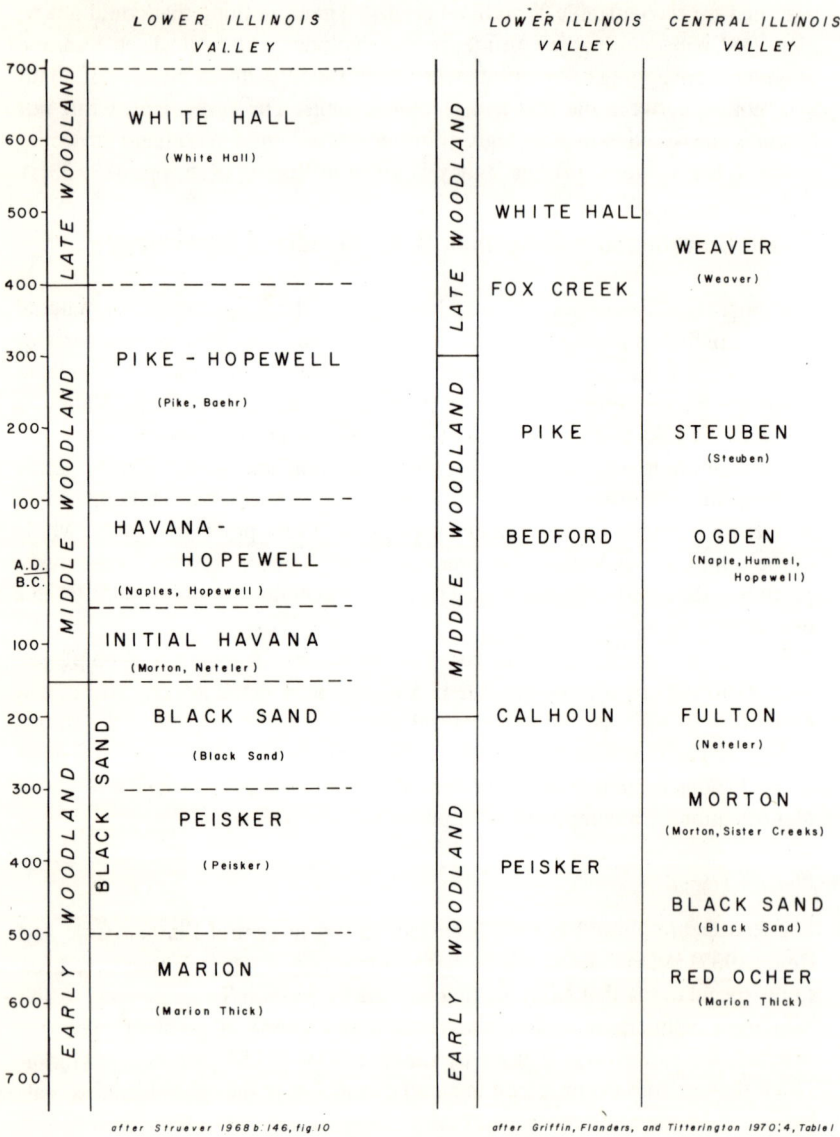

Fig. 3. Chronological Frameworks for Illinois Woodland.

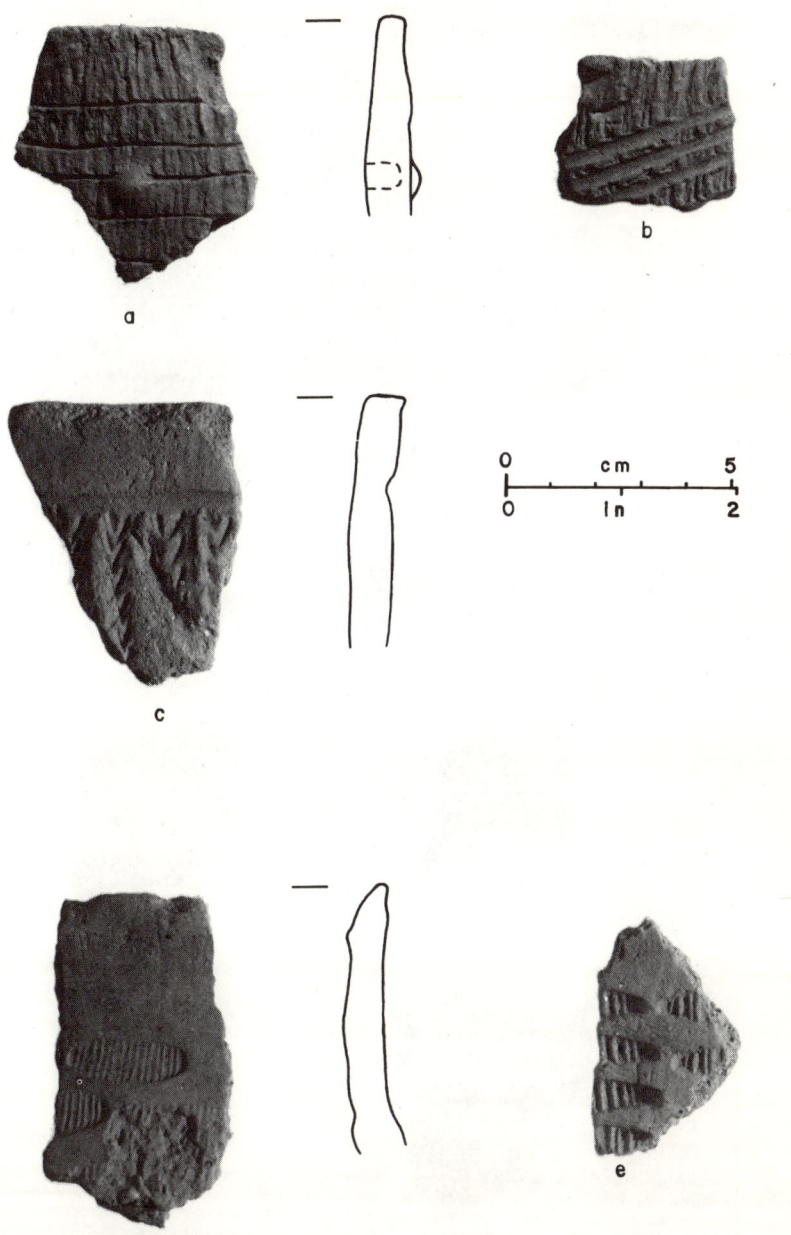

Plate 1. Early and Middle Woodland Pottery: a,b Black Sand Incised; c Morton Incised; d,e Naples Ovoid.

Plate 2. Middle Woodland Pottery: a,b Neteler Stamped var. Dentate; c Neteler Stamped var. Plain; d Havana Zoned var. Cord-Wrapped-Stick; e Steuben Punctate.

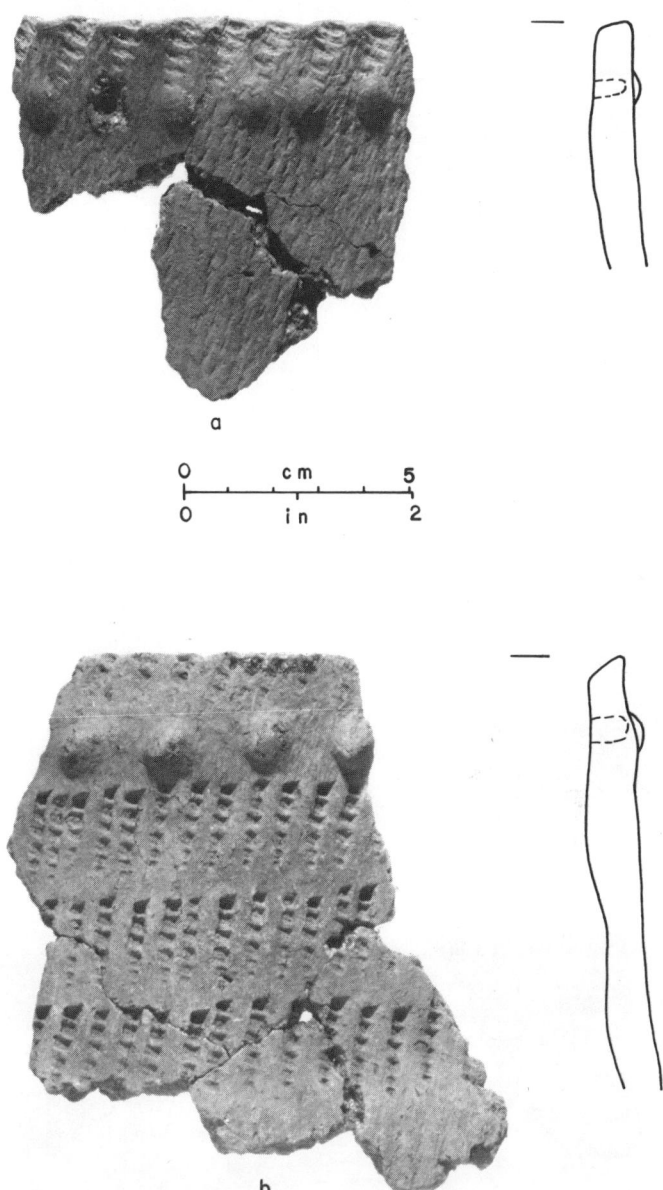

Plate 3. Middle Woodland Pottery: a Naples Stamped var. Cord-Wrapped-Stick; b Naples Stamped var. Dentate.

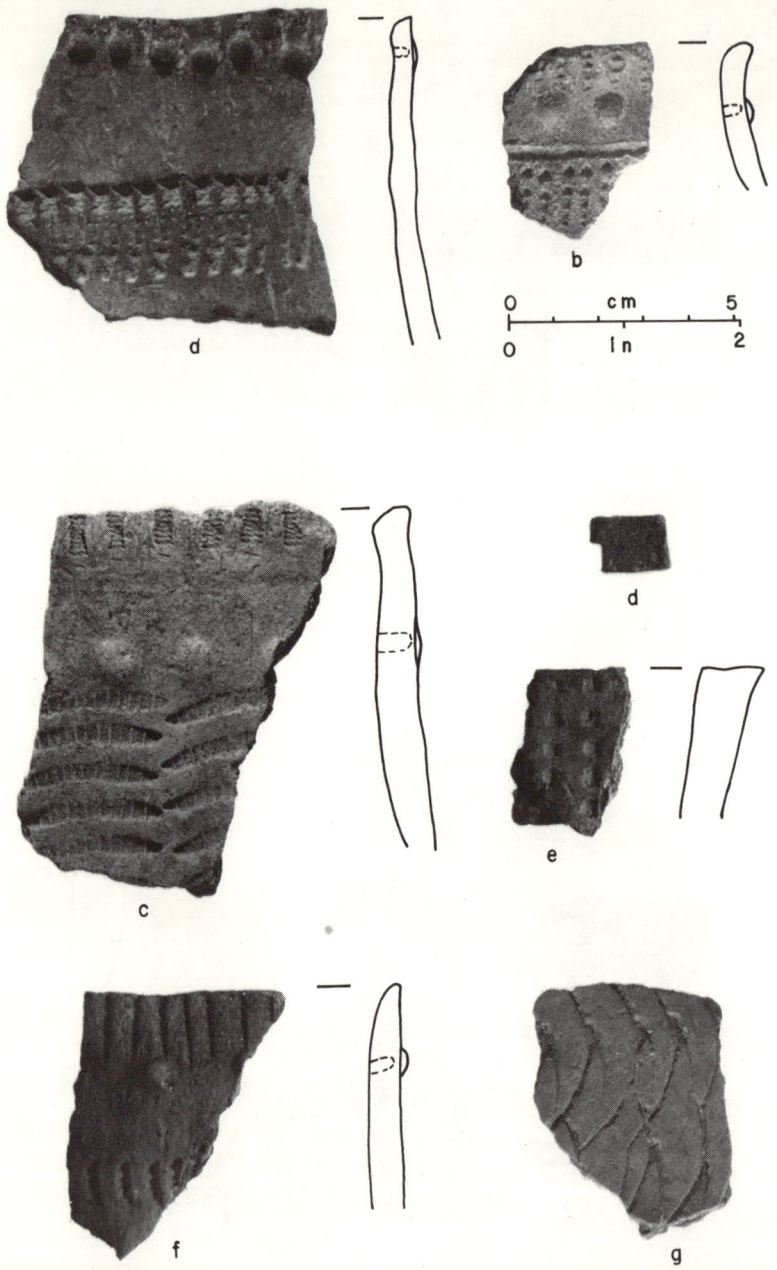

Plate 4. Middle Woodland Pottery: a Hummel Rocker var. Dentate; b,e,f Naples Stamped var. Dentate; c Hummel Stamped var. Dentate; g Hummel Rocker var. Plain; d galena cube.

SETTLEMENT PATTERN MODELS IN CENTRAL ILLINOIS 31

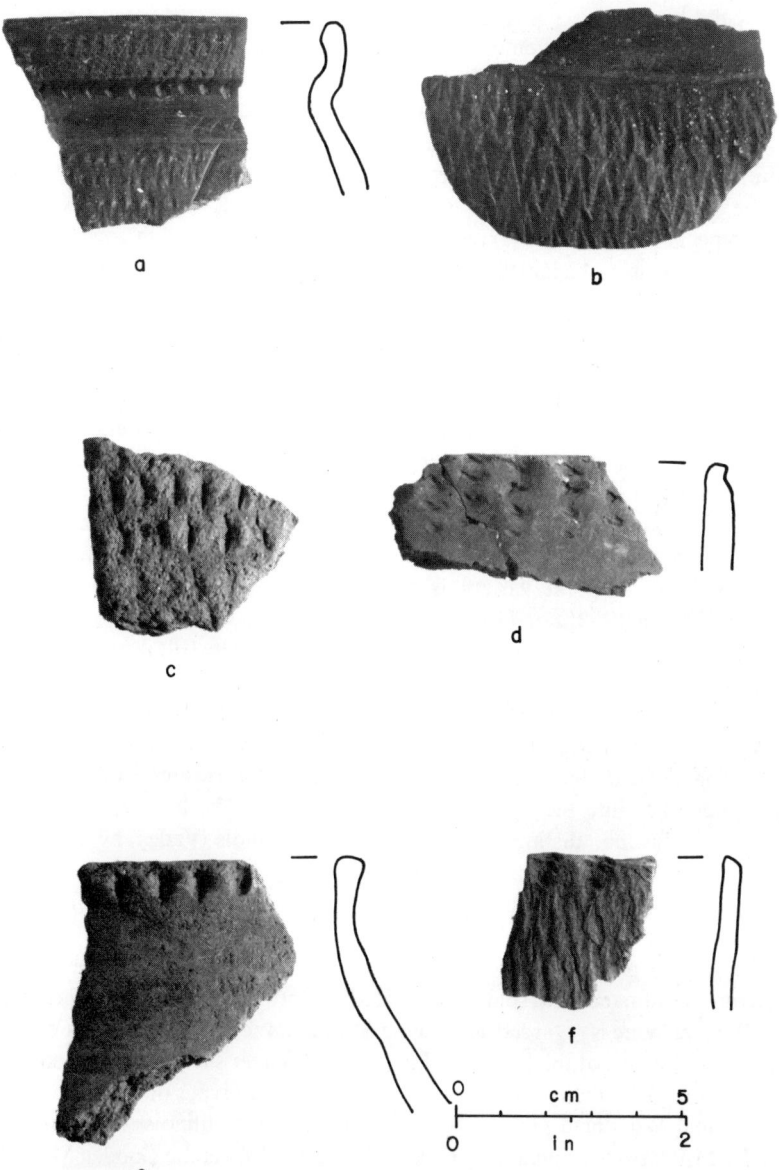

Plate 5. Hopewell and Weaver Pottery: a,b Hopewell Rocker var. Dentate; c Montezuma Punctate; d Weaver Plain var. Cord-Wrapped-Stick; e Weaver Plain var. Plain Stamped; f Weaver Cordmarked.

designs, placed over an unsmoothed cordmarked surface (Pl. 1a,b). On some vessels, a single row of bosses or nodes appears on the surface, several cm below the lip.

Morton is a ceramic complex following Black Sand (Griffin 1970: p. 5). Diagnostic ceramic types are Morton Incised, characterized by closely spaced short lines often in herringbone or other geometric patterns over a cordmarked surface (Pl. 1c), and by Sister Creeks Punctate, characterized by circular or annular punctates often over a cordmarked surface.

The succeeding Fulton phase is distinguished by Neteler Stamped pottery. This type is recognized by crescent-shaped stamps applied in rows on the smoothed rim area of a jar (Pl. 2a–c). Griffin (1970: p. 6) regards this phase as "the period and cultural level in the central Illinois Valley associated with early forms of the Havana ceramic tradition."

The Ogden phase is characterized by a variety of styles of the Havana Ceramic tradition (Naples, Hummel, Naples Ovoid, etc.; Pl. 1d,e; 2d; 3; 4a–c,e–g) as well as Hopewell ware types (Pl. 5a–c). The Havana types retain the idea, first seen in the Neteler pottery, of a plain or dentate stamp, now in a variety of shapes, applied over a plain, cordmarked, or smoothed cordmarked surface (Griffin 1952: pp. 104–14). Hopewell ceramics are often, but not always, limestone-tempered, and are thinner and harder than Havana ware. A great variety is found in the decoration on Hopewell vessels (Griffin 1952: pp. 114–21).

The Steuben phase is characterized by Steuben Punctate (Pl. 2e) ceramics as well as early Weaver Ware (Griffin, 1970: pp. 8–9). Steuben is a Havana Ware type characterized by two to four rows of hemiconical, D-shaped punctates applied over a plain surface. Weaver will be mentioned below. Griffin is somewhat unclear, but apparently would include "intrusions" of Pike and Baehr ceramics into the central valley at this time. Pike is a separate ware similar to Havana, distinguished in the lower Illinois Valley by Struever (1968b: p. 166). It is the diagnostic ceramic group of the Pike phase (Griffin 1970: p. 8), roughly equivalent to the Steuben phase in the central valley (see Fig. 3). Baehr is a Hopewell Ware type.

The Weaver phase is marked by Weaver Ware ceramics. Weaver sherds are thin, often cordmarked but seldom decorated except on or just below the lip (Pl. 5 d-f). Weaver Ware is regarded as showing a "gradual shift" from Havana Ware. Indeed, the ranges of thickness of Havana and Weaver sherds overlap, sometimes making it virtually impossible to separate the two types of body sherds.

The final Woodland phase recognized in the central Illinois Valley is the Maples Mills, first designated by Cole and Deuel (1937) at the Gooden Mound group in Fulton County. Maples Mills ceramics (also referred to as Canton, Tampico, or Gooden) are characterized by globular jars, with vertical collared rims. The collar is decorated with cord impressions applied in geometric forms (Pl. 6a–d). Occasionally, cord-impressed designs are also applied to the lip.

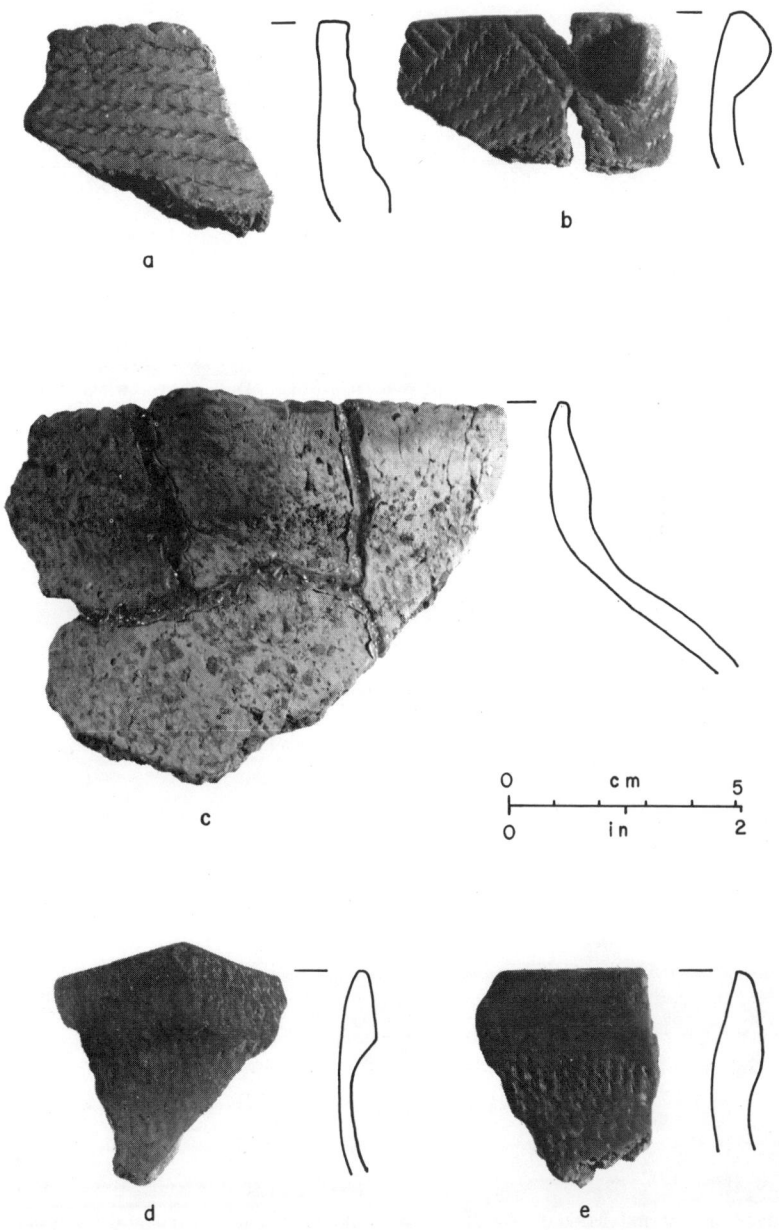

Plate 6. Late Woodland Pottery: a,b Maples Mills; c-e Albee Cordmarked.

Plate 7. Early and Middle Woodland Projectile Points: a-c Kramer; d-f Dickson Broad-Bladed; g-i Snyders group.

The Woodland Period in the Sangamon River Valley

Mortuary material of the Red Ochre phase is not known in the Sangamon Valley, nor has Marion Thick pottery been identified in the Sangamon survey collections. However, at least five Kramer points (Pl. 7a–c) have been identified. The Kramer point is thought to be associated with Marion Thick pottery (Munson 1966; Linder 1974).

Only three sites in the present study have Black Sand pottery. On all three sites, however, Black Sand sherds occur in small frequencies. Further, two of the sites—Mn^{v}75 and Mn^{v}117—are close to the Illinois River Valley. Mn^{v}75 is at the point of junction of the Sangamon and Illinois valleys, while Mn^{v}117 is slightly over two miles upriver.

In comparison with the remainder of Illinois, the scarcity of Black Sand ceramics in the Sangamon Valley is not surprising. Farnsworth found only one site with Black Sand ceramics in the Macoupin Valley. This site had only five sherds of Black Sand and the related Peisker types and was only 800 meters from the point at which Macoupin Creek joins the Illinois River Valley (Farnsworth 1973: p. 18). Munson (1971) and Harn (1971), working in the Wood River Terrace and the American Bottoms of the Mississippi River, also found sparse Black Sand material. Rackerby found scarce evidence of Black Sand in the Carlyle Reservoir area of the central Kaskaskia River (1968: p. 80), and W. M. Gardner (undated letter postmarked 28 February 1974) found none in the upper Kaskaskia Valley. Wilson (1961: p. 27) noted only sparse amounts of Black Sand pottery in the upper central Spoon River Valley and Winters (1967: p. 36) located only a few sherds in the Wabash Valley.

In larger valleys, Black Sand ceramics have been recognized in greater quantities not only in the central Illinois Valley (McGregor 1957; Munson and Harn 1966), but also the lower Illinois Valley (Struever 1968b, c; Perino 1966; Rackerby 1973), upper Illinois Valley (Brown 1964; Schnell 1974), and the Iowa River Valley (Logan 1958; Anderson 1971). Thus, the major distribution of Black Sand ceramics appears to be confined to some of the major waterways within the southern portion of the Prairie Peninsula.

Pottery characteristic of the Morton and the Fulton phases is not prominent in the Sangamon Valley. Morton ceramics occur at only two sites and in extremely low frequencies. Neteler occurs at more sites, also in low frequencies, but is somewhat more abundant in terms of percentage than Morton.

Ogden phase ceramics are well represented in the Sangamon River Valley by both a variety of Havana types, and the presence, in small numbers, of Hopewell sherds. Havana ceramics have been recognized at 28 sites. Hopewell sherds were collected from ten of these sites. Both Havana and Hopewell are scattered throughout the Sangamon Valley (Fig. 4), including upriver from the eastern boundary of the area under consideration here (Wright 1973).

It has been observed that the widely dispersed Havana ceramics are of styles equivalent to those popular at the time of the Ogden phase. McGregor's (1957)

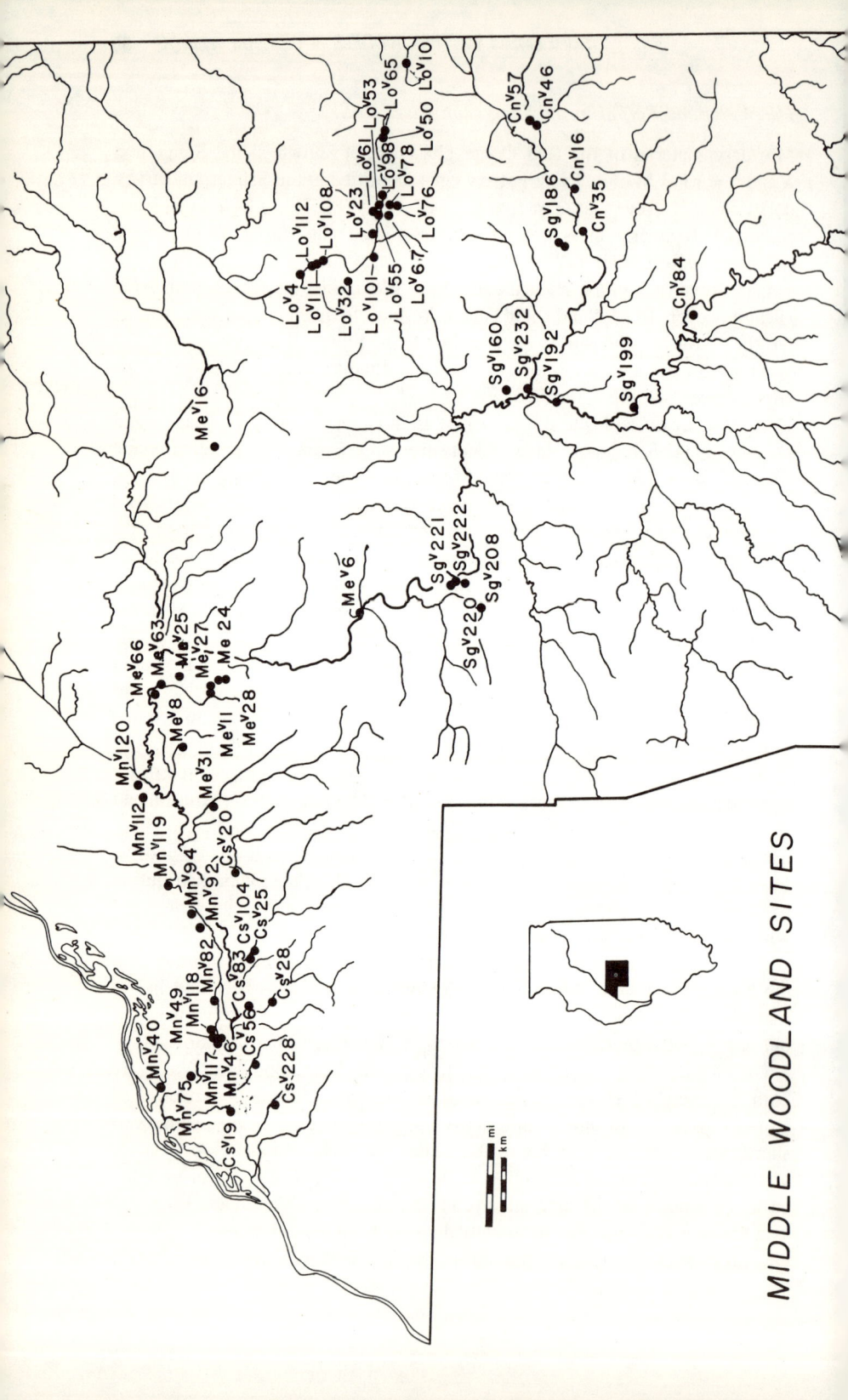

distribution study showed "Early Hopewell" (roughly the same as the central Illinois Valley Ogden phase and the lower Illinois Valley Bedford phase) to be present throughout the Illinois Valley and its tributaries. Subsequent work has shown material related to the Ogden and Bedford phases to be present in the Spoon (Wilson 1961), Macoupin (Farnsworth 1973), upper Kaskaskia (Gardner 1969), middle Kaskaskia (Rackerby 1968), Wabash (Winters 1967), and Sangamon valleys. In addition, Havana is present in northeastern Illinois (Brown 1964, Schnell 1974), northwestern Indiana (Faulkner 1961, 1972), southwestern Michigan (Bettarel and Smith 1973; Fitting 1970), southern Wisconsin (Freeman 1969; Mason 1966; Hurley 1974), northwestern Illinois (Bennett 1945), and northeastern Iowa (Logan 1958; Anderson 1971).

In addition to small quantities of Hopewell ceramics, other Hopewell items are found in the Sangamon Valley. One obsidian flake and a galena cube (see Pl. 4d) were found on the surface of 11Mn^{V}120. Imported cherts are present. Blue-grey Dongola chert is found on nearly all Middle Woodland sites, and other exotic cherts regularly occur. A Snyders group point from 11Me^{V}16 is made of Knife River flint; a Dickson Broad-Bladed point, also of Knife River flint, is in the private collection of the owner of 11Me^{V}8. Some evidence of mortuary activity is also present. The writer has seen mounds in every county in the survey area, and it is known that at one time more were present (e.g., Snyder 1883, Wickersham 1885). Presence of mounds is not in itself evidence of Hopewell mortuary activity since mounds were built at other times but, unfortunately, no mound in the Sangamon Valley has ever been professionally investigated or reported. The Noten-Wiseman or Kingfisher Hill mound (11 Me^{0}1) is known to be Hopewell, however (Baker et al., 1941: p. 5). A skull with copper stains on the mastoids, reportedly from this mound, is in the collections of the Illinois State Museum. A Havana Zoned vessel from the mound is in a private collection. Other Hopewell material has been seen in other private collections from the Sangamon Valley, and it is probable that other mounds are also Hopewell.

Steuben phase ceramics are also poorly represented in the Sangamon Valley and, when Steuben sherds are present, they occur in low frequencies. Pike ceramics are absent, and only one Baehr sherd was observed in the entire survey collection.

Weaver phase ceramics are represented at seven sites in this study. Six of these sites are in Mason County, and the other is directly across the river in Cass County. Two of the sites have been tested (11Mn^{V}94 and 11Cs^{V}20) and found to have deep middens. In addition, 11Mn^{V}94 contained a large number of pit features. Both had excellent faunal and floral preservation. Analysis of both sites is still in progress. A single radiocarbon date on 11Mn^{V}94 of A.D. 1050 ± 100 (GX 2765) is probably rather late for Weaver. [Note: Continuing surveys while this study was in preparation recorded several Weaver sites in Menard County. Two Weaver rim sherds, probably from the same vessel, were also identified in the collection from the Airport Site (11 Sg^{V}280) in Sangamon County (Roper 1978).]

The distribution of Weaver is not well known. On the basis of only six sites, McGregor (1957: p. 273) confined Weaver to the central Illinois and Spoon River valleys. Griffin (1970: p. 10) also implies a central Illinois Valley locus for Weaver. Munson (1971) and Harn (1971), however, both report "Weaver-like" ceramics from the American Bottoms and Wood River Terrace in the East St. Louis area, and Anderson (1971) reports "Weaver-like" ceramics from the Iowa River Valley. Evidence from surveys in tributaries of the Illinois is primarily negative except for the Spoon and the Sangamon.

Maples Mills is quite well represented in the Sangamon Valley. Maples Mills ceramics were recovered from nineteen sites distributed through the valley (Fig. 5), as well as upriver from the area under consideration in this study (Lewis 1975).

Several other types of ceramics occur with Maples Mills in the Sangamon Valley. Every site in the Sangamon Valley which has Mississippian ceramics also has Maples Mills ceramics, but the reverse is not true. Such an association of Maples Mills and Mississippian is also reported elsewhere. Smith reports Maples Mills ceramics to be stratigraphically below the Mississippian pottery at the Crable Site in Fulton County (1951: pp. 30–31). Wray (1952: pp. 156–57), however, reports mixing of Maples Mills and Mississippian at the Garren site, also in Fulton County.

Several other Late Woodland types also occur with Maples Mills. Albee Cordmarked (see Pl. 6*d–e*) and Starved Rock Collared (Pl. 6*c*) occur with Maples Mills at two sites in Logan County and the Hood site (11M^{v}56) in Macon County (Lewis, 1975: p. 19). Every site with Albee and Starved Rock also has Maples Mills, but the reverse is not true.

Although Griffin does not show it in his table, he recognizes in his text a Maples Mills phase, placed at about A.D. 700-900, in the central Illinois Valley (Griffin, 1970: p. 9). If these dates are correct, however, Maples Mills should not occur with Mississippian ceramics, which should date later (ca. A.D. 900–1450). Three radiocarbon dates have been obtained for Maples Mills and associated ceramics in the Sangamon Valley. At site 11Sg^{v}113 (not included in this study), reported to have had Maples Mills pottery, a single radiocarbon sample gave a date of 840 ± 100 years B.P.; A.D. 1110 (GX 0759). At the Hood site (11M^{v}56) in Macon County, two dates were obtained: 1000 ± 100 B.P.; A.D. 950 and 1230 ± 115 B.P.; A.D. 720 (Lewis 1975: p. 5).

The distribution of Maples Mills ceramics is not well known. A number of Maples Mills sites were reported in the Peoria area by Schoenbeck (1946). When McGregor (1957) made his study of site locations in the Illinois Valley, he reported only two Maples Mills sites in that valley. Several more sites are now known there (e.g., Munson and Harn 1966). Interestingly, McGregor (1957) did tentatively project the distribution of Maples Mills up the Sangamon River, although he did not indicate the basis for this inference.

In summary, ceramics diagnostic of what in the central Illinois Valley would be the Ogden, Weaver, and Maples Mills phases are the most abundant

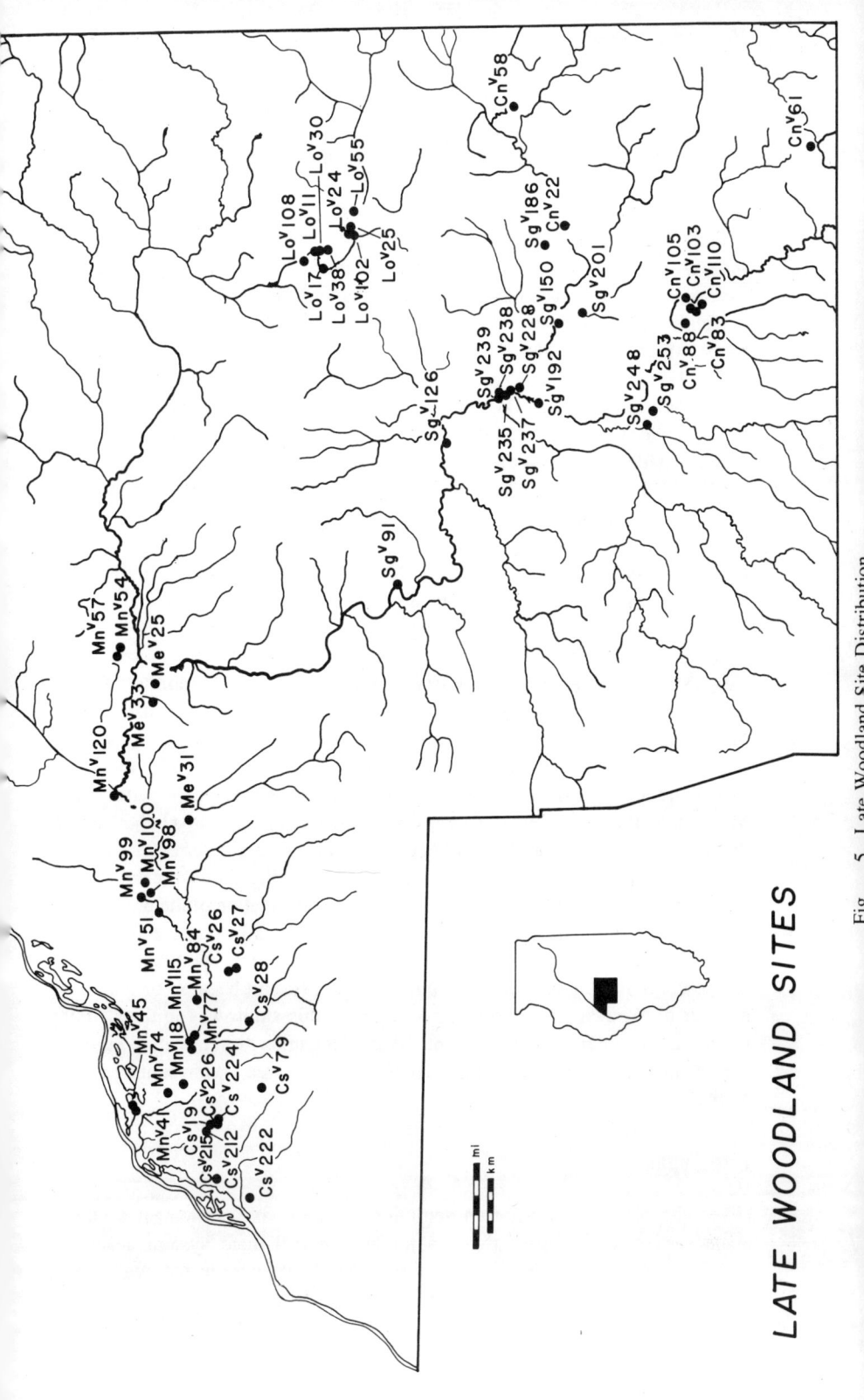

Fig. 5. Late Woodland Site Distribution

Woodland types in the Sangamon River Valley. Other Havana types are present in small numbers.

It is obvious in the foregoing discussion that the phases described are defined entirely on the basis of ceramics, with the presence of Hopewell items (e.g., copper, obsidian, mortuary practices) entering into the definition of some Middle Woodland phases. Other items are, however, of potential use as indicators but are not part of the phase definitions. Projectile points are of especially great use. The major problem with them, however, is that they do not correlate well with the ceramic phases, but rather with the gross temporal units: Early, Middle, and Late Woodland periods.

The first column of Fig. 3 lists the division of the Woodland sequence into Early, Middle, and Late Woodland periods. For present purposes, we find manifestations of only the Middle and Late Woodland periods in the Sangamon Valley. Ogden phase is well within the Middle Woodland period. Weaver and Maples Mills are both Late Woodland. Projectile point types do not break down quite the same, however, and Weaver is indistinguishable from Middle Woodland. Six types were employed as "type fossils" in this study: Kramer, Snyders, Steuben (Lowe), Dickson, Madison, and Late Woodland. Kramer (see Pl. 7*a-c*) is Early Woodland; Snyders, Steuben and Dickson (Pl. 7*d-i*, 8*a-c*) are all Middle Woodland; Madison (Pl. 8*h-k*) and Late Woodland (Pl. 8*d-g*) are Late Woodland and Mississippian. Steuben, however, carries over from Middle Woodland into Weaver. Because of the continuity of both ceramics and projectile points from Havana into Weaver, and because the size of the sample of Weaver sites is too small to stand alone, Weaver sites are included with the Middle Woodland sites in this study, and the designation Late Woodland includes sites with Maples Mills, Albee, Mississippian pottery, and Madison and/or the general category Late Woodland points. It is believed that this lumping does no violence to the potential of the data in terms of the finer phase division just reviewed. Since *all* Middle Woodland sites are dominated by ceramics of the Ogden phase, and since the interpretation of the presence of Morton and Fulton phase ceramics is unclear, virtually nothing is lost by lumping phases into periods. Including Weaver with Middle Woodland is based on the continuity of ceramics and projectile points, and because of the small number of Weaver sites identified at the time this study was initiated. Furthermore, if our present interpretations of Sangamon River Valley culture-history are correct, it appears that there is a hiatus between Weaver and Maples Mills.

Site Types

Given the distinctions between settlement patterns and settlement systems made earlier, it is apparent that although the settlement system normally segments itself, producing two or more "types" of sites, in fact we cannot know these system components until after detailed analysis of site contents.

Meanwhile, settlement pattern analysis normally differentiates sites into two or more types on the basis of some arbitrary set of criteria. Although it is to be hoped that such types will prove to have behavioral validity, such a correspondence is to be demonstrated rather than assumed.

For the present purposes, the Sangamon River sites have been divided into four classes of what might be called "material evidence types," based on the kinds of identifiers used: (1) those with diagnostic ceramics (or ceramics and points of the same period), (2) those with diagnostic points but with only undiagnostic ceramics, (3) those with diagnostic points only and with no ceramics, and (4) those with non-diagnostic pottery only and with no diagnostic

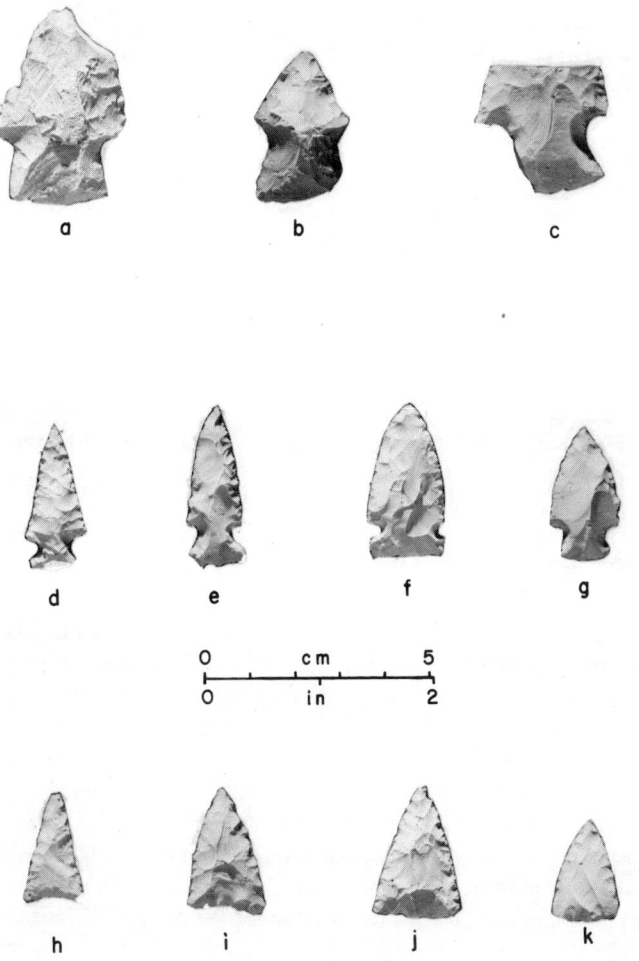

Plate 8. Middle and Late Woodland Projectile Points: a-c Stcuben Expanding Stemmed (Lowe Flare Base); d-g Late Woodland; h-k Madison.

points. Combined with designations of Middle and Late Woodland, seven categories of sites are recognized: (MW-1) Middle Woodland ceramic sites, (MW-2) Middle Woodland projectile points and undiagnostic ceramics (or with other ceramics), (MW-3) Middle Woodland points and no ceramics, (LW-1) Late Woodland ceramics, (LW-2) Late Woodland projectile points and undiagnostic ceramics (or with other ceramics), (LW-3) Late Woodland points and no ceramics, and (W) non-diagnostic pottery only and no diagnostic points (the grit-tempered ceramics, however, assign the site to Woodland). The individual sites assigned to each of these categories are listed in Table 2.

A conservative assignment strategy was used: if a site had points indicative of two different periods, it was assigned to both; the same held for pottery. If it had pottery diagnostic of, for example, Middle Woodland and also some Late Woodland points, it was assigned as a Middle Woodland ceramic site and also a Late Woodland projectile point site. In this sense, the "undiagnostic" ceramics should read "undiagnostic and/or other." Fortunately, very few sites had both. Note then that the present use of the term "sites" is more correctly stated as "components."

IV. THE BIOPHYSICAL ENVIRONMENT

The Prairie Peninsula

The Sangamon River study area is located within the southeast portion of the Prairie Peninsula, a great wedge of grassland extending east from the Great Plains into the deciduous forest, and encompassing parts of Iowa, Indiana, Illinois, Michigan, Missouri, and Minnesota, with outliers in Ohio (Fig. 6). Climate and vegetation set off this area from the deciduous forest into which it intrudes. Brown (1965) has shown that this area prehistorically was also culturally distinct.

The exact origin of the Central North American grassland has been the subject of some discussion, in particular whether the prairies are the natural product of low precipitation and high temperature, or whether they are man-made as a result of firing. The subject has been reviewed in the archaeological literature by Wedel (1957) and by Winters (1969: pp. 6–10). The general conclusion reached by both archaeologists and botanists is that the prairies are natural, and the fire had little to do with prairie origins: "Fire as an ecological factor seems to boil down to this: that in forest climates it retards development, and may result in scrub, but it does not result in prairie. In a prairie climate it helps to maintain and perhaps rarely enlarges the prairie" (Transeau 1935: p. 434).

A vast prairie interspersed with forest in areas of relief was the scene described by an early traveller in Illinois:

SETTLEMENT PATTERN MODELS IN CENTRAL ILLINOIS 43

TABLE 2

Material Evidence Types

MW-1	MW-2	MW-3	LW-1	LW-2	LW-3	Sites with no diagnostic material—with grit-tempered ceramics	
Mnᵛ40	Mnᵛ49	Meᵛ16	Mnᵛ41	Mnᵛ51	Mnᵛ54	Mnᵛ42	Mnᵛ114	Meᵛ18	Cnᵛ79
Mnᵛ46	Mnᵛ118	Meᵛ24	Mnᵛ45	Mnᵛ98	Mnᵛ57	Mnᵛ43	Mnᵛ116	Meᵛ19	Cnᵛ94
Mnᵛ75	Csᵛ56	Meᵛ28	Mnᵛ77	Mnᵛ100	Mnᵛ74	Mnᵛ44	Csᵛ54	Meᵛ30	Cnᵛ107
Mnᵛ82	Csᵛ83	Sgᵛ160	Mnᵛ115	Mnᵛ118	Mnᵛ84	Mnᵛ47	Csᵛ60	Meᵛ68	Cnᵛ111
Mnᵛ92	Csᵛ104	Cnᵛ16	Mnᵛ120	Csᵛ27	Mnᵛ99	Mnᵛ48	Csᵛ72	Sgᵛ128	Cnᵛ119
Mnᵛ94	Csᵛ228	Cnᵛ57	Csᵛ19	Csᵛ79	Csᵛ215	Mnᵛ53	Csᵛ84	Sgᵛ149	Loᵛ12
Sgᵛ186	Sgᵛ178	Loᵛ23	Csᵛ26	Csᵛ222	Csᵛ224	Mnᵛ72	Csᵛ88	Sgᵛ177	Loᵛ18
Sgᵛ199	Sgᵛ192	Loᵛ32	Csᵛ28	Meᵛ25	Csᵛ226	Mnᵛ73	Csᵛ97	Sgᵛ197	Loᵛ20
Sgᵛ220	Sgᵛ208	Loᵛ50	Csᵛ212	Meᵛ33	Sgᵛ126	Mnᵛ76	Csᵛ107	Sgᵛ207	Loᵛ21
Sgᵛ221	Loᵛ10	Loᵛ53	Meᵛ31	Sgᵛ186	Sgᵛ150	Mnᵛ78	Csᵛ214	Sgᵛ211	Loᵛ29
Sgᵛ222	Loᵛ76	Loᵛ61	Sgᵛ91	Sgᵛ201	Sgᵛ253	Mnᵛ85	Csᵛ216	Sgᵛ233	Loᵛ54
Sgᵛ232	Loᵛ78	Loᵛ65	Sgᵛ192	Sgᵛ235	Cnᵛ58	Mnᵛ87	Csᵛ217	Sgᵛ234	Loᵛ70
Csᵛ19	Loᵛ108	Loᵛ67	Sgᵛ228	Sgᵛ238	Cnᵛ61	Mnᵛ88	Csᵛ218	Sgᵛ249	Loᵛ71
Csᵛ20		Loᵛ98	Sgᵛ237	Sgᵛ239	Cnᵛ88	Mnᵛ89	Csᵛ219	Sgᵛ280	Loᵛ73
Csᵛ25		Loᵛ101	Sgᵛ248	Cnᵛ22	Cnᵛ105	Mnᵛ95	Csᵛ220	Cnᵛ9	Loᵛ74
Csᵛ28		Loᵛ111	Loᵛ11	Cnᵛ83	Loᵛ25	Mnᵛ96	Csᵛ221	Cnᵛ14	Loᵛ82
Cnᵛ35		Loᵛ112	Loᵛ17	Cnᵛ103	Loᵛ38	Mnᵛ103	Csᵛ223	Cnᵛ48	Loᵛ85
Cnᵛ46			Loᵛ30	Cnᵛ110	Loᵛ102	Mnᵛ104	Csᵛ225	Cnᵛ64	Loᵛ86
Cnᵛ84			Loᵛ108	Loᵛ24		Mnᵛ107	Csᵛ227	Cnᵛ68	Loᵛ87
Loᵛ4				Loᵛ55		Mnᵛ109	Csᵛ229	Cnᵛ78	Loᵛ105
Loᵛ55						Mnᵛ110			Loᵛ114
Meᵛ6									
Meᵛ8									
Meᵛ11									

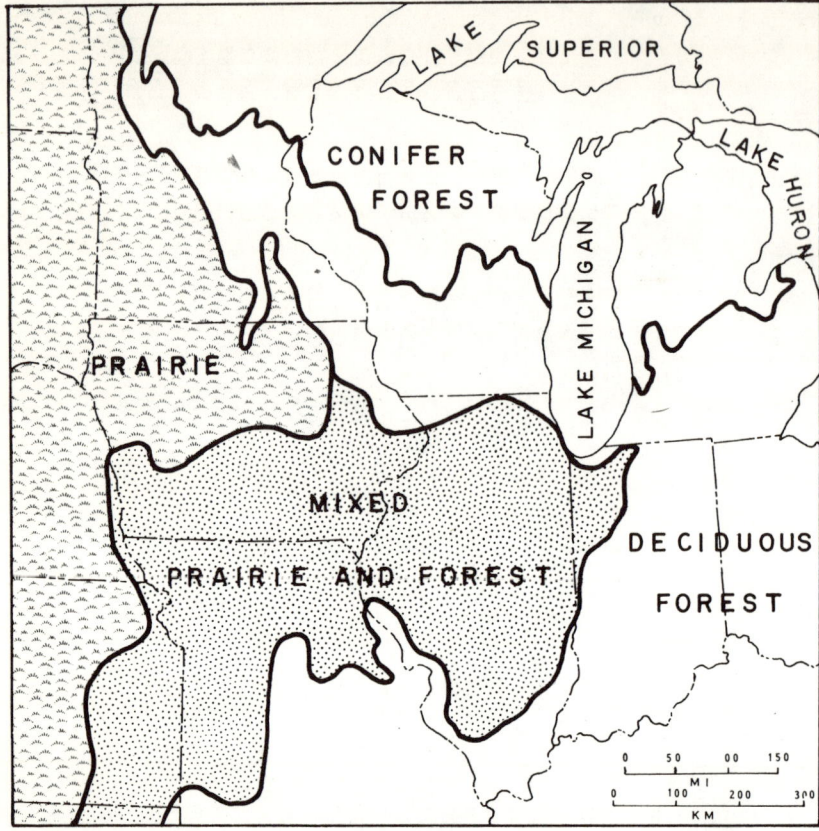

Fig. 6. The Prairie Peninsula (after Wright, 1968: p. 79).

> In all this distance, the margins of the streams are almost the only places where timbered land is found; and the streams have only narrow skirts of wood. . . . Their [prairie] borders are by no means uniform, but are intersected in every direction by strips of forest land advancing into and receding from the prairie towards the water-courses, whose banks are always lined with timber, principally of luxuriant growth. Between these streams, in many instances, are copses and groves of timber, containing from 100 to 2000 acres, in the midst of the prairies, like islands in the ocean. (Mitchell 1837: pp. 10, 12)

Climate

Rainfall

A number of climatic factors are characteristic of the prairie: (1) less rain and fewer heavy rains in winter than in the deciduous forest to the southeast; (2) less snowfall than the continental interior to the north; and (3) increase from west to east in intensity of summer rainfall (Borchert 1950). Much of the annual rainfall on the Prairie Peninsula occurs during the summer months in marked contrast to the deciduous forest. This fact may be demonstrated by a comparison of rainfall distribution at Springfield, in the center of the study area, and at Cairo, in the deciduous forest at the southernmost extremity of Illinois. Figure 7 plots mean monthly precipitation for Springfield and Cairo over the 67-year period from 1880–1946 (data from Page 1949). A comparison of monthly rainfall distribution using a t-test of the differences of means (Fig. 8; see Blalock, 1960: pp. 170–76) confirms that the winter months have significantly lower rainfall on than off the Prairie Peninsula. The monthly means for summer rainfall do not differ significantly (Fig. 8).

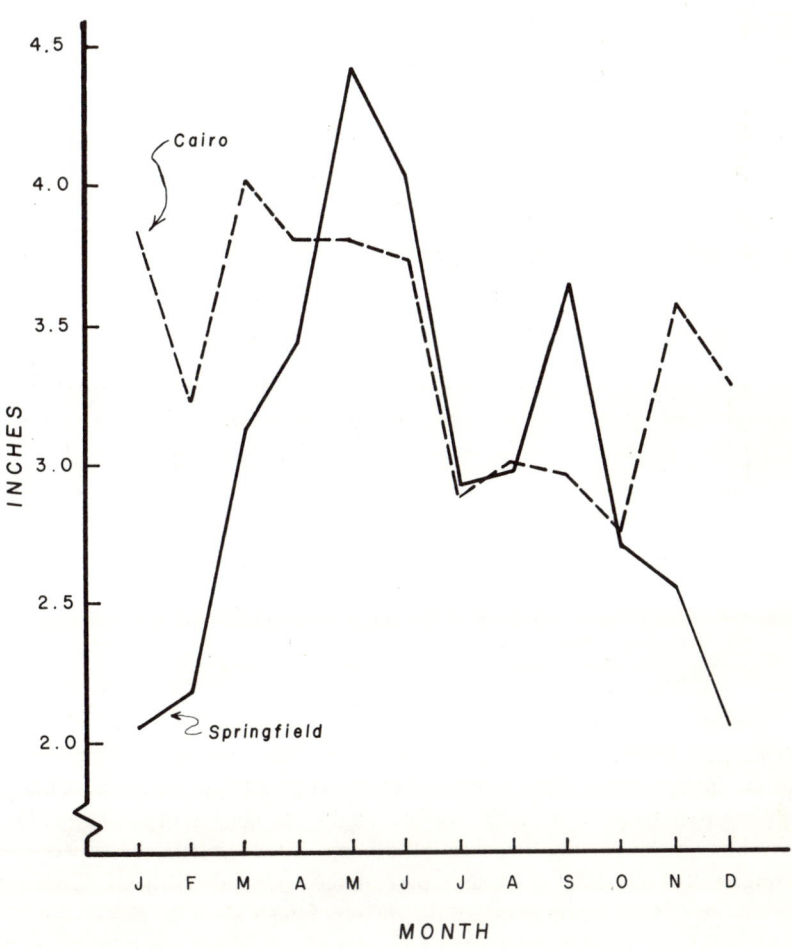

Fig. 7. Mean Monthly Precipitation at Springfield and Cairo.

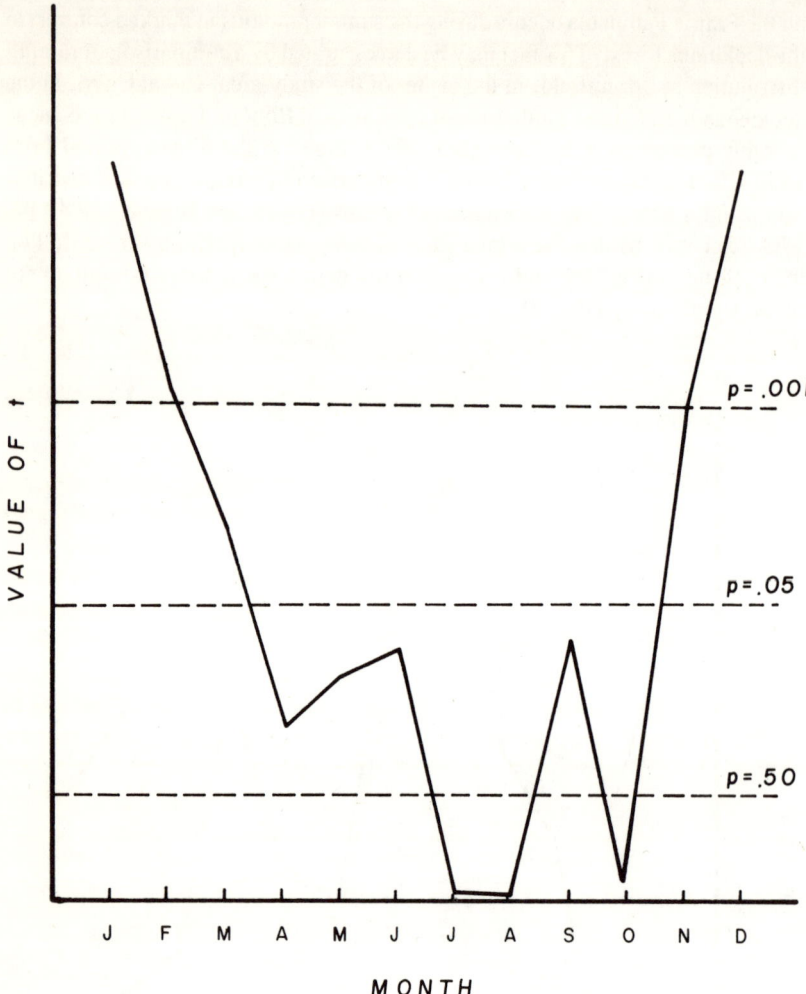

Fig. 8. Difference of Means of Precipitation at Springfield and Cairo.

Another important characteristic of the Prairie Peninsula is the variability in its summer (June to August) rainfall. Since long-term average precipitation is no less in the prairie than in the rest of the Midwest, the greater variability implies more frequent and more severe drought than in areas of similar rainfall surrounding the prairie (Borchert, 1950: pp. 10–11). It is these periodic droughts that give the grasslands part of their special character. Drought conditions favor the persistence of prairie over forests since the grasses have a superior ability to utilize available moisture in the deeper layers of the soil (Transeau, 1935: p. 433).

Temperature

Latitude is the most important geographical consideration in temperature distribution throughout Illinois (Page, 1949: p. 114). Springfield follows the normal Illinois pattern in yearly temperature variation, i.e., July is the warmest average month, and January the coldest (Fig. 9). On a year-to-year basis however, Borchert (1950: p. 16) has shown that there is an inverse correlation between rainfall and temperature during the summer in the grassland. When July rains fail, drought is widespread and temperatures soar.

The growing season, like temperature, is controlled by both latitude and altitude, but in general, shortens from south to north. At the latitude of the Sangamon River area, the average frost-free season is 180 days (Table 3).

Plant Communities

Three lines of evidence were used in reconstructing the composition and distribution of plant communities: (1) the ecological literature, (2) a study of the proto-Euro-American phytogeography of the Sangamon River Valley by J. Johnson (1972), based on the records of the Federal Land Surveys in the Archives of the State of Illinois, and (3) such limited travellers' accounts as are available. The second of these is by far the most useful.

Both forest and prairie in Illinois can be divided into a number of communities on the basis of composition and topography. These in turn can be related to hydrology and soil distributions, which should influence the distribution of fauna, and ultimately of human communities.

Forests are divided into upland and floodplain or bottomland forests. Mitchell (1837: p. 16) described the different composition of these forests:

TABLE 3

Average and Extreme Dates of Frosts for Selected Stations in and near the Sangamon River Study Area, Through 1944

Station	No. Years	Average Date Last Frost	Average Date First Frost	Frost-Free Period
Decatur	51	Apr. 24	Oct. 18	177
Havana	51	Apr. 17	Oct. 18	184
Jacksonville	49	Apr. 23	Oct. 14	174
Lincoln	50	Apr. 28	Oct. 15	170
Pana	45	Apr. 24	Oct. 20	179
Springfield	65	Apr. 15	Oct. 19	187

(Data from Page, 1949: p. 128)

> The growth of the bottom lands consists of black walnut, ash of several species, hackberry elm [sic] (white, red and slippery), sugar-maple, honey-locust, buck-eye, catalpa, sycamore,

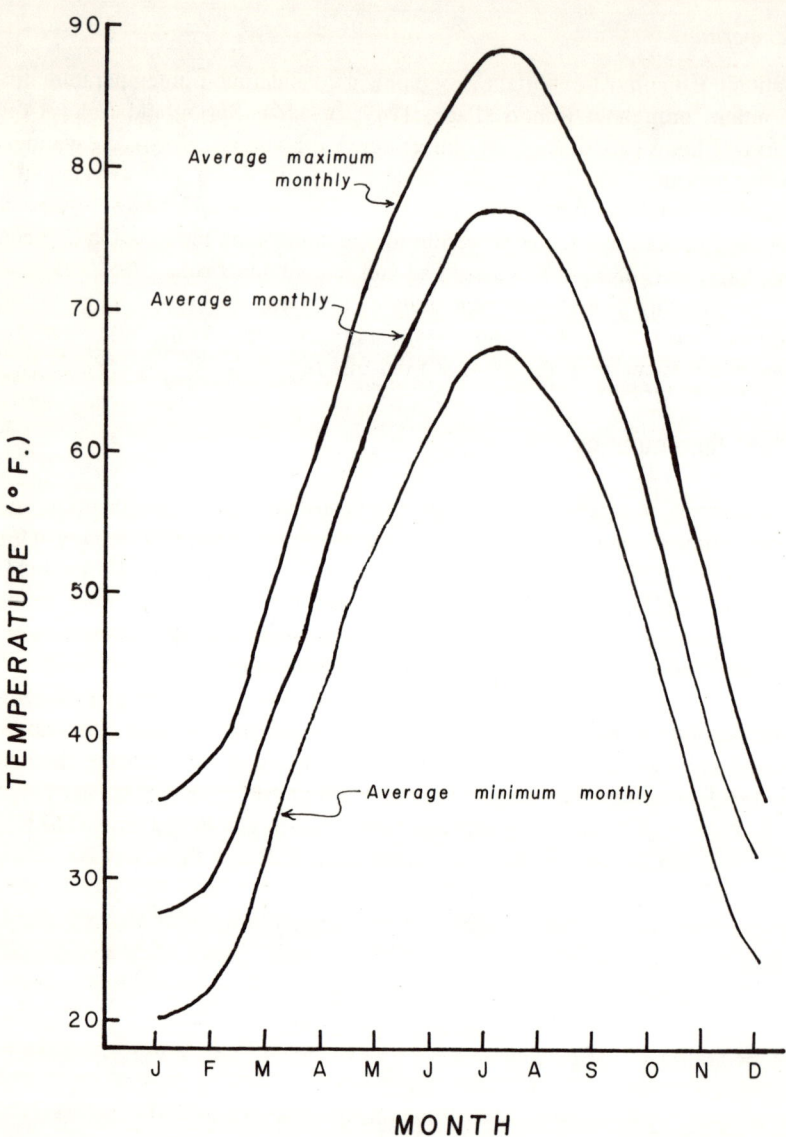

Fig. 9. Average Monthly, Average Minimum Monthly, and Average Maximum Monthly Temperatures, Springfield, 1880–1946.

cottonwood, pecan, hickory, mulberry; several oaks—as, overcup, burr-oak, swamp or water oak, white, red, or Spanish oak; and of the shrubbery are red-bud, papaw, grape-vine, dogwood, spice-bush, hazel, greenbrier, & c. Along the margins of the streams the sycamore and cottonwood often predominate, and attain to an amazing size. . . .

The uplands are covered with various species of oak, amongst which is the post-oak, a valuable and lasting timber for posts; white oak, black oak of several varieties, and the black jack, a dwarfish gnarled looking tree, good for nothing but fuel, for which it is equal to any tree we have: of hickory, both the shagbark and smoothbark, black walnut in some parts, white walnut or butternut, Lynn, cherry, and many of the species produced in the bottoms.

For the Sangamon drainage, the best records of the pre-modern vegetation are the records of the Federal Land Surveys. Instructions in force at the time (1818–1823) specified the following in regard to recording:

> You will be careful to note in your field *book* all the courses and distances you shall have run, the names and estimated diameters of all corner or bearing trees, and those trees which fall in your line called *station or line trees* notched as aforesaid, together with the courses and distances of the bearing trees from their respective corners, with the letters and numbers marked on them as aforesaid; also all rivers, creeks, springs and smaller streams of water, with their width, and the course they run in crossing the line of survey, and whether navigable, rapid, or mountainous; the kinds of timber and undergrowth with which the land may be covered, all swamps, ponds, stonequarries, coal beds, peat or turf grounds, uncommon, natural or artificial productions, such as mounds, precipices, caves, etc. all rapids, cascades or falls of water; minerals, ores, fossils, etc. the quality of the soil and the true situation of all mines, salt licks, salt springs and mill seats, which may come to your knowledge are particularly to be regarded and noticed in your field books (Tiffin 1815, emphasis in the original).

Also, the point at which the surveyor entered and left prairies, groves, forests, etc. was to be noted (Bourdo, 1956: p. 759).

Using the wealth of information contained on the vegetation and its distribution in the Sangamon River Valley, a reconstruction of the proto-Euro-American vegetation has been compiled by Johnson (1972). Johnson divided the drainage into four geographic divisions: Division One, the central portion of the drainage, including the South Fork of the Sangamon River; Division Two, the lower Sangamon from its mouth at the Illinois River to its junction with the Salt Creek; Division Three, the Salt Creek drainage; Division Four, the area around the junction of Salt Creek and the Sangamon River, a division transitional to the other three. A series of topographic zones were recognized: floodplain, terrace, valley slope, rolling slope, upland, and undefined riparian. (The designation "undefined riparian" refers to the Illinois River bottomlands at the mouth of the Sangamon.) All four divisions have floodplain, terrace, slope, and upland zones. Only the third has rolling slope, a designation created to account for the gently rolling Illinoian topography east of the Buffalo Hart moraine. In total, then, there are eighteen zones in the Sangamon drainage.

Vegetation within these zones reflects the varying topographic and microenvironmental conditions. Based on forest composition, Johnson derived eight macroforest groups based on the four most numerous species in each zone: (1) elm, hickory, black oak, sycamore; (2) black oak, elm, hickory, white oak; (3) sycamore, elm, black oak, ash. All three groups are found only on the floodplains. The other five macroforest groups are found only above floodplains: (4) black oak, hickory, white oak, blackjack; (5) black oak, white oak, hickory, walnut; (6) black oak, white oak, hickory, elm; (7) black oak, hickory, white oak, s oak (probably for shingle oak); (8) elm, black oak, hickory, walnut.

The question is often raised in archaeological uses of Federal Land Survey records of how well the Federal Land Survey maps can be construed to model prehistoric plant communities.

In other words, how closely do proto-Euro-American prairie-forest borders approximate the prehistoric boundaries, and how similar is the composition of the nineteenth century and prehistoric forests?

The question of correspondence in distribution of modern and prehistoric plant communities is important to a study employing site catchment techniques, and is a matter that must be evaluated for a region prior to each application (cf. Roper n.d.). The importance of climate in persistence of the Prairie Peninsula has already been noted. Except for minor fluctuations, however, climatic change was probably not a factor in forest-prairie distribution during the Woodland period. Wood (1976) has considered the effects of climatic change on forest distribution and concluded that Federal Land Survey records are most accurately used for the precise period of time under study here. Although King and Roper (1976: pp. 148–49) have suggested that a climatic fluctuation may have been responsible for a shift in observed floral remains at two Sangamon Valley Woodland sites, it would not have been necessary for major distribution changes to have occurred to account for the shifting availability of resources. Further, the character of a soil reflects the vegetation under which it is formed. Given adequate soil maps, it is therefore possible to compare similarity of prairie-forest borders and prairie soil-timber soil borders. In the Sangamon River drainage, the correspondence is very high. Forests invading prairie soils comprise most exceptions.

The question of correspondence of forest composition is more difficult to evaluate. Grüger's (1972) pollen studies in Fayette County suggest the presence of an oak-hickory forest at least since the close of the Wisconsinan. Similarly, pollen records from Minnesota and Ohio also show a sudden increase in oak and hickory after the close of the Pleistocene (Wright 1968: pp. 83–86). Floral remains from the Koster site in the Illinois River Valley indicate the use of oak-hickory deciduous forest products from at least Horizon 11, dated at around 5100 B.C. (Asch, Ford, and Asch 1972). Thus, there is no reason to doubt that forests in central Illinois in Woodland times were oak-hickory forests. Floral remains from Woodland sites also reflect utilization of oak-hickory forest products. For example, at the Eilers and Griffie sites, both Woodland sites in the Sangamon River Valley (11Cs^{v}20 and 11Mn^{v}94), floral remains include black walnut, hazelnut, acorn, hickory, hackberry, persimmon, wild plum, and black locust (King and Roper, 1976: p. 145). Thus, we can assume a correspondence of general forest composition.

If major distributional differences between nineteenth century and aboriginal forest-prairie distributions are ruled out, and general compositional similarity of forest is assumed, the reconstruction of early nineteenth century vegetation of the Sangamon River drainage (J. Johnson 1972) seems to provide the best available model of resource availability for study of prehistoric settlement distribution.

Analysis of Land Survey Data

Since local conditions of topography, soil, and hydrology affect the distribution of forest communities, whether nineteenth century or time-of-Christ forests, it is useful to examine the nineteenth century composition of the forests and the distribution and relative frequencies of the various species recorded in the land surveys. For this analysis, principal components analysis was performed. The input data consisted of the frequencies of species in each of the eighteen topographic zones defined by Johnson (1972). Of the 52 species listed in the land surveys for this area, only 37 occur at corner points. For the purposes of this analysis, the 12 numerically dominant species were used: white oak, black oak, hickory, elm, black walnut, s oak, hackberry, ash, maple, pin oak, sycamore, and blackjack oak. The other 25 species were totalled into a thirteenth variable called "other." In 12 of 18 cases, this category included less than 10% of the total forested corner recording points in the zone, and of the 6 cases over 10%, 5 of these had total sample sizes of under 100. Frequencies are listed in Table 4.

Program FACTOR (Veldman 1967) was employed for principal components analysis with varimax rotation of the principal components. The varimax rotated loadings are listed in Table 5 and displayed as histograms in Fig. 10. Four factors were retained and interpreted, collectively accounting for 84.3% of the rotated variance. The first rotated factor accounts for 41.7% of the variance and probably represents the general oak-hickory forest which characterizes this portion of central Illinois (Shelford, 1963: p. 57; Braun, 1950: p. 185). Black walnut, white oak, hickory, elm, hackberry, "other," and pin oak all have loadings of 0.69 or greater on this factor and tend to occur together in topographic zones.

The second factor represents bottomland forest. Maple has the highest loading, followed by ash. Interpretation of this factor with the aid of the factor scores, i.e., the correlations of the cases with the factors (Table 6) indicate that it is describing the undefined riparian zone at the confluence of the Sangamon and Illinois Rivers.

Factor III shows high loadings for blackjack oak and black oak. Most other species load very low on this factor. Blackjack is an indicator of dry soil (Harlow, 1957: p. 164), a condition also tolerated by black oak (Harlow, 1957: p. 159). It would thus seem reasonable to label this factor as representative of a dry variant of the oak-hickory forest.

The fourth factor is another bottomland forest factor. Sycamore dominates the factor, followed in order by ash, hackberry, and elm.

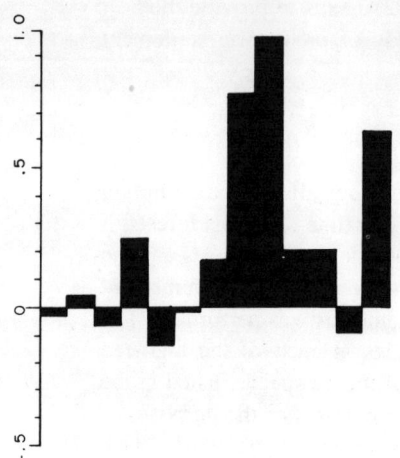
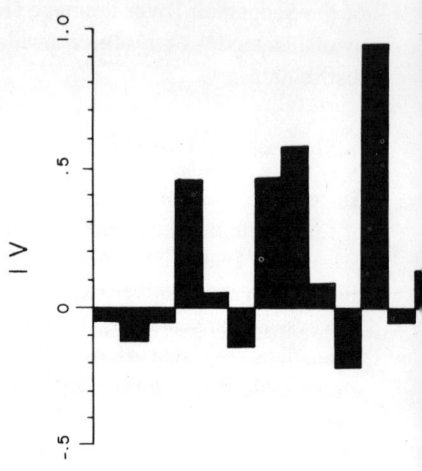
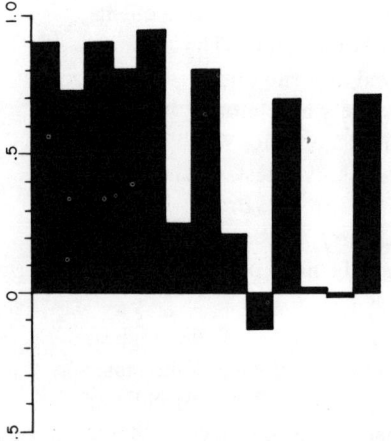
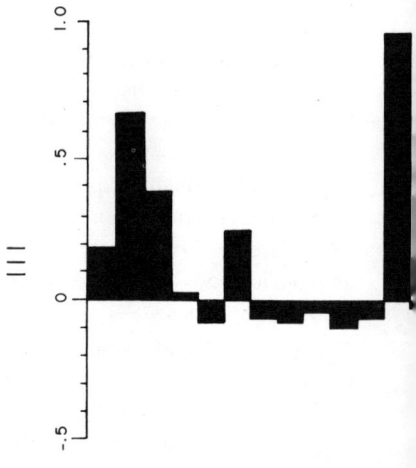

SETTLEMENT PATTERN MODELS IN CENTRAL ILLINOIS 53

TABLE 4
Frequencies of Selected Species

Zones	White Oak	Black Oak	Hickory	Elm	Black Walnut	S Oak	Hackberry	Ash	Maple	Pin Oak	Sycamore	Blackjack	Other	Total
Div 1 Bottomland	11	18	22	43	5	0	6	9	7	2	13	0	15	151
Div 1 Terrace	2	5	5	6	5	0	3	0	0	3	0	0	4	33
Div 1 Slope	181	196	92	57	17	2	12	6	1	6	2	3	47	622
Div 1 Upland	29	79	57	13	6	0	2	2	0	8	0	1	6	203
Div 2 Bottomland	8	19	10	12	3	0	0	7	6	0	3	2	13	83
Div 2 Terrace	11	118	16	2	0	0	0	1	1	0	0	28	2	179
Div 2 Slope	86	161	61	13	6	6	1	1	0	0	1	30	10	376
Div 2 Upland	4	39	18	2	2	0	0	0	0	0	0	5	0	70
Div 2 Illinois Riverine	3	34	3	15	0	1	2	10	34	3	2	0	34	141
Div 3 Bottomland	4	7	1	10	2	1	5	7	8	0	13	0	9	57
Div 3 Terrace	3	9	3	1	1	2	4	1	0	0	0	0	1	22
Div 3 Slope	69	64	19	14	9	4	0	2	0	0	0	3	14	199
Div 3 Rolling Slope	12	7	9	4	6	2	0	2	0	0	0	0	4	46
Div 3 Upland	6	9	8	0	2	3	0	0	0	3	0	0	0	31
Div 4 Bottomland	3	2	5	3	2	1	0	2	0	0	0	0	4	22
Div 4 Terrace	1	3	1	4	0	0	0	0	0	0	0	0	1	10
Div 4 Slope	61	39	8	5	4	0	0	0	0	0	0	0	8	125
Div 4 Upland	10	11	8	2	2	0	0	0	0	0	0	0	2	35

TABLE 5

Varimax Rotated Factor Loadings

Species	I	II	III	IV*	h^2
White Oak	0.89	−0.04	0.18	−0.04	.93
Black Oak	0.72	0.03	0.66	−0.11	.98
Hickory	0.89	−0.06	0.38	−0.05	.94
Elm	0.81	0.25	0.00	0.46	.94
Black Walnut	0.94	−0.13	−0.08	0.05	.95
S Oak	0.24	−0.01	0.24	−0.14	.84
Hackberry	0.80	0.17	−0.07	0.47	.92
Ash	0.21	0.75	−0.08	0.58	.95
Maple	−0.12	0.97	−0.04	0.09	.98
Pin Oak	0.69	0.20	−0.09	−0.21	.82
Sycamore	0.01	0.20	−0.05	0.95	.95
Blackjack	−0.00	−0.09	0.96	−0.06	.99
Other	0.72	0.63	−0.02	0.14	.95
% variance	41.7	16.3	12.5	13.7	
Cum % variance	41.7	58.0	70.5	84.2	

(*Factor IV is reflected)

TABLE 6

Varimax Rotated Factor Scores

Zones	I	II	III	IV*
Div 1 Bottomland	0.28	0.19	−0.18	2.82
Div 1 Terrace	0.04	−0.59	−0.72	−0.44
Div 1 Slope	3.62	0.21	−0.08	0.23
Div 1 Upland	1.06	−0.27	0.19	−1.17
Div 2 Bottomland	−0.47	0.61	−0.13	0.44
Div 2 Terrace	−0.78	−0.22	2.81	−0.09
Div 2 Slope	0.39	−0.21	2.59	−0.16
Div 2 Upland	−0.51	−0.62	0.31	−0.30
Div 2 Illinois Riverine	−0.43	3.90	−0.15	−0.85
Div 3 Bottomland	−0.62	0.19	−0.21	2.45
Div 3 Terrace	−0.60	−0.37	−0.54	−0.27
Div 3 Slope	0.46	−0.21	−0.66	−0.36
Div 3 Rolling Slope	−0.27	−0.39	−0.83	−0.29
Div 3 Upland	−0.31	−0.31	−0.64	−0.86
Div 4 Bottomland	−0.58	−0.32	−0.53	−0.08
Div 4 Terrace	−0.70	−0.51	−0.37	−0.28
Div 4 Slope	−0.08	−0.52	−0.46	−0.46
Div 4 Upland	−0.51	−0.57	−0.40	−0.34

(*Factor IV is reflected)

Floodplain Forest. These factors are easily interpreted in light of what is already known of forest compositions in Illinois. Telford's (1926) forest survey of Illinois recognized three types of bottomland forest, two of which are applicable to central Illinois. He distinguishes a "mixed hardwoods of the main stream" type and a "mixed hardwoods of secondary streams" type (Telford,

1926: p. 9). Telford notes (1926: p. 66) that the division between these two is based upon flood conditions, the main streams having floodplains inundated for a longer portion of the year. Commenting on bottomland compositions of these two types of forests, Telford (1926: p. 16, 31) notes the following:

> Certain bottomland species which are not sensitive to excessive moisture, such as elm, soft maples, and sycamore, may be found well represented in each type; others, such as pecan, are naturally adjusted to protracted flood conditions, and are limited to the main bottoms; while others, such as black walnut, tulip, and basswood, do not grow well under conditions of protracted flooding, and are more characteristic of the bottoms of the secondary streams.
>
> It [secondary stream floodplain type] is a type intermediate between the association of the flood-plains of the large rivers and the upland types; and in general more nearly conforms to the sandy loam associations of the upland hardwood type than to any other. Such characteristically bottomland species as river birch, cottonwood, sycamore, and silver maple are associated with such typically upland species as basswood, hard maple, tulip-poplar, and red oak; or certain species common to both bottomland and upland, such as elm, hackberry, and honey locust, grow best on these well-drained bottoms.

Examining factor scores for factors II and IV in light of Telford's discussion is interesting. Factor II attains its highest scores in the undefined riparian, i.e., Illinois River bottomlands area, while Division 2, lower Sangamon floodplain, is second. It will be remembered that this factor had high loadings on maple, ash and "other." Other is a category which includes such species as pecan, which occurred in low frequency. Factor II attains its highest scores in the floodplain of Johnson's Division 1 and Division 3. Both of these divisions are upriver from the Salt Creek-Sangamon River confluence, in the area Telford considers as having better drained soils. It is interesting to note then that elm and hackberry, two of the species common to both upland and bottomland, are important in describing this fourth factor. This would seem to reaffirm Telford's assessment of this secondary stream floodplain type as being intermediate between a main river floodplain type and an upland type, and is further supported by the position of the factor scores of the Division 1 slope on factor II and of Division 2 bottomland factor IV. Both of these cases show a slight tendency in the direction of the factor, even though their highest scores are on other factors.

In summary, the factor analysis for the floodplain of the Federal Land Survey data indicates that the forest composition of the floodplains in the early nineteenth century fits Telford's description of bottomland forests in Illinois, and reflects changing hydrographic conditions as one moves up the Sangamon from its confluence with the Illinois. The topographic, hydrographic, and soil conditions leading to this difference will be examined shortly.

Upland Forest. In the Prairie Peninsula and in Illinois in general, a number of types of upland forest are distinguished. These are generally related to soil and topography (Braun, 1950: p. 189). For Illinois, Telford (1926: pp. 9, 54) distinguished several types of upland forest, of which two are applicable to the Sangamon River study area: scrub oak, and upland hardwood, subtype oak-hickory.

The first factor corresponds quite closely to Telford's upland hardwood subtype oak-hickory forest. He describes it thus:

> These oak-hickory stands are usually even-aged, and occur as narrow strips along the slopes and as isolated wood-lots. Shingle oak may occur, but the commonest tree in the central region is black oak; . . . (Telford, 1926: p. 55).

Indeed, although white oak correlates more highly than black oak with the first factor, black oak is always more frequent than white oak in the zones that have high scores on this factor (Table 4). Telford (1926: p. 55) also notes that in the oak-hickory forests in the central and northern parts of the state, oak and hickory often make up over 90% of the stand. This extreme is approached by the trees sampled in the Federal Land Surveys. For example, in Division 1 slopes, oak-hickory account for 77% of the witness trees, and for 86% on the uplands in the same division; in Division 4 slopes, oak and hickory together account for 86% of the witness trees. The high loadings of other species on the first factor is undoubtedly due to the fact that these species, although small in percent anywhere, occur in the greatest numbers in the upland forests covering these terrace and above landforms.

Factor III is a good reflector of the conditions Telford (1926: p. 37) describes as scrub oak forest. He notes that "of the trees native to the sand areas, black oak (*Q. velutina*) is the commonest. In the southern areas black-jack oak (*Q. marilandica*) is common, . . ." (While the Sangamon River area is not in southern Illinois, the scrub oak forest that Telford maps for Mason County is the southernmost area of the scrub oak forest type.) Again, while black oak is the most common oak in these stands, blackjack oak is found almost exclusively, for the Sangamon Valley, in these stands. Forests of this type are present today in the Sangamon Valley as a recent ecological summary of the area shows:

> Upland areas of light-colored, well drained soil types are commonly dominated by species of oak and hickory. Within this broad vegetation type, several diverse associations can be recognized in the Sangamon River basin. In the dry sandy soil of the western portion of the basin, blackjack oak and post oak are the dominant tree species. The rich woods of the eastern portion, on the other hand, are dominated by white oak and black oak in their more xeric phases and by red oak, sugar maple, and basswood in more mesic phases (Jones and Bell, 1974: p. 4).

In summary, upland forest associations revealed by principal components analysis of the Federal Land Surveys data have distinguished the same two upland forest types in the early nineteenth century as were present in the early twentieth century (Telford 1926) and at present (Jones and Bell 1974). These different types of forest are indicated on the general vegetation distribution map (Fig. 11). The two different forest types in the uplands (a term here including

SETTLEMENT PATTERN MODELS IN CENTRAL ILLINOIS 57

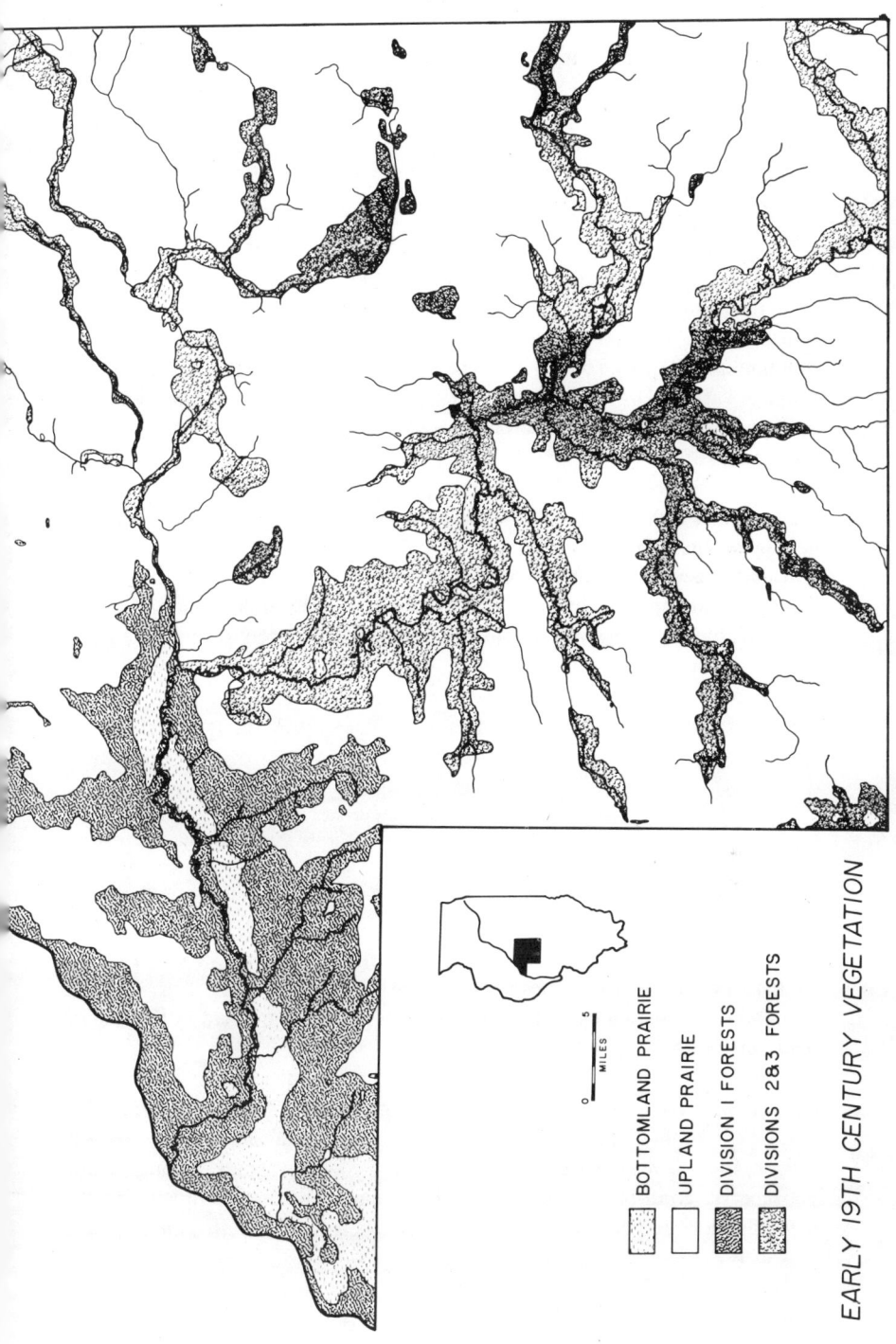

Fig. 11. Distribution of Forests and Prairies in the Sangamon Valley, Early Nineteenth Century.

not only true uplands, but also terraces and slopes) are distinguished from one another by soil, topography and drainage conditions. Although it is perhaps risky to assume too close a correlation between early nineteenth century and aboriginal forest compositions, it seems reasonable that some of the underlying conditions influencing the distribution of the different forest types in historic times were also reflected in the forests present in Woodland times.

Undergrowth

Unfortunately, the detail the surveyors put into listing the undergrowth did not match that of the forests themselves. Although the surveyors' instructions require them to list undergrowth (Tiffin 1815), these instructions do not mention the detail with which it is to be recorded. Consequently, there is a wide range of variation from surveyor to surveyor on the care expended in describing undergrowth while seasonal variation probably also affected what species were recognizable and recorded. The best that can be done with the land survey records, therefore, is simply to list the species that were recorded, and supplement this list with such details as may be gleaned from travellers' accounts and ecological literature.

Table 7 lists undergrowth species specifically mentioned by the surveyors. This list is broken down by three of four divisions, and by floodplain and upland forest within the divisions. Seedlings of the species that constitute the canopy are also included in the undergrowth.

Accounts in the travellers' literature or ecology literature are scarce. In describing early Springfield, in Division 1, Enos (1909: p. 190) writes:

> This location was in the middle of a handsome undulating prairie nook, a mile in length east and west and a half mile north and south, thoroughly drained by never failing spring branches and bordered on the north and west by heavy timber and on the south by a number of beautiful groves of young forest trees, of pin oak, elm, cherry and hackberry, which were festooned with grape nuts, alders and blackberries, and encircled by millions of strawberry vines.

In an upland forest a little up the Sangamon from Division 1, Koelz (1936: p. 7) lists the following shrubs: coral-berry, gooseberry, sassafras, redbud, greenbriars, haws—a list not too different from those compiled by the federal land surveyors.

Jones and Bell's (1974: pp. 4, 3) recent summary of vascular plants of the Sangamon River basin lists the following as understory: red elm, hophornbeam, redbud, pawpaw, sassafras, climbers such as Virginia creeper, poison ivy, several species of grape, and shrub species among which gooseberry, coral-berry, and hazel are common. For the floodplain forests, they mention: red mulberry, red haw, elderberry, wahoo, bladdernut, and poison ivy.

The forests of Division 2, however, are of somewhat different character. In their evaluation of the forests, and the land that was "unfit for cultivation," the

TABLE 7

Undergrowth Species Listed by Land Surveyors

DIVISION 1		
Floodplain Forest		
Willow vines	Grape vines	Briars
Spice bush	Greenbriars	Plum bushes
Hazel vines	Sassafras	Crabthorn
Pawpaw		
Bottomland Prairie Groves		
Walnut	Ash	Plum
Crabapple	Vines	Hazel
Hackberry	Locust	Elm
Pricklie ash	Briar	
Upland Forest—slope and upland		
Hazel	Sassafras	Dogwood
Pricklie ash	Redbud	Haw
Locust	Spice bush	Grape
Black briars	Gooseberry	Plum
Crabapple	Greenbriar	Apple
DIVISION 2		
Bottomland		
Pawpaw	Briars	Nettles
Brush	Vines	Flags
Upland Forest		
Hazel	Vines	Red root
Briars	"Grass and weeds"	Grapes
DIVISION 3		
Bottomland Floodplain		
Pawpaw	Spice bush	Swamp ash
Swamp bushes	Vines	
Upland Forest—terrace, rolling slope, valley slope		
Hazel	Swamp willow	Vines
Plum	Briars	Onions
Sassafras	Pricklie ash	Brush

land surveyors frequently referred to the land as "thinly timbered," occasionally using the term "barrens" to describe the vegetation. Mitchell (1837: p. 15) describes barrens, a well recognized plant association, thus:

> This term is used in the west to designate a species of land which partakes, as it were, at once of the character of the forest and prairie. The surface is generally dry and more uneven than the prairies, and is covered with scattered oaks, interspersed at times with pine, hickory, and other forest trees, mostly of stunted and dwarfish size, . . . They rise from a grassy turf, seldom incumbered with brushwood, but not unfrequently broken by jungles of rich and gaudy flowering plants, and of dwarf sumach.

This mixed character, with little undergrowth of brush, seems to be noted by others. Gleason (1907: p. 173) remarks of the blackjack forest on the sand areas of Mason County that: "The underbrush consists mainly of young trees of hickory and the two oaks (black and blackjack) with occasional clumps of *Rhus aromatica* (fragrant sumac). Other shrubby species of less prominence occur."

Barrens are technically defined by ecologists as having more than one tree per acre, but less than half the total area covered by the tree canopy (Curtis 1959: p. 262). Zawacki and Hausfater (1969: p. 18) note that the characteristic structure of oak-hickory barrens in Illinois is an "opening surrounded by a strip of brush composed of seedling hazelnut (*Corylus americana* Walt.) and other species which extended the margin of the groves from 15 to 100 feet beyond the tree line proper." Note then in Table 7 that few species are listed for Division 2 forests. It is perhaps possible that this is not a reflection of a failure of the surveyors to give detail, but rather the lack of much forest undergrowth. Unfortunately, there is no way to evaluate the situation.

Prairie

The other major biome represented in the Sangamon River area is, of course, the prairie. The account of the prairie given here is neither long nor detailed, even though there is a vast literature on the subject. The major purpose of providing the summary is to survey the distribution and availability of the relatively few potential food resources.

Three types of prairies are recognized in the ecological literature: (1) "hill prairies" (Evers 1955), also known as "xeric prairies" (Curtis 1959); (2) the upland prairie which Curtis (1959: p. 276) refers to as "mesic prairie" and is the famous grassland that gives Illinois its nickname of the "Prairie State"; and (3) bottomland prairie. The composition of each is somewhat different.

Hill Prairie. Because of their small size and scarcity, the hill prairies are of little consequence for present purposes. They are isolated, occurring "on loess bluffs, on mounds, on steep, rocky slopes of glacial drift, or on any other steep slopes" (Evers, 1955: p. 367). In the study area, they occur only in Cass County, along the Sangamon River bluff line, and in Mason County.

Upland Prairie. These prairies occur on "flat or gently rolling land forms. The level sites are frequently on glacial outwash with a stratified and very porous subsoil of sand or gravel while the undulating sites may be on glacial till of recessional moraines or on residual or loessial soils on the rolling surfaces of dolomitic bedrock" (Curtis, 1959: p. 282). Thus, the flat to gently rolling Illinoian till plains of central Illinois with their deep loess deposits are preferred type of habitat for the upland prairie.

Upland prairies were an important factor in the European settlement of Illinois and probably also were important in prehistoric settlement. Their importance may come not so much from their composition, but from the fact that they presented something of an obstacle of virtually useless land to people without a steel plow.

Shelford (1963: p. 330) places the Prairie Peninsula within the tall-grass grassland of the Northern Temperate Grassland. The dominant plants of this grassland are: porcupine grass, prairie dropseed, little bluestem, side-oats grama, Junegrass, western wheatgrass, plains muhly, panic grass, and sedge (Shelford, 1963: p. 334). Seeds of some of these were occasionally eaten in the west, but none are recorded in eastern United States (Yanovsky 1936). Also present were a number of herbaceous plants with edible products. For upland prairie zones of the Lower Illinois Valley, Zawacki and Hausfater (1969: p. 16) list the following herbs: milkweed, butterfly-weed, love-grass, wild strawberry, yellow oxalis, and prairie clover. These are supplemented by three woody plants: hazelnut, smooth sumac, and common elder. This list could probably be somewhat expanded (F. B. King n.d.), but not to the point of making the prairie a very productive resource zone for human exploitation.

Bottomland Prairie. Floodplain prairies were perhaps more useful to the prehistoric inhabitants of Illinois. There are no studies specifically of the bottomland prairies of the Sangamon River Valley, and of course, the Federal Land Surveys do not record the species present in them. Therefore, a discussion of the resources in this zone must be projected from what is known of bottomland prairie elsewhere in Illinois. Basically, however, we find ourselves in the same position as Zawacki and Hausfater (1969: p. 41), who remark that: "The early surveyors did not record the vegetation of the *Floodplain Prairie*, requiring us to rely heavily on Turner's description of the area. Even so, Turner acknowledges the difficulty of any reconstruction of the *Floodplain Prairie*, . . ." From species lists provided by Turner (1934), Zawacki and Hausfater (1969: pp. 40–41) list four plants with possible economic use: sedge, marshelder, pinkweed, and blue vervain. In the absence of any evidence to the contrary, it will be presumed that the same plants were available in the Sangamon River Valley.

Summary of Vegetation

To summarize the vegetation of the Sangamon River Valley, it is apparent that the best information is for the arboreal constituents of the forests. Data are available in the original Federal Land Surveys, accounts by early travellers in Illinois, and the wealth of ecological literature. The nature of forest undergrowth is not as well documented. The Federal Land Surveys may be inconsistent from surveyor to surveyor as to the detail with which undergrowth is recorded, but travellers' accounts and the ecological literature are much less detailed. The result is a somewhat sketchy and minimal listing of available plants. It should be noted, however, that there is a degree of consistency among these various sources as to presence of certain species of undergrowth vegetation. The upland prairies have been sparsely treated, not for dearth of literature, but rather because of their relative unimportance as a source of food to prehistoric peoples. Floodplain prairies, probably more important to prehistoric peoples, are also sketchily treated, because of a lack of available literature.

Physiography

The physiography of the Sangamon River study area is largely shaped by events that took place during the Pleistocene. Although the area is underlain by bedrock of Pennsylvainian age, very little of this bedrock is exposed. Topography, soils, and drainage are all a product of glacial action. Of the four major glacial advances of the Pleistocene, two—the Kansan and Illinoian—covered the area. A third, the Wisconsinan, stopped just short of the area, but had a profound influence on the character of the river valleys because of the tremendous outwash deposits disgorged through the streams, and the thick loess accumulations in the uplands.

Both the Liman and Monican substages of the Illinoian advance completely covered the area, creating an extremely flat till plain (Willman and Frye, 1970: p. 27). These upland till plains were later blanketed with thick loess deposits during the Wisconsinan stage Woodfordian advance, which reached to the headwaters of the Sangamon system. Sixty-five to 75% of the loess in the uplands is Peoria loess, formed during Woodfordian times beyond the limits of the glacial advance. In the Sangamon River area, loess thickness varies from over 300 inches (about 8m) along the lower portions of the river and adjacent parts of the Illinois Valley, to 75–100 inches (1.9–2.5m) in southern Sangamon County and the middle of Christian County (Willman and Frye, 1970: pl. 3).

These flat upland till plains are the primary location of the upland prairie association. Soils on this landform thus reflect both the deep loess parent material, and the prairie grass cover. The Joy-Tama-Muscatine-Ipava-Sable soil association (Soil Association A; Fehrenbacher et al., 1967: p. 8) is found on these moderately sloping to nearly level areas. These soils are silty, moderately permeable, and dark in color, indicating development under prairie grass.

During the third, or Jubileean, substage of the Illinoian, the ice advanced to a position represented by the Buffalo Hart moraine which cuts across northwest Sangamon County, as well as portions of Mason, Logan, and Christian counties. The Sangamon River drainage system was probably formed during this advance. It has been suggested that during Jubileean times, a proglacial lake, Lake Williams, was formed. The outlet channel of Lake Williams became deeply entrenched and later developed into the present valley of the Sangamon River (Miller, 1973: pp. 1, 3).

Later, during the Woodfordian substage of the Wisconsinan stage, ice advanced to a position at the headwaters of the Sangamon drainage system. Melting of the glacier caused increased discharge into the Sangamon Valley, with resultant scouring of previous deposits in the middle and upper portions of the valley. Thus, Miller (1973: p. 28) in his study of the Quaternary history of the middle portion of the valley found no terraces of any age along this segment of the valley.

The lower segment of the river has a slightly different Quaternary history. An early Woodfordian advance to the position represented by the Bloomington moraine, near the present city of Bloomington, sent an immense fan-shaped outwash deposit down the Illinois River Valley—the Bloomington outwash (Wanless, 1957: p. 143). Subsequent Woodfordian advances sent lesser deposits down the valley, which had the effect not so much of deposition as of reworking the earlier Bloomington deposits. Four superimposed terraces rising as much as 80 feet above the floodplain were created by this reworking: the Manito, Havana, Bath, and Beardstown terraces (Wanless, 1957: p. 146). North of the Sangamon valley, most of Mason County is a part of the nearly 500 square mile (195 sq km) Illinois River terrace system created by Woodfordian glacial events. Subsequent to formation, winds reworked the sands of these glacial deposits, and dunes of the Parkland sand formation were created on the terraces (Wanless, 1957: p. 149; Willman and Frye, 1970: p. 35).

As would be expected, soils on these terraces are derived from sandy outwash deposits. Fehrenbacher et al. (1967: p. 29ff.) classify the soils on the Illinois River terraces as being of the Hagener-Ridgeville-Bloomfield-Alvin soil association (Soil Association X). These are sandy soils, moderately-rapidly to very-rapidly permeable. Their color varies, suggesting that native vegetation on this terrace system was mixed. In places, an upland prairie association prevailed, in others vegetation was the scrub oak forest, dominated by black oak and blackjack, described earlier.

On the south side of the Sangamon, directly across from the Mason County terrace system, the terraces are much less extensive. Only the Havana terrace extends farther upriver than the middle of Cass County. In the lowest portions of the valley, terraces are about two miles wide. Moving up the Sangamon valley, the Havana terrace gradually narrows and finally becomes discontinuous shortly before the junction of Salt Creek with the Sangamon River. However, unmodified Bloomington outwash deposits form an extensive wide terrace extending up the Salt Creek.

Unlike the terraces to the north of the Sangamon, those on the south side of the river do not have sand dunes. Aeolian deposition has, however, mantled the slopes with sand and created a few small patches of sand dunes on the bluffs (Wanless, 1957: p. 149), which are reflected in the soil and vegetation covering. The Havana terrace along the south side of the Sangamon and the unmodified Bloomington outwash terraces along Salt Creek are both covered by the bottomland prairie association noted earlier. The soils of this landform are of the Littleton-Proctor-Plano-Camden-Hurst-Ginat association (Soil Association W; Fehrenbacher et al., 1967: p. 26ff.). In general, these soils are developed from medium to fine textured water-deposited materials and range in color from light to dark. It might be noted, however, that most of the Littleton-Proctor-Plano-Camden-Hurst-Ginat soils in Cass and Menard counties are dark, which is to be expected given the high correlation of the terraces with bottomland prairie. Most are moderately permeable silt loams. Small portions of the Hagener-Ridgeville-Bloomfield-Alvin association (Soil Association X) also occur (Fig. 12), corresponding with the areas of sand accumulation.

The slopes and bluff crests in this portion of the valley are also covered with the scrub oak, black oak, blackjack forest type. The soil association is the

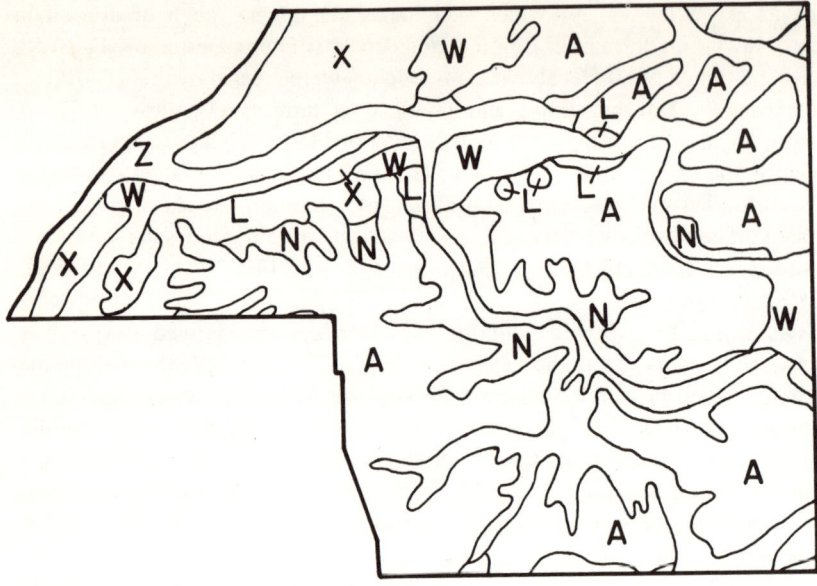

Fig. 12. Soil Associations in the Sangamon River Drainage (after Fehrenbacher et al., 1967; see text for identification of lettered associations).

Seaton-Fayette-Stronghurst association (Soil Association L; Fehrenbacher et al., 1967: pp. 16–17), developed in thick loess under forest or mixed forest-prairie conditions. Thus, the soils are light to moderately dark. Virtually all are silt loams, and most are moderately permeable.

The soil association on the slopes in the middle portions of the Sangamon Valley, as well as that of the South Fork, is the Clary-Clinton-Keomah association (Soil Association N; Fehrenbacher et al., 1967: pp. 18–19), an association similar to the preceeding. These soils are also developed from thick loess under forest or mixed forest-prairie vegetation. They too are all silt loams, usually with moderately slow permeability due to their somewhat heavier textured subsoil. The forests of this slope landform in this portion of the valley are Telford's (1926) oak-hickory upland forest type, described earlier.

The uppermost deposits of the stream floodplains are those of the Cahokia alluvium (Miller, 1973: p. 7). This alluvium began to accumulate as soon as the valleys were freed of ice and thus rests on previous glacial deposits (Willman and Frye, 1970: pp. 75–77; see also Miller, 1973: fig. 3–8 for cross sections of the Sangamon valley showing the position of the Cahokia alluvium on the Sangamon River floodplain). Soils on the floodplains are of the Lawson-Beacoup-Darwin-Haymond-Belknap association (Soil Association Z; Fehrenbacher et al., 1967: pp. 32–34). All are weakly developed soils, varying in texture, color, and natural drainage.

The soil association map of the Sangamon area (see Fig. 12) therefore reflects the Quaternary history of the drainage. More localized conditions of slope, drainage, soil texture, permeability, parent material, vegetation, and several other characteristics are reflected in the more detailed county soil survey maps.

Although detailed, the county soil maps vary in quality from county to county, due primarily to the fact that they have been published over a span of 62 years. Nevertheless, enough detail can be summarized from them to depict spatial variability in several classes of soil variables. The primary soil variable which will be used in this study is soil texture. Soils are classed by the proportions of the sizes of individual particles in the soil, i.e., clay, silt, and sand. These are ordered in terms of increasing proportions of coarse particles: clay, silty clay, sandy clay, silty clay loam, clay loam, sandy clay loam, silt, silt loam, loam, very fine sandy loam, fine sandy loam, sandy loam, and sand (Soil Survey Staff, 1951: pp. 205-13). The distribution of these soil texture classes varies over space. Each soil listed in "Soil Type Acreages for Illinois" (Runge, Tyler, and Carmer 1969) for the six-county area within the study area was classified using the county soil maps and "Soils of Illinois" (Fehrenbacher et al. 1967). The acreage of soils of each texture class were totaled, percentages calculated, and plotted by zone (Fig. 13). Definite distributional trends can be noted. While silt loams are by far the predominant soil types in each zone, the distribution of the remainder of the soils varies. Floodplains and upland prairies tend to have finer soils. Bottomland prairies and upland forests, usually associated with terraces and valley slopes, respectively, tend toward coarser soils such as sandy loams and sands.

Drainage

Surface water resources are also of importance in the study of settlement patterns. Of course, presence of water is important for a number of reasons, such as providing drinking water for both man and the animals he hunts, for providing avenues for transportation, and as a resource zone in its own right, providing fish, mussels, and some species of turtles and mammals. But not all surface water resources are of equal value for all purposes. The main channel of the Sangamon River is quite a different thing from one of its smallest headwater feeder streams. Both may provide drinking water, but both will not be equal in terms of resources they may provide, nor in terms of their relations to the surrounding terrain, nor even in the reliability of their availability.

Using this difference in a multivariate study requires quantitative description of the drainage. Such a technique is available in the stream ranking system used by quantitative geomorphologists, and recently introduced into the archaeological literature by Weide and Weide (1973). Such a technique not only allows systematic differentiation of different magnitudes of streams, but also relates the drainage network to the terrain through a series of stream laws specifying relations among the streams and basin areas, slopes, etc. (see Strahler 1964; Leopold, Wolman, and Miller, 1964; Leopold, 1974: pp. 63-67). Weide and

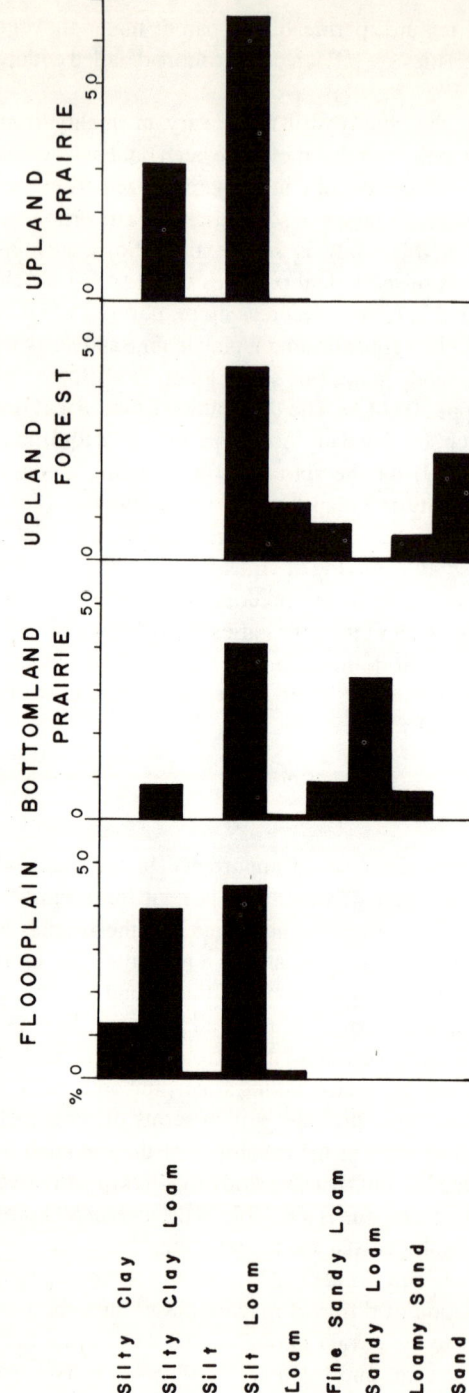

Fig. 13. Soil Texture in Relation to Vegetation Zones.

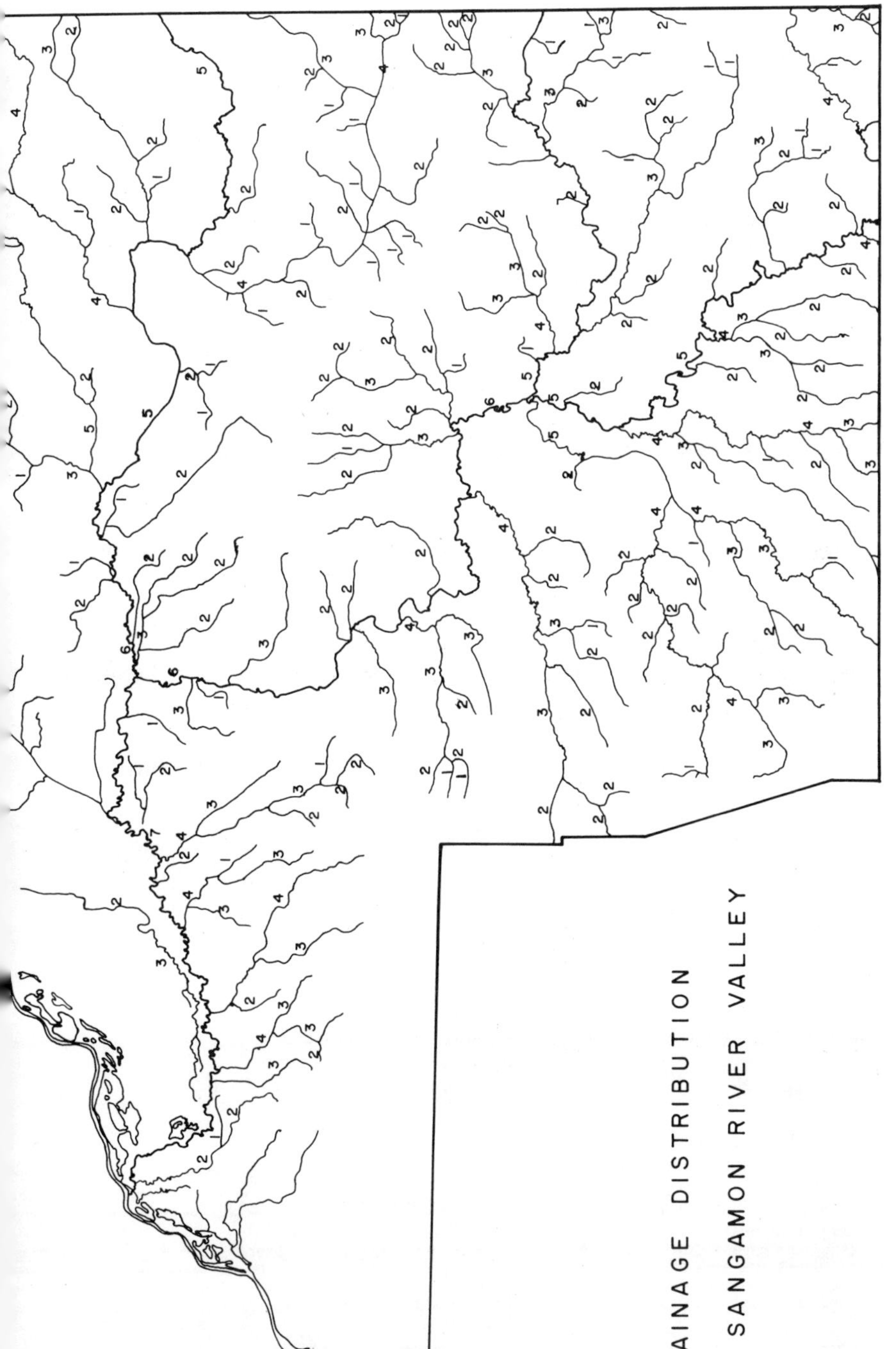

SETTLEMENT PATTERN MODELS IN CENTRAL ILLINOIS   67

Fig. 14. Drainage Ranks of Major Streams.

DRAINAGE DISTRIBUTION
SANGAMON RIVER VALLEY

Weide (1973) have discussed some of the anthropological implications of using this system.

A stream with no tributaries is designated as a stream of the first order. When two first order streams join, a second order stream is created, when two second order streams join, a third order stream is created, etc. Note, however, that a stream of lower order joins a higher order stream with no change in the rank of either stream. Note also that the system is dependent upon the scale of the map upon which the ranking is carried out. Fig. 14 summarizes the ranking of the Sangamon River drainage, and represents the spatial distribution of streams of the various ranks. (Note: not all streams are shown.)

Fauna

The data analyzed in the present study were derived from maps of topography, drainage, soil, and vegetation. If it were possible to plot a faunal map in the same way as a vegetation or soil map, it would be included here; but, alas, animals do not stay put. Yet human interaction with the natural environment includes close interaction with the faunal as well as the floral communities and for this reason, fauna cannot be ignored.

Fortunately many species show preferences for specific types of habitat, be that forest, prairie, or whatever. These preferences can be used to discuss, at least simplistically, the probable distribution of animals in the Sangamon River area.

Table 8 lists potentially available species and their preferred habitats.

TABLE 8

Potentially Available Animal Species, with Habitats

Species	Habitat
MAMMALS:	
Opossum	woodlands near streams, not too active in winter, nocturnal
Eastern mole	meadows, open woodlands, stream banks
Short-tailed shrew	forest edge, meadow, nocturnal
Least shrew	weedy fields, brush
Black bear	wooded and swampy areas, inactive in winter
Racoon	wooded river bottoms, nocturnal, not too active in winter
Long-tailed weasel	brushland, woodland
Mink	along streams and lakes, nocturnal
River otter	along streams and lakes, nocturnal
Striped skunk	edge of woods, nocturnal
Badger	open country, prairie, nocturnal, not too active in winter

TABLE 8 (Continued)

Species	Habitat
Red fox	semi-open woodlands, forest edge, nocturnal
Gray fox	forest, river bottom and bluffs, nocturnal
Coyote	open country, nocturnal
Timber wolf (gray wolf)	(not listed)
Bobcat	wooded sections, especially timbered bluffs and slopes
Woodchuck	forest edge, inactive in winter
Thirteen-lined ground squirrel	grassy area, hibernates in winter
Franklin's ground squirrel	grassy areas, hibernates in winter
Eastern chipmunk	brushy woods, wooded bluffs, hibernates
Eastern gray squirrel	wooded streams, heavy timber
Eastern fox squirrel	woods with openings
Southern flying squirrel	heavily wooded areas, nocturnal
Plains pocket gopher	open lands, prairie
Beaver	in and along streams, rivers, marshes
Western harvest mouse	prairie
Deer mouse	prairie
White-footed mouse	forests, brushlands, river bottoms
Prairie vole	prairie
Pine vole	woods
Muskrat	rivers, streams, etc., near water
Meadow jumping mouse	bank of stream or pond, open grassy area, nocturnal, undergoes prolonged winter sleep
Eastern cottontail	forest edge, dry bottomlands
Elk (wapiti)	wooded streams, open woods
White-tailed deer	woods and thickets, forest edge

AMPHIBIANS AND REPTILES:

Small-mouthed salamander	woodland, prairie, nocturnal
American toad	probably prairie
Fowler's toad	"all suitable habitats"
Western chorus frog	temporary pools and ditches
Northern leopard frog	streams, ponds, lakes
Snapping turtle	aquatic, stream or lake bottom, muddy
Stinkpot turtle	aquatic, mud bottoms of ponds and streams
Illinois mud turtle	silty bottoms of ponds and sloughs
Blanding's turtle	aquatic
Ornate box turtle	prairie
Midland painted turtle	aquatic
Red-eared turtle	aquatic
Smooth soft-shell turtle	aquatic, clean sand, stream margin

TABLE 8 (Continued)

Species	Habitat
Eastern spiny soft-shell turtle	aquatic, clean sand, stream margin
BIRDS:	
Turkey	forest
Prairie chicken	prairie
Sandhill crane	prairie
Wood duck	aquatic, March-November
Hooded merganser	aquatic, June-October
Mallard	aquatic, November-March
Black duck	aquatic, November-March
Canada goose	aquatic, October-March
Lesser scaup	aquatic, November-April
Pintail	aquatic, October-March
Ringneck	aquatic, November-March
Canvasback	aquatic, November-March
Blue/Snow goose	aquatic, October-April
Bufflehead	aquatic, November-December, February-March
Gadwall	aquatic, October-November, March-April
Baldpate	aquatic, September-October March-April
Shoveler	aquatic, November-December, March-April
Redhead	aquatic, November-December, February-March
Coot	aquatic, November-December, March-April
Green-winged teal	aquatic, October-December, March-April
Blue-winged teal	aquatic, September-November, March-April
Ruddy duck	aquatic, October-November, March-April
FISHES:	all aquatic
Long-nosed gar	aquatic
Short-nosed gar	aquatic
Bowfin	aquatic
Gizard-shad	aquatic
Channel catfish	aquatic
Yellow bullhead	aquatic
Common bullhead	aquatic
Black bullhead	aquatic
Mud-cat	aquatic
Stonecat	aquatic
Tadpole cat	aquatic
Brindled stonecat	aquatic
Big-mouthed buffalo	aquatic
Small-mouthed buffalo	aquatic
River carp	aquatic
Blunt-nosed carp	aquatic
Quillback carp	aquatic
Common sucker	aquatic

TABLE 8 (Continued)

Species	Habitat
Stoneroller	aquatic
Chub-sucker	aquatic
Spotted sucker	aquatic
White-nosed sucker	aquatic
Common red-horse	aquatic
Short-headed red-horse	aquatic
Silvery minnow	aquatic
Black-headed minnow	aquatic
Blunt-nosed minnow	aquatic
Golden shiner	aquatic
Bullhead minnow	aquatic
Spot-tailed minnow	aquatic
Redfin	aquatic
Silverfin	aquatic
Common shiner	aquatic
Shiner	aquatic
Sucker-mouth	aquatic
Spotted shiner	aquatic
Silver chub	aquatic
Storer's chub	aquatic
River chub	aquatic
Striped top-minnow	aquatic
Common top-minnow	aquatic
Trout-perch	aquatic
Pirate perch	aquatic
White crappie	aquatic
Black crappie	aquatic
Rock bass	aquatic
Warmouth	aquatic
Green sunfish	aquatic
Long-eared sunfish	aquatic
Orange-spotted sunfish	aquatic
Bluegill	aquatic
Pumpkinseed	aquatic
Small-mouthed bass	aquatic
Large-mouthed bass	aquatic
Pike-perch	aquatic
Sauger	aquatic
Yellow perch	aquatic
Black-sided darter	aquatic
Green-sided darter	aquatic
Sand darter	aquatic
Banded darter	aquatic
Rainbow darter	aquatic
Fantailed darter	aquatic
White bass	aquatic
Yellow bass	aquatic
Fresh-water drum	aquatic

Mammals

The list of mammals is summarized from the *Fieldbook of Illinois Mammals* (Hoffmeister and Mohr 1972), and excludes bats (*Chiroptera*) and such introduced species as the Norway rat and the house mouse. Habitat and habit listings are supplemented by the more complete discussions in Schwartz and Schwartz (1959).

The major mammals of the Sangamon floodplain are mink, muskrat, racoon, cottontail, skunk, flying squirrel, white-footed mouse, and weasel (Shelford, 1963: pp. 114–17). Koelz (1936: p. 35) noted that the diversity of species of mammals on the floodplain was not as great as on the slopes, but found that mammals were more abundant on the floodplain.

Shelford (1963: p. 59) found that few mammals have large populations in the deciduous forest. Bear and gray fox occur in low numbers, gray squirrels are somewhat more abundant. Fox squirrels, racoons, opossums, and striped skunks all range through the woods but prefer other habitats.

Similarly, the prairies were the preferred habitat of a few mammals present in Illinois. The western harvest mouse, deer mouse, prairie vole, and thirteen-lined ground squirrel had fairly large populations in a prairie area studied in Kansas (Shelford, 1963: p. 336), but none of these species (nor several others that may also have been present in the Illinois prairies) are particularly meaty. Some believe the elk was once at home on the prairies, as well as in open woods (Hoffmeister and Mohr, 1972: p. 201). Bison are known to have been in Illinois in small numbers, but it is probable that they appeared no earlier than late prehistoric times (J. W. Griffin and Wray 1945). They do not appear in archaeological faunal assemblages as anything other than an occasional fragment prior to Mississippian, and then are not common (J. W. Griffin and Wray 1945). Badgers were apparently not common, and coyotes and gray wolfs make use of other habitats.

Certainly the most prolific area for mammals is the forest edge. Shelford (1963: pp. 314–15) lists cottontails, elk, white-tailed deer, racoon, red fox, coyote, striped skunk, meadow jumping mouse, and Franklin's ground squirrel as important animals in the forest edge. Several of these are large, meaty animals and are known to have been important prehistorically. Deer in particular has been a meat staple throughout Illinois prehistory, while the cottontail and racoon are also regular constituents of archaeological faunal assemblages.

Amphibians and Reptiles

Amphibians and reptiles are summarized from Philip W. Smith's *Amphibians and Reptiles of Illinois* (1961). Only species whose ranges include all or part of the Sangamon River drainage are included (omitting snakes). Except for salamanders, toads, and box turtles, which are all prairie inhabitants, all species listed are aquatic.

Birds

Birds are abundant and many species live in central Illinois. Most of these are not included in Table 8. Lists can be found in Koelz (1936: pp. 55–60) in which the species are listed by zone and season.

One of the most important forest birds was the wild turkey, which may have had its largest populations in the oak-hickory forest (Shelford, 1963: p. 59). In addition, Cleland (1966: p. 245) lists the broad-winged hawk, long-eared owl, tanager, nuthatch, and several species of woodpecker as preferring a forest edge habitat.

Of the prairie birds, the prairie chicken and sandhill crane were among the species most important to prehistoric inhabitants. In addition to these species, the meadowlark, dickcissel, and horned lark (Shelford 1963: p. 336), short-eared owls, several curlews, and hawks (Cleland 1966: p. 245) also show a preference for grasslands.

As with mammals, the diversity of forest-edge birds is also high. Shelford (1963: pp. 315–16) lists 20 forest edge species, Cleland (1966: p. 245) lists 17, although the lists overlap. Many are small birds such as sparrows, cardinals, and crows.

Other than turkey, prairie chicken, and sandhill crane, the most important bird species are the migratory waterfowl (see e.g., faunal lists in Munson, Parmalee, and Yarnell 1971; or Parmalee, Paloumpis, and Wilson 1972). The Sangamon River study area is near the Great Mississippi Flyway. Within this flyway, the Mississippi River Corridor has the greatest density of dabbling ducks (mallards, pintails, baldpates, green-winged teals, gadwalls, shovelers) of any waterfowl migration corridor east of the Rockies (Bellrose, 1968: p. 8). Diving ducks (lesser scaup, ringneck, canvasback) occur in far smaller numbers (Bellrose, 1968: p. 11). Several species of geese are also found in the flyway.

Because of their migration patterns, seasonal availability of waterfowl is variable. B. D. Smith (1974: p. 282) has summarized the seasonal availability of 22 species of waterfowl in the central portion of the flyway. The list in Table 8 draws on Smith's summary.

Fish and Mussels

Even in these modern times of water pollution, there are many species of fish in the Sangamon River system (P. W. Smith, 1971: p. 6). The list of fishes in Table 8 is drawn from Forbes and Richardson (1920). Fish are known to have made significant contributions to the diet of Illinois Woodland populations (see e.g., Parmalee, Paloumpis and Wilson 1972 for an analysis of the faunal remains from the Apple Creek site in Greene County, where fish made up nearly 40% of the estimated meat). Many species are known to have been taken, at least in the Illinois River Valley, possibly a result of harvesting fish from backwater ponds and sloughs (Parmalee, Paloumpis and Wilson, 1972: p. 18).

Finally, the aquatic habitat provided large quantities of freshwater mussels

Although abundant at some Woodland sites, mussels have low food value and it has been proposed that they never provided more than a dietary supplement (Parmalee and Klippel, 1974: p. 432). Although each species has its own habitat requirements, rivers and streams have a larger mussel population than lakes (Parmalee, 1967: p. 13).

Seasonal Variability

Except for the fauna, the foregoing discussion has concentrated on the spatial distribution of resources but has neglected the seasonal or temporal variability.

Plants

A list of the potentially available food plants has been compiled by Frances B. King (n.d.) based on Jones and Bell (1974). Each species is listed by habitat(s), season(s), part(s) used, with references documenting use in early historic times in the Great Lakes area. Jones and Bell (1974) and King (n.d.) use a zonal division slightly different from the one used by Johnson (1972) adopted here. They use a six-fold division: floodplain forest, upland forest, open woodland, prairie, marshes/aquatic habitats, and disturbed ground. The first two correspond to the floodplain forest and upland forest categories here; open woodland refers to the "barrens" (not delineated on Johnson's maps); prairie evidently includes both upland and bottomland prairie, although Jones and Bell are not clear on this; marshes/aquatic habitat is a category entirely unaccounted for vegetationally in the Federal Land Surveys; and disturbed ground is of course also unaccounted for. It should be noted, however, that disturbed ground is a potentially very useful category. While we cannot assess the amount of disturbed ground available to the prehistoric inhabitants of the Sangamon, we can consider the possibility that a site itself, and its surrounding biodeterioration zone, might provide the habitat for disturbed ground plant communities.

Seasonal availability of edible plant products is summarized in Fig. 15. The bars represent counts of species in each habitat, season, and part. Thus, if a species is available at several times of the year in several habitats, and/or several parts were used, it is counted each time. Note also that this is based upon simple counts with no attempt to weight the counts by the relative importance or abundance of the product. Thus, for example, hickory nuts (which were an important part of the diet of the Woodland inhabitants of central Illinois) and pollen (of which only a few species may have been used and which did not form an important part of the diet) are each weighted the same in this graph.

Hydrology

Another seasonal factor in selecting sites is hydrological conditions, particularly flooding. Any place flooded for part of the year is obviously uninhabitable at that time.

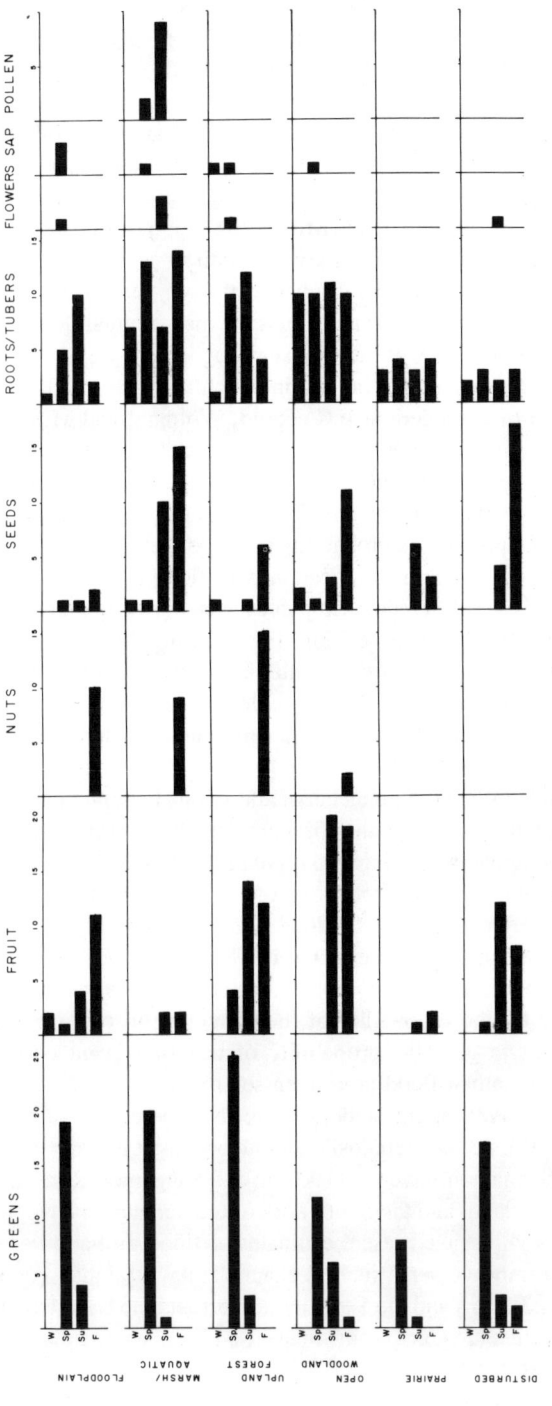

Fig. 15. Seasonal and Spatial Availability of Plant Foods.

Flooding, defined as a stream flow in excess of bank-full, is a normal, expected characteristic of rivers (Leopold, 1974: p.73). The largest flood in each year is called the annual flood. The magnitude of this flood varies from year to year. Hydrologists treat the variation of this magnitude as a random variable, and study it as a probability problem. All annual floods may thus be described in terms of a probability distribution, on the premise that floods occurring during any given period of time are a sample of an indefinitely large population (Leopold, Wolman, and Miller, 1964: p. 63). The probability of the annual flood taking place during a given month or season can thus be calculated. Tabulation of the highest discharge of each year at each station, and calculation of the mean of this series yields the mean annual flood. Plotting the position of each of these events on semi-log paper yields the recurrence interval, i.e., the average interval within which a flood of a given magnitude will be equalled or exceeded once (Leopold, Wolman, and Miller, 1964: pp. 65–66). Further, measurements of gage height or stage of annual floods are available. The gage height can, of course, be converted into a height above mean sea level of the gage datum. We only need to know the recurrence interval, or its reciprocal, the probability of a flood reaching a given height, in order to be able to compare site location with flood risk.

As one should expect, a relationship does exist between the gage height and discharge of the stream. This relationship, known as the rating curve, is an empirical relationship. It is fully logarithmic and is normally derived for each station from current-meter readings (Leopold, 1974: p. 41). The stability of the relationship is, however, a function of the physical characteristics of the stream (Leopold, Wolman, and Miller, 1964: p. 168); thus, rating curves are not normally linear. Plotting the rating curve allows one to obtain the discharge for a given gage height and to enter this discharge into the curves of the relationship of the discharge to recurrence interval (given in Carns 1973). The reciprocal of the recurrence interval is the probability of a flood of given magnitude in any year. With the height of the flood known, and the probability of its occurrence in any year established, an assessment of flood risk for a site at any given elevation may be made. This assessment may be further refined by multiplying this probability by the probability of the annual flood occurring in a given month or season to give the probability of the joint event of a site being inundated by the annual flood at a given season.

Records from five gaging stations were used here: the Illinois River at Beardstown (now listed as Meredosia, the station was at Beardstown from 1879 to 1938); the Sangamon River at Oakford; the Sangamon River at Riverton; Lake Fork at Cornland; and the South Fork of the Sangamon River at Kincaid. Three problems will make present estimates of flood probabilities somewhat crude: (1) river improvements such as channelizing, straightening, diversion, etc., on both the Illinois and the Sangamon rivers and the Lake Fork Creek will affect the discharge; (2) topographic maps used for assessing elevation of sites are drawn with at least 10 foot contour intervals, making elevation assessment for each site subject to some variation; (3) moving upstream or downstream from gaging stations, the elevation of the river changes, thus probabilities will exhibit some variation. Still, a rough estimate can be made.

Table 9 is the approximation of the probability of the annual flood reaching a given elevation corresponding to the elevations of contours on U.S.G.S. topographic maps. Sites are classified by flood probability to the extent possible.

In summary, this chapter provides a very general seasonal and spatial model of floral and faunal resource availability and of habitation potential relative to soil and flooding characteristics. Although general, this model is sufficiently detailed to be usable in making inferences concerning a site's position in a settlement system.

V. ANALYSIS

The data in this study were collected and analyzed to answer several research questions.

1. Do people seem to be selecting particular types of situations and sites for habitation?

2. Are ceramic and projectile point sites in different types of situations?

3. How are these situations different? What are the characteristics of the different situations?

4. How greatly does spatial variation within the Sangamon drainage affect site location?

5. Do Middle and Late Woodland settlement patterns differ?

6. If they do, how do they differ? Does there seem to be change in the structure of the settlement pattern itself? If so, what is the nature of this change?

The Environmental Variables

At the outset, it was established that the most relevant environmental categories would be those of topography, drainage, soil, flora, and fauna—characteristics that were given the most attention in Chapter IV. The discussion now focuses on how they are to be used in answering the research questions.

To state that all sites are located on landforms is to state the obvious. Choice of landform for a site location, while related to soil and vegetation features, does have some importance in itself. As we have seen, flooding of a greater or smaller portion of the floodplain of any river is virtually inevitable at some time of the year, rendering at least a portion of the floodplain uninhabitable when it occurs. Similarly, flat upland plains may also become uninhabitable because of lack of runoff during periods of heavy rainfall. Steep slopes are in general probably not too conducive to normal day-to-day activities. For such reasons, prehistoric and historic man chooses the landforms on which he lives.

TABLE 9
Seasonal Flood Probabilities at Given Elevations with Sites Assigned to Contour Intervals

Elevation	Site Number			Probabilities				
	Middle Woodland	Late Woodland	Unknown	Winter	Spring	Summer	Fall	Annual
ILLINOIS RIVER AT BEARDSTOWN:								
460'	Mn^{v}82	Mn^{v}74	Mn^{v}47	>.01	>.01	>.01	>.01	>.01
	Cs^{v}28	Mn^{v}84	Cs^{v}88					
	Cs^{v}228	Mn^{v}115	Cs^{v}97					
		Cs^{v}28	Cs^{v}227					
		Cs^{v}79	Cs^{v}229					
440'	Mn^{v}40	Mn^{v}41	Mn^{v}42 Cs^{v}60	.100	.288	.057	.014	.459
	Mn^{v}46	Mn^{v}45	Mn^{v}43 Cs^{v}72					
	Mn^{v}49	Mn^{v}77	Mn^{v}44 Cs^{v}84					
	Mn^{v}75	Mn^{v}118	Mn^{v}48 Cs^{v}214					
	Mn^{v}117	Cs^{v}19	Mn^{v}73 Cs^{v}216					
	Mn^{v}118	Cs^{v}212	Mn^{v}76 Cs^{v}217					
	Cs^{v}19	Cs^{v}215	Mn^{v}78 Cs^{v}218					
	Cs^{v}56	Cs^{v}224	Mn^{v}87 Cs^{v}219					
	Cs^{v}83	Cs^{v}226	Mn^{v}114 Cs^{v}220					
			Mn^{v}116 Cs^{v}223					
			Cs^{v}225					
430'		Cs^{v}222	Mn^{v}72	.229	.558	.131	.033	.951
			Cs^{v}54					
			Cs^{v}221					
SANGAMON RIVER AT OAKFORD:								
480'	Mn^{v}94	Mn^{v}51	Mn^{v}53 Me^{v}18	<.01	<.01	<.01	<.01	<.01
	Mn^{v}112	Mn^{v}54	Mn^{v}85 Me^{v}19					
	Mn^{v}119	Mn^{v}57	Mn^{v}89 Me^{v}30					
	Mn^{v}120	Mn^{v}98	Mn^{v}95 Me^{v}68					
	Cs^{v}20	Mn^{v}99	Mn^{v}96					
	Cs^{v}25	Mn^{v}100	Mn^{v}103					
	Me^{v}6	Mn^{v}120	Mn^{v}104					
	Me^{v}8	Cs^{v}26	Mn^{v}107					

SETTLEMENT PATTERN MODELS IN CENTRAL ILLINOIS

460'	Me^{v}11 Me^{v}16 Me^{v}24 Me^{v}25 Me^{v}27 Me^{v}28 Me^{v}31 Me^{v}63 Me^{v}66	Cs^{v}27 Me^{v}25 Me^{v}31 Me^{v}33	Mn^{v}109 Mn^{v}110 Cs^{v}107					
	Mn^{v}92 Cs^{v}104		Mn^{v}88	.223	.447	.186	.093	.949
SANGAMON RIVER AT RIVERTON:								
540'	Sg^{v}178 Sg^{v}186 Sg^{v}208 Sg^{v}220	Sg^{v}91 Sg^{v}126 Sg^{v}186	Sg^{v}128 Sg^{v}149 Sg^{v}197 Sg^{v}207 Sg^{v}211 Sg^{v}280 Sg^{v}177	<.01	<.01	<.01	<.01	<.01
530'	Sg^{v}160	Sg^{v}150 Sg^{v}201 Sg^{v}228		.062	.129	.078	.021	.290
520'	Sg^{v}221 Sg^{v}222 Sg^{v}232	Sg^{v}235 Sg^{v}237 Sg^{v}238 Sg^{v}239	Sg^{v}231 Sg^{v}233 Sg^{v}234	.204	.424	.255	.068	.951
SOUTH FORK AT KINCAID:								
570'	Cn^{v}84	Cn^{v}61 Cn^{v}83 Cn^{v}88 Cn^{v}103	Cn^{v}9 Cn^{v}14 Cn^{v}48 Cn^{v}64 Cn^{v}94 Cn^{v}107 Cn^{v}119	<.01	<.01	<.01	<.01	<.01
560'	Cn^{v}110			.025	.072	.044	.009	.150
550'	Cn^{v}105		Cn^{v}111	.163	.470	.286	.061	.980

TABLE 9 (Concluded)
Seasonal Flood Probabilities at Given Elevations with Sites Assigned to Contour Intervals

Elevation	Site Number			Probabilities			
	Middle Woodland	Late Woodland	Unknown	Winter	Spring	Summer	Fall	Annual

Elevation	Middle Woodland	Late Woodland	Unknown	Winter	Spring	Summer	Fall	Annual
LAKE FORK NEAR CORNLAND:								
580'	Lo^v4	Lo^v24	Lo^v21	<.01	<.01	<.01	<.01	<.01
	Lo^v10	Lo^v25	Lo^v29					
	Lo^v23	Lo^v55	Lo^v54					
	Lo^v50	Lo^v102	Lo^v71					
	Lo^v53	Lo^v108	Lo^v73					
	Lo^v55		Lo^v74					
	Lo^v61		Lo^v82					
	Lo^v65		Lo^v85					
	Lo^v98		Lo^v86					
	Lo^v108		Lo^v87					
			Lo^v105					
570'	Lo^v32	Lo^v17	Lo^v17	.089	.268	.238	.030	.625
	Lo^v67	Lo^v30	Lo^v18					
	Lo^v76		Lo^v20					
	Lo^v78		Lo^v114					
	Lo^v101							
	Lo^v111							
	Lo^v112							
560'		Lo^v11	Lo^v12	.136	.407	.362	.045	.950
		Lo^v38						

However, sites are placed not only on landforms, but in relation to other landforms. To say that a village is located so as to have some natural protection from the wind is to say more than it is located on, for example, a river terrace. It is to imply that hills rise to the windward of the village, affording it natural protection. For this reason, it is appropriate to analyze not only a landform-on variable, but also the topographic situation of a site.

Situation characteristics are easily considered by considering not a point, but an area. As an arbitrary starting point, a circle of one-mile radius was superimposed on each site, and the areas of each of the four major landforms—floodplain, terrace, slope and upland—were measured using a planimeter.

In light of the previous discussion of human exploitation of the natural environment, it might be surmised that vegetation and its distribution is one of the most important variables in site location. Strictly speaking, both flora and fauna are probably important, but the prehistoric availability of fauna is quite difficult, if not impossible, to assess today in the same way as flora. Since fauna and flora are highly correlated anyway, the availability of fauna is omitted.

A series of concentric circles was used, centered on the site. These circles represented one-, two-, and three-mile radii. It was reasoned that even though this seems to incorporate a high degree of redundancy, such redundancy might permit some assessment of size and distance considerations in the assessment of available resources. In other words, it permitted a more accurate assessment of immediately available resources, as well as those that were somewhat farther away. For example, if upland forest were rather important, it might consistently occur within the one-mile radius in some perhaps rather large proportion of the area within that circle, while upland prairie, for example, might be of less importance and not be present at all within three miles of the site, or perhaps not show up until the 2–3 mile radius circle.

Four vegetation zones—upland and floodplain forest, and upland and bottomland prairie—were employed. The areas of each of these four zones within one-, two-, and three-mile radii were measured for each site using a planimeter.

Drainage is important for several reasons. First, bodies of water provide drinking water. Second, bodies of water are resource zones in themselves, providing fish, mussels, some species of turtles, and providing the preferred habitats for some mammals, reptiles, amphibians, and plants. Third, some bodies of water are potential avenues of transportation.

The hydrographic variable is already partially accounted for in the evaluation of topographic situation, i.e., floodplain proximity is considered. Evaluation of water resources in the present study was based on the stream order designations discussed in the previous chapter. Each site was scored for the rank of the largest stream within one, two, and three miles, a set of variables similar to those used for vegetation. In addition, the rank of the nearest stream and horizontal and vertical distance to that stream were evaluated for each site.

Finally, the soil variable is given somewhat more cursory treatment here than it perhaps deserves. There is probably more to the selectivity of soils for habitation than just fact that it is correlated with landform and vegetation, or its agricultural potential. Several other soil variables can be just as important; for example, coarseness or fineness of the soil. A heavy textured, fine particle, clayey soil on a flat surface (e.g., a floodplain or till plain) will hold water on the surface longer than will a coarser textured soil which will usually be somewhat more permeable. It might be reasoned that for reason of comfort, for example, a site would be located on a soil of at least moderate permeability, on not too great a soil slope.

Unfortunately, obtaining comparable soil information in the Sangamon area from county to county is difficult for all categories of information. Soil texture class was the only soil variable on which it was possible to obtain completely consistent and usable information. These are ordered by the U.S.D.A. (Soil Survey Staff, 1951: p. 207) into fourteen classes on the basis of increasing proportions of fine particles. Each site was scored for soil texture.

In addition to these variables used in the analysis of site locations, three other variables were held as independent variables: temporal period (i.e., Middle or Late Woodland); material evidence type (see Chapter III); and a spatial variable—the natural division of Illinois, taken from a map of "The Natural Divisions of Illinois" (Schwegman n.d.) issued by the Illinois Department of Conservation (Fig. 16).

Analysis of Middle Woodland Sites

Cluster Analysis

Raw data on each of the 23 variables for each of the 63 Middle Woodland sites were standardized, and a matrix of Euclidean distances among the cases in the 23-dimensional hyperspace was computed. This matrix was used as the basis for both cluster analysis and non-metric multidimensional scaling.

The distance matrix was first clustered using three separate clustering routines: unweighted pair-group method, weighted pair-group method, and complete linkage (performed using programs in the Numerical Taxonomy System [Rohlf, et al. 1972]; see Sneath and Sokal, 1973: pp. 222–35 for details of the differences of these different clustering techniques). The matrix of cophenetic values was obtained and used along with the original distance matrix to compute a cophenetic correlation coefficient (Sokal and Rohlf 1962) for each of the three clustering solutions.

The cophenetic correlation coefficient was used for two purposes: (1) as a guide in choosing the best clustering solution (cf. Sneath and Sokal, 1973: pp. 279–80), and (2) as a numerical measurement of the ability of the cluster analysis to adequately portray the structure of the data (cf. Rohlf and Fisher 1968, Kaesler 1970).

The cophenetic correlation coefficients obtained from clustering the Middle Woodland sites data with the three clustering techniques listed above are given

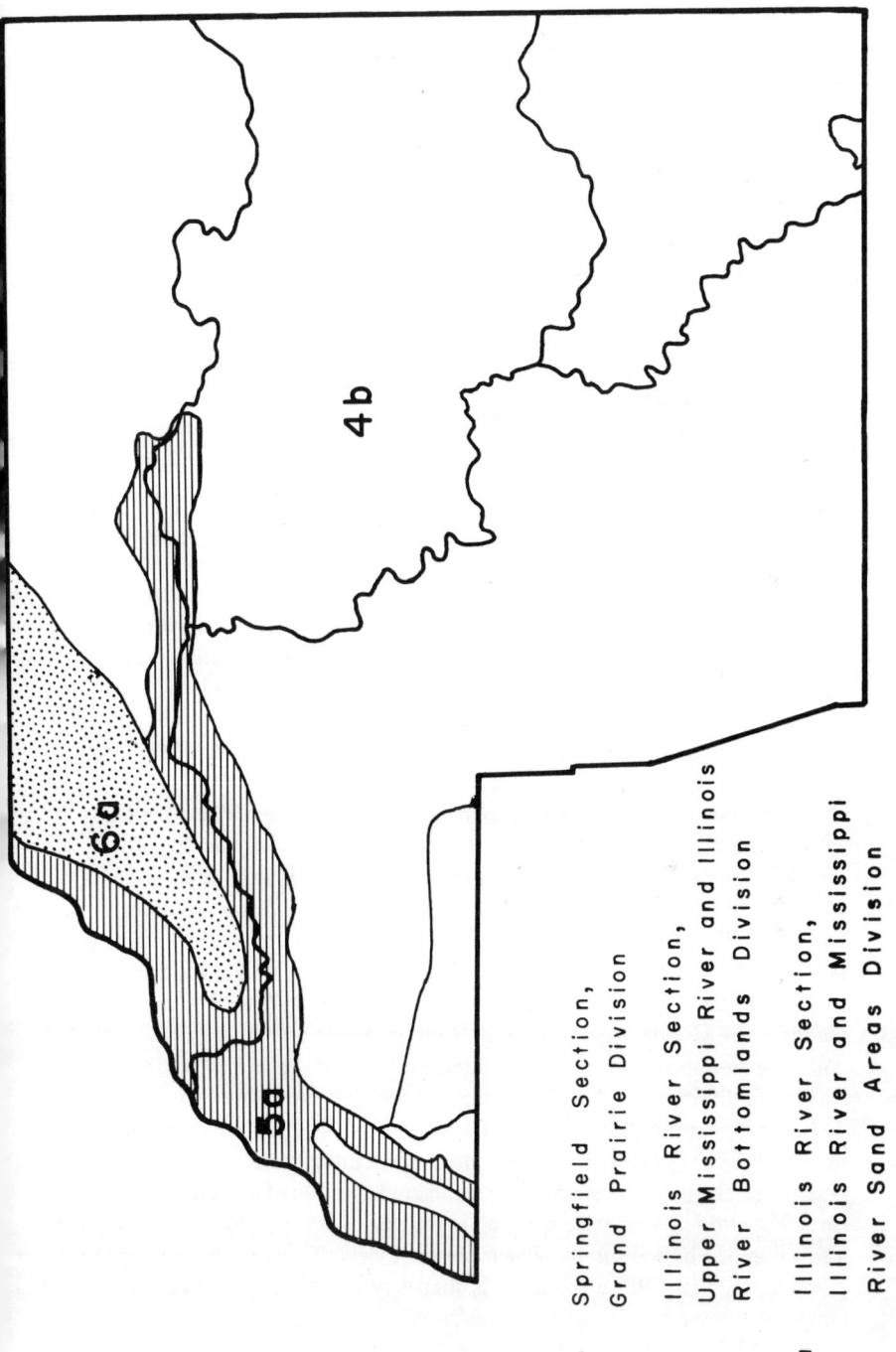

Fig. 16. Natural Divisions of Illinois within the Study Area (after Schwegman n.d.).

4b Springfield Section, Grand Prairie Division

5a Illinois River Section, Upper Mississippi River and Illinois River Bottomlands Division

6a Illinois River Section, Illinois River and Mississippi River Sand Areas Division

in Table 10, and suggest that the complete linkage analysis achieved the best clustering solution for this problem. The dendrogram for this solution is given in Fig. 17.

TABLE 10
Cophenetic Correlations, Middle Woodland

Clustering Technique	Correlation
Unweighted pair-group method	.73
Weighted pair-group method	.63
Complete linkage	.74

It is suggested that six clusters, formed at a distance level of 7.75 or lower are an optimal number for interpretation. One of these (#4) is subdivided. These clusters and subclusters are indicated on the dendrogram.

Table 11 presents a three-way cross tabulation of cluster composition, material evidence type, and natural division. Several things are apparent in the distribution of the sites in the table. First, there is a marked concentration of ceramic sites in Natural Divisions 5a and 6a, i.e., at the lower end of the Sangamon River, and a concentration of projectile point only sites (those with no ceramics at all) in Natural Division 4b, the Grand Prairie. Second, clusters are not randomly distributed within the natural divisions. Specifically, the first three clusters are overrepresented in Natural Divisions 5a and 6a, while the cluster 4, 5, and 6 sites occur only in Natural Division 4b. Third, all projectile point only sites occur in clusters 4, 5, and 6, while a large number of the ceramic sites of both types occur in all clusters.

Three preliminary conclusions are drawn: (1) Middle Woodland peoples did select particular types of situations for locating functionally distinct sites; (2) the placement of functionally equivalent types, i.e., ceramic sites, appears to vary with the structure of the natural environment; (3) different portions of the Sangamon River drainage were differently used. Specifically, the upper portions of the drainage, here represented by Natural Division 4b (the Springfield Section of the Grand Prairie Division) have more than their share of sites identified as Middle Woodland only from projectile points, with no ceramics collected during our survey. Of course, this could be a function of biased survey, and further work will be necessary in order to reject this possibility. This is not to imply, however, that the upper portion of the river valley within the study area is devoid of ceramic sites. They are present, although they are perhaps somewhat more sparse than in the lower portion of the drainage. Again, further controlled work will be necessary to rule out the possibility of this being a function of a biased survey. The traditional view of small sites, perhaps with projectile points well represented, is that they are a hunting camp, occupied temporarily by a portion of the male population. Ceramic sites, on the other hand, are often thought to represent habitation sites, i.e., more permanently established residences. If this is roughly true of Middle Woodland, we might

SETTLEMENT PATTERN MODELS IN CENTRAL ILLINOIS 85

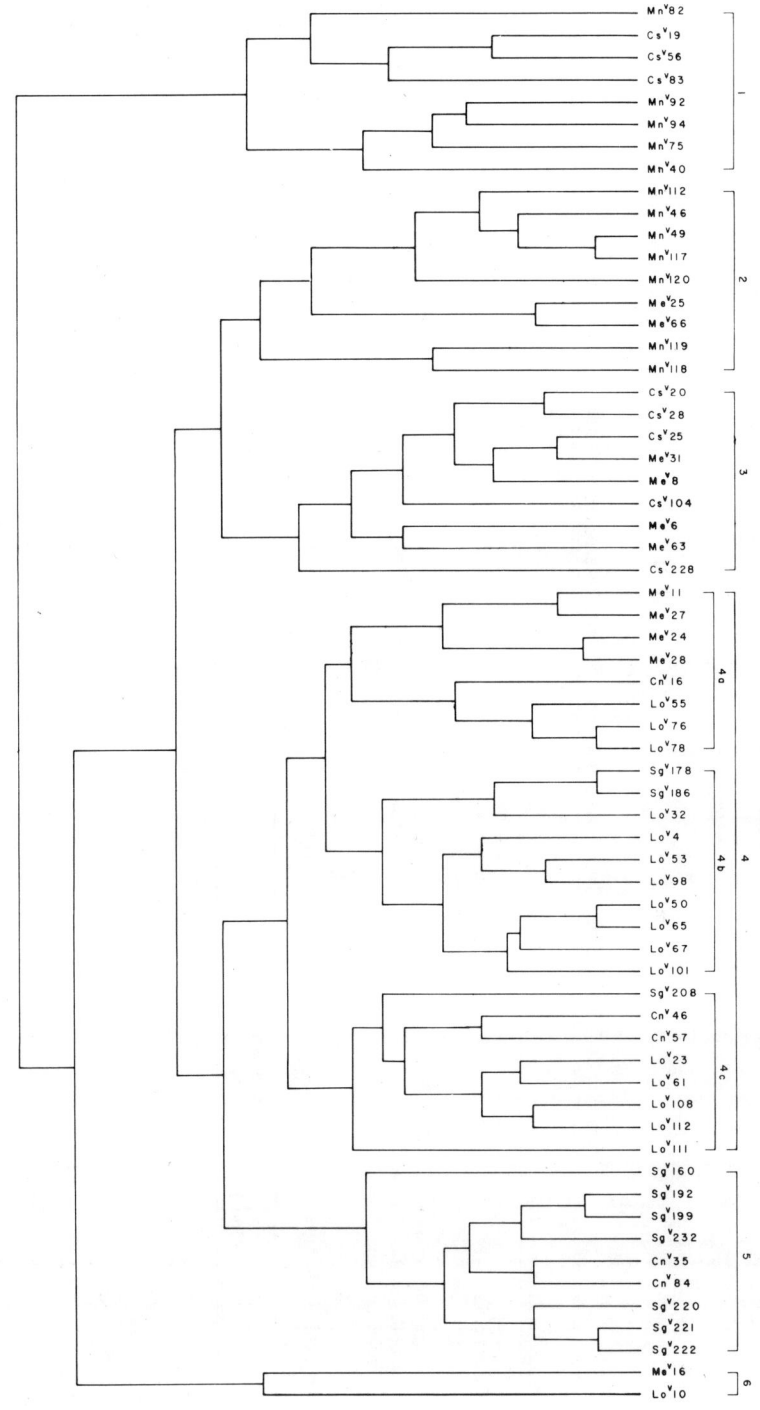

Fig. 17. Dendrogram of Cluster Analysis, Middle Woodland.

TABLE 11
Three-Way Contingency Table, Cluster, Natural Division, Material Evidence Type, (Middle Woodland Sites)

Material Evidence Type	Natural Division	Cluster						Row Total
		1	2	3	4	5	6	
Ceramic Sites	4b-Grand Prairie	0	1	1	6	7	0	33
	5a-Bottomlands	2	1	6	0	0	0	
	6a-Sand Areas	4	5	0	0	0	0	
Undiagnostic Ceramics with diagnostic Projectile Points Sites	4b-Grand Prairie	0	0	0	5	1	1	13
	5a-Bottomlands	2	0	2	0	0	0	
	6a-Sand Areas	0	2	0	0	0	0	
Projectile Point Sites	4b-Grand Prairie	0	0	0	15	1	1	17
	5a-Bottomlands	0	0	0	0	0	0	
	6a-Sand Areas	0	0	0	0	0	0	
Block Totals		8	9	9	26	9	2	63
Column Total		$ND_1=39$	$ND_2=13$	$ND_3=11$				

suspect that the upper portions of the drainage were somewhat more sparsely inhabited on a permanent basis (although this area was not devoid of habitation) and were instead used primarily for hunting.

The cluster analysis, however, only shows that the sites vary, it does not show how they vary. Inasmuch as functionally different sites appear to be in different types of places, and since spatial variability in the Sangamon River environment probably also affects site placement, it will be of interest to know what variables differentiate the situations of sites both over space and function. For this, multidimensional scaling is employed.

Multidimensional Scaling

The same distance matrix used in the cluster analysis was also used in the multidimensional scaling, performed using Kruskal's MDSCAL program (version contained in the Numerical Taxonomy System of Multivarate Programs—NTSYS [Rohlf, et al. 1972]). Two measures for evaluation of the solution were computed: (1) Kruskal's stress (Kruskal 1964: p. 9), a measure of how well the configuration fits the data, and (2) the correlations between the original and reconstructed distances, a measure equivalent to the cophenetic correlation of cluster analysis or the amount of variance explained by a factor analysis.

All dimensional solutions from 9 through 2 were obtained. Stress values and correlations for these are plotted in Fig. 18. Plotting the stress values sometimes will show a distinct elbow or break in the curve, suggesting an appropriate number of dimensions. Several considerations should enter into determining the appropriate number of dimensions: stress, interpretability, and visualizability (Shepard, 1972: pp. 9–10; Kruskal, 1964: p. 16). In the present case, the curve of stress values shows no distinct elbow, falling rather sharply and smoothly from 2 dimensions through 7 before more or less leveling out. The correlation curve does, however, show more of a pronounced break after three dimensions. At this point, which is, of course, the maximum number of dimensions which is readily visualizable, the stress is 22.5%, which on Kruskal's (1964: p. 3) verbal evaluation scale would rate as "poor." The correlation, however, is 0.968, or nearly 94% of the variance explained. This solution is also more highly interpretable than the higher dimensional solutions in which the additional dimensions are trivial. The three-dimensional configuration is given in Table 12.

Interpretation of the multidimensional scaling was facilitated by a canonical correlation between the original variables and the multidimensional configuration. The most useful part of such an analysis, therefore, is the correlations between the original variables (program CANONA [Veldman 1967]) and the canonical variables. This matrix is given in Table 13 for the canonical correlation of the three dimensional solution of the Middle Woodland site locations with the original variables. A further aid in interpretating the results of the

TABLE 12
Varimax Rotated Multidimensional Scaling Configuration
(Middle Woodland)

Site No.	I	II	III
Mn^{v}82	−0.646	−0.656	−0.730
Mn^{v}92	−0.993	−0.758	0.104
Mn^{v}94	−0.932	−0.491	0.033
Mn^{v}112	−0.717	0.408	−0.115
Mn^{v}119	−0.406	0.692	−0.744
Mn^{v}40	−1.330	−1.121	0.212
Mn^{v}46	−0.984	−0.003	−0.068
Mn^{v}49	−0.925	0.145	0.168
Mn^{v}75	−1.477	−0.404	0.095
Mn^{v}117	−0.911	0.187	0.173
Mn^{v}118	−0.876	0.037	−0.599
Mn^{v}120	−0.747	0.381	0.428
Cs^{v}19	−1.748	−0.011	−1.094
Cs^{v}20	0.049	1.103	−0.035
Cs^{v}25	−0.175	0.947	0.224
Cs^{v}28	−0.095	0.974	−0.008
Cs^{v}56	−1.401	0.361	−0.666
Cs^{v}83	−1.054	0.286	−0.379
Cs^{v}104	−0.678	0.917	−0.125
Cs^{v}228	0.472	1.128	−0.466
Me^{v}6	0.062	0.801	0.656
Me^{v}8	0.060	0.712	−0.034
Me^{v}11	0.335	0.201	−0.257
Me^{v}16	1.483	−0.329	−0.857
Me^{v}24	−0.067	0.095	−0.103
Me^{v}25	0.019	0.684	−0.723
Me^{v}27	0.190	0.298	−0.272
Me^{v}28	−0.024	0.055	−0.087
Me^{v}31	−0.098	0.958	0.331
Me^{v}63	−0.415	0.564	0.177
Me^{v}66	−0.346	0.767	0.058
Sg^{v}160	−0.285	−0.385	0.897
Sg^{v}178	0.688	−0.424	−0.494
Sg^{v}186	0.706	−0.366	−0.473
Sg^{v}192	0.026	−0.233	0.500
Sg^{v}199	0.117	−0.273	0.393
Sg^{v}208	0.883	0.355	0.148
Sg^{v}220	0.096	0.236	0.693
Sg^{v}221	0.005	0.197	0.861
Sg^{v}222	−0.013	0.162	0.829
Sg^{v}232	−0.249	−0.372	0.378
Cn^{v}16	−0.128	−0.566	−0.089
Cn^{v}35	0.061	0.047	0.349
Cn^{v}46	0.108	−0.045	−0.110
Cn^{v}57	0.496	0.126	−0.073
Cn^{v}84	0.202	−0.026	0.367
Lo^{v}4	0.488	−0.187	0.143
Lo^{v}10	1.080	−1.331	−0.602
Lo^{v}23	1.018	−0.062	0.074
Lo^{v}32	0.876	−0.701	−0.302
Lo^{v}50	0.763	−0.574	−0.080
Lo^{v}53	0.796	−0.077	0.058
Lo^{v}55	0.366	−0.450	0.103

TABLE 12 (Continued)
Varimax Rotated Multidimensional Scaling Configuration
(Middle Woodland)

Site No.	I	II	III
Lo^{v}61	0.867	−0.096	0.020
Lo^{v}65	0.703	−0.638	−0.136
Lo^{v}67	0.770	−0.394	0.080
Lo^{v}76	0.478	−0.723	−0.068
Lo^{v}78	0.448	−0.633	−0.016
Lo^{v}98	0.804	−0.323	−0.020
Lo^{v}101	0.673	−0.502	0.081
Lo^{v}108	0.728	0.012	0.313
Lo^{v}111	0.628	−0.407	0.640
Lo^{v}112	0.659	−0.276	0.245

TABLE 13
Correlations of Original and Canonical Variables (Middle Woodland)

Variable	I	II	III
ORIGINAL:			
1—Bottomland Prairie-1 mi (BP1)	−.20	−.73	.25
2—Upland Prairie-1 mi (UP1)	−.16	.29	−.80
3—Floodplain Forest-1 mi (FF1)	−.45	.35	.41
4—Upland Forest-1 mi (UF1)	.82	−.04	.04
5—Bottomland Prairie-2 mi (BP2)	−.13	−.83	.30
6—Upland Prairie-2 mi (UP2)	−.08	.48	−.69
7—Floodplain Forest-2 mi (FF2)	−.67	.00	.35
8—Upland Forest-2 mi (UF2)	.85	.07	.31
9—Bottomland Prairie-3 mi (BP3)	−.20	−.84	.22
10—Upland Prairie-3 mi (UP3)	.00	.60	−.53
11—Floodplain Forest-3 mi (FF3)	−.55	−.23	.41
12—Upland Forest-3 mi (UF3)	.77	−.00	.25
13—Floodplain (FP)	−.72	.16	.49
14—Terrace (T)	−.14	−.73	.22
15—Valley Slope (VS)	.72	.07	.05
16—Upland (U)	.27	.45	−.60
17—Closest Water Source (W)	.53	.45	.12
18—Horizontal Distance (H)	.10	.09	−.40
19—Vertical Distance (V)	.42	−.30	−.15
20—Largest Water Source-1 mi (W1)	−.05	.36	.55
21—Largest Water Source-2 mi (W2)	−.36	−.38	.45
22—Largest Water Source-3 mi (W3)	−.25	−.52	.38
23—Soil Texture (S)	.05	−.56	.17
DIMENSION:			
1	.61	.27	−.74
2	.69	−.58	.44
3	.32	.73	.60

multidimensional scaling is to plot the configurations, two dimensions at a time, and to superimpose the clusters derived from the cluster analysis (Fig. 19 a-c). Discussion of the multidimensional scaling will refer to the positions of the clusters on the dimensions as represented in the plots. The reader should

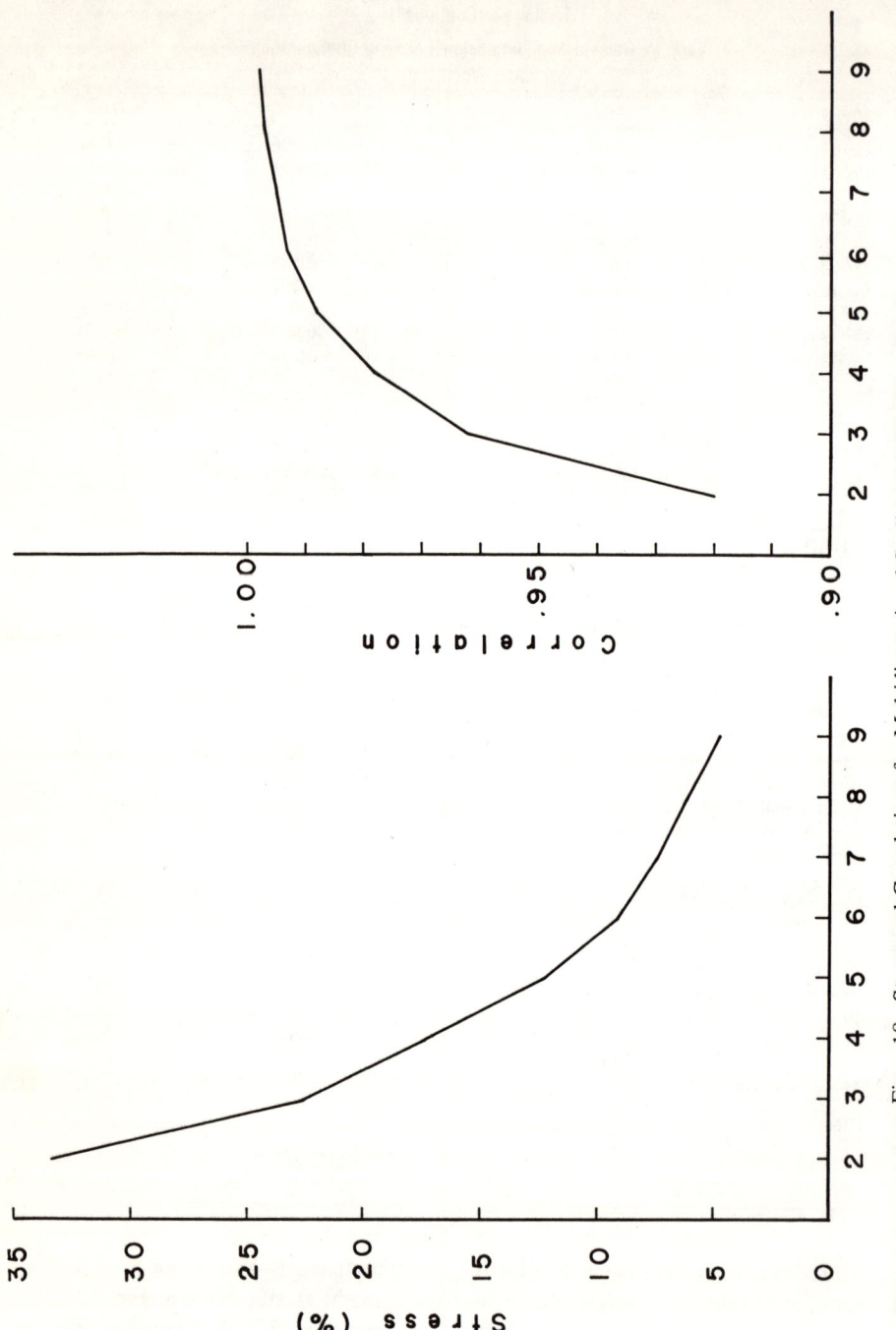

Fig. 18. Stress and Correlations for Multidimensional Scaling, Middle Woodland.

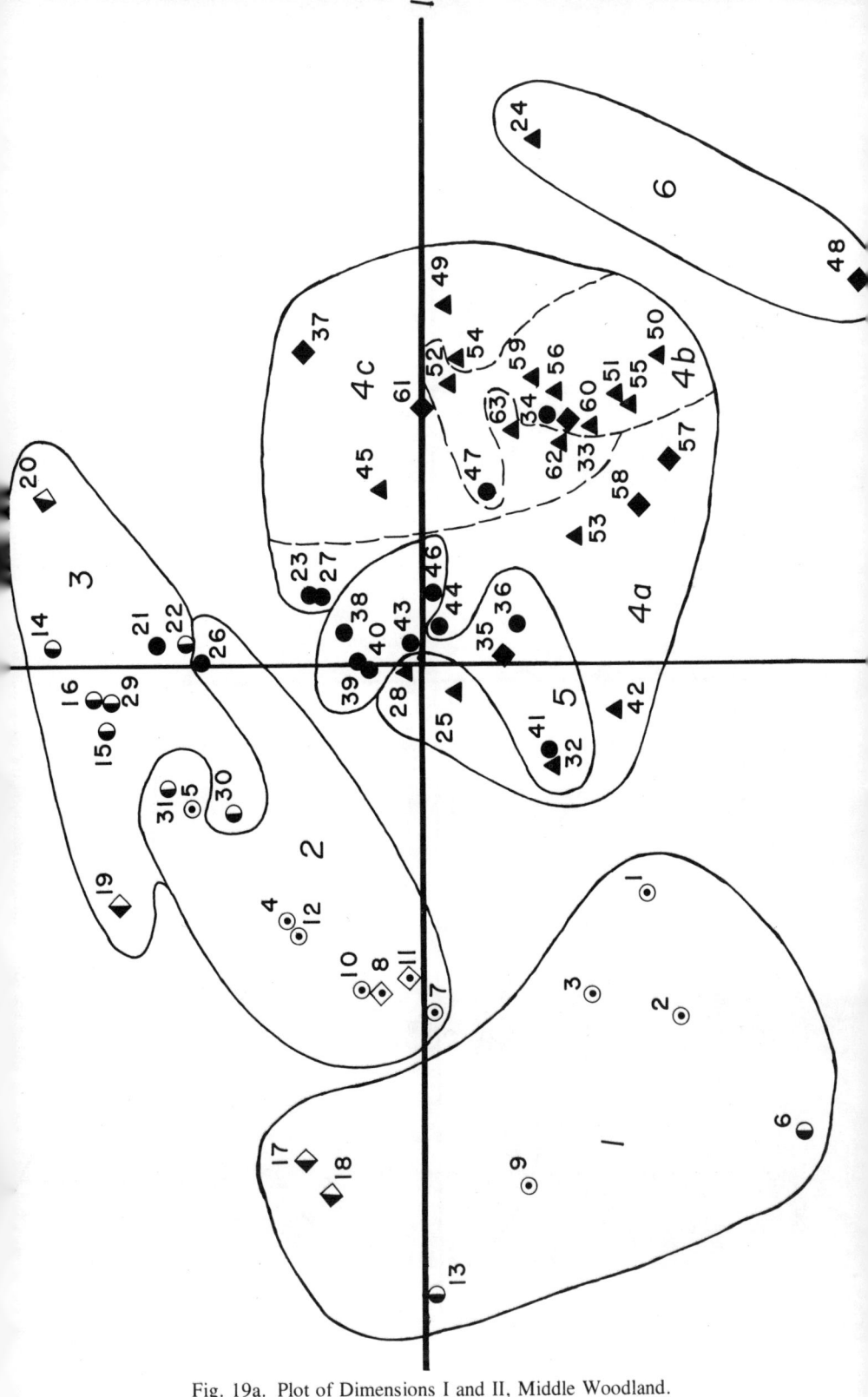

Fig. 19a. Plot of Dimensions I and II, Middle Woodland.

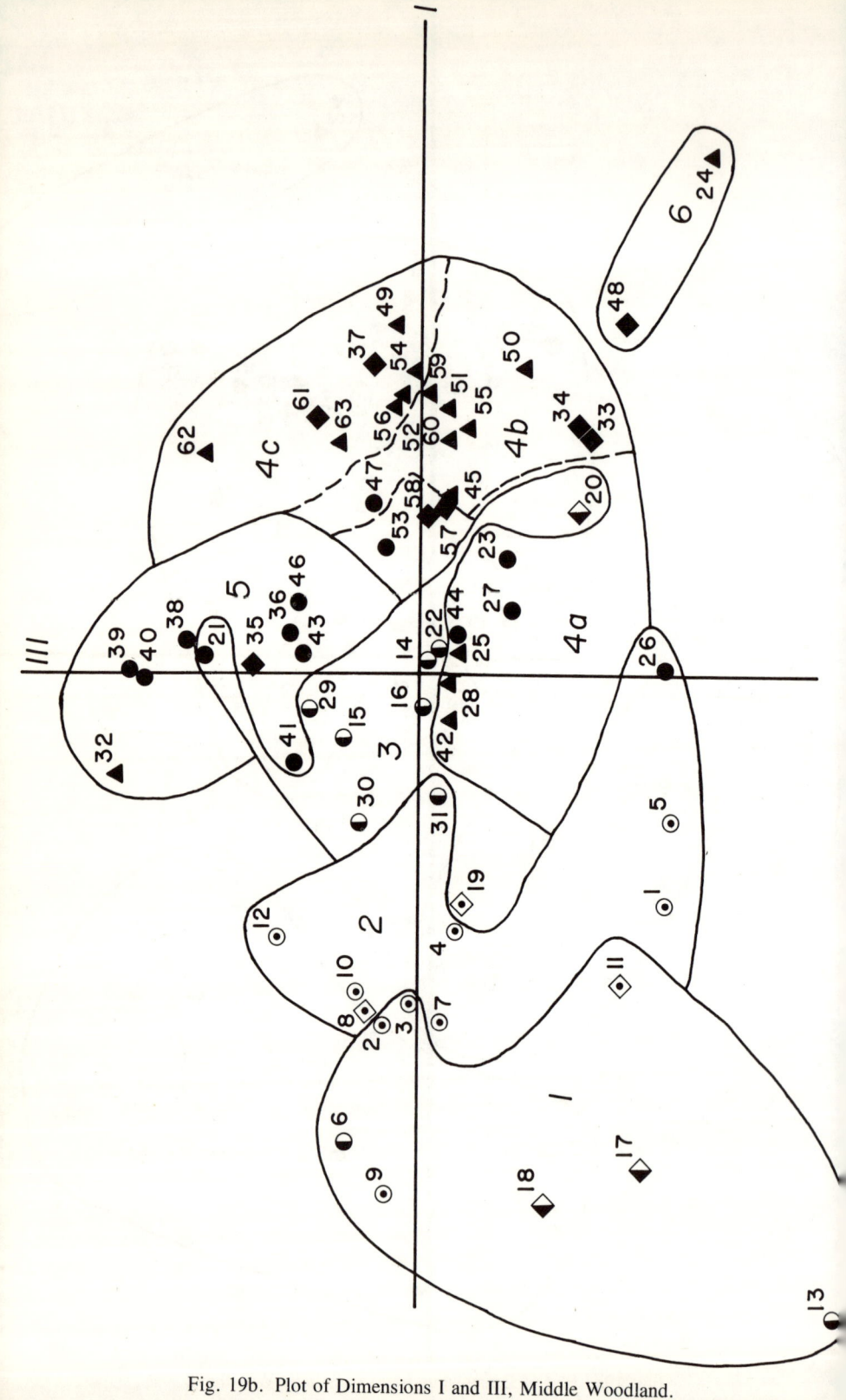

Fig. 19b. Plot of Dimensions I and III, Middle Woodland.

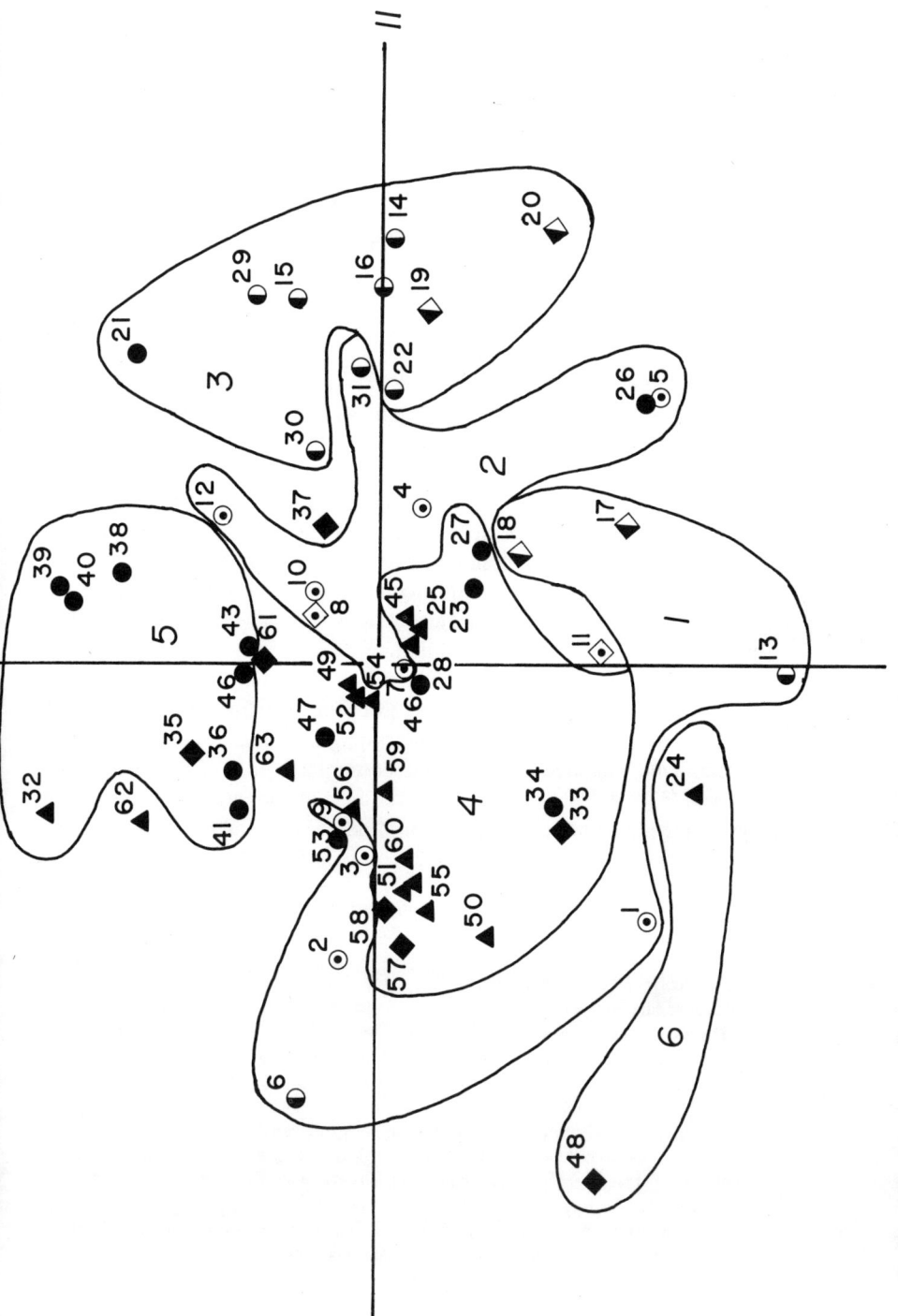

Fig. 19c. Plot of Dimensions II and III, Middle Woodland.

bear in mind when inspecting these figures that although a given plot may appear to entangle cases belonging to several clusters, the clusters may actually be widely separated on the particular dimension not given in the plot.

The first dimension is readily identified as a contrast between uplands, including valley slopes, and floodplain. Both upland prairie and upland forest as well as valley slope and uplands have a positive correlation and contrast with the floodplain and floodplain forest. Rank of nearest watersource also correlates positively, although perhaps somewhat weakly, as does vertical distance to water.

The second dimension contrasts the combination of terrace and valley slope with the floodplain. Correlating with the terrace and valley slope, as expected, are bottomland prairie and upland forest, while, predictably, the floodplain forest correlates with the floodplain. Watersources, especially within three miles, and soils both correlate, although somewhat weakly with this dimension.

The third dimension generally correlates negatively with both upland and bottomland prairie. The second canonical root suggests a moderately strong negative correlation with bottomland prairie, while the third canonical root suggests a somewhat weaker negative correlation with uplands and upland prairies, particularly upland prairie within one mile. Soil and water variables also correlate somewhat more strongly with this dimension than with the second dimension, but in a negative direction.

In short, this analysis derives a multidimensional configuration very similar to that derived in the pilot study (Roper 1974). That study employed R-mode principal components analysis of the 12 vegetation variables only, and extracted 3 factors: (1) a forest factor, contrasting upland and floodplain forest, (2) bottomland resources, contrasting bottomland prairie with floodplain forest, and (3) avoidance of upland prairie. In summarizing the results of that analysis, three hypothetical strategies of Middle Woodland site location in the Sangamon River Valley were defined. To quote from that report:

> The first strategy was restricted in distribution to the south side of the river drainage below its junction with Salt Creek and bears resemblances to the strategy noted within other areas within the range of the Havana Tradition. Sites are on a slope, bluff-base, or back of a terrace, near a tributary entering the Sangamon Valley. In such a position, they are within upland forest but near its edge and within two or three miles of all major environmental zones along the river.
>
> The second strategy is a modification of the first and is employed where no linear terrace intervenes between the valley wall and the floodplain. Sites located according to this strategy are also generally on a slope but are not on a tributary entering the valley. Rather, they are near the river itself, which could well have been near the valley wall at the time the sites were occupied. The floral context of these sites, is, however, variable. . . .
>
> All sites located according to the third hypothetical strategy are below the Sangamon-Salt confluence but are on the north side of the river. They are placed at the front edge of a terrace, near lakes, . . . No true uplands exist . . . These sites for the most part do not have the access to upland forest that sites located according to the first two strategies have and are very much more bottomland oriented in regard to immediately available resources (Roper 1974: p. 19).

The location of cluster 3 sites in the present analysis is similar to that described in the first strategy outlined above. The position of the cluster 3 sites on the first dimension is intermediate, i.e., the sites are neither particularly toward the slope and uplands, nor toward the bottomland. They do, however, correlate highly with the second dimension, indicating a large combination of terrace and valley slope as well as upland forest and bottomland prairie. As such, the sites are a mile or two back from the river, due to the broad terrace. It will be remembered that the watersource variables also correlate with the second dimension. The value of closest watersource for sites in this cluster is low, but increases markedly as a distance of three miles from the site is reached. Since sites are back from the river because of the intervening terrace, they are placed next to a watersource of low rank. As increasingly large radii around the site are considered, the rank of the largest watersource rises as the Sangamon River itself is included in the circles. Since the cluster 3 sites are at the edge of the forest, their position on the third dimension, away from the prairies, is neither particularly high, nor particularly low. Thus, the forest surrounding the site must be fairly broad, since if there were a large amount of upland prairie, the site would score low on the third dimension.

All sites in cluster 3 are ceramic sites. Seven of them (Cs^v20, Cs^v25, Cs^v28, Me^v6, Me^v8, Me^v31, Me^v63) have diagnostic Havana ceramics (some of them also have Hopewell ceramics) the other two (Cs^v104, Cs^v228) are identified as Middle Woodland on projectile point evidence but have undiagnostic ceramics. All but one of the sites are in Natural Division 5a—the Illinois River Section of the Upper Mississippi River and Illinois River Bottomlands Division. This division has a series of linear microenvironmental zones, including a rather broad terrace, paralleling the river. Site Me^v6 is in Natural Division 4b, the Grand Prairie Division, although near the lower end of it, and is not far from the sites in Division 5a.

In sum, cluster 3 sites occupy that portion of the Sangamon River Valley that is physiographically most like the Illinois River Valley. It will be shown in Chapter VI that the site location pattern in this portion of the Sangamon valley is similar to the location pattern in the Illinois River Valley. However, the present study has been able to not only discern the topographic and hydrographic placement of the sites, but has discerned the vegetational context of the sites as well. For the most part, the sites are at the edge of the forest, i.e., they are within the forest, but are near the bottomland prairie. As such, they occupy a middle position on the first, or forest dimension; score highly on the second or valley slope-terrace dimension; and occupy an intermediate position on the third, or prairie dimension due to the fact that they are placed away from the upland prairie.

Cluster 5 sites correspond to those defined in the second strategy in the previous analysis. All of these sites, however, are in Natural Division 4b—the Springfield Section of the Grand Prairie Division. The major difference between cluster 3 and cluster 5 is their position on the second and third dimensions. On the first dimension, these sites differ very little from those in cluster

3, i.e., they are in a rather intermediate position. In other words, the sites, like those of cluster 3, are neither particularly toward the slope and upland, nor toward the terrace and floodplain.

The second dimension clarifies the position of the sites in relation to the bottomland and slope. Although the sites are near small amounts of terrace, they score in an intermediate position on the dimension. Most of the land surrounding the site that is not slope or upland is floodplain. The average amount of terrace is the lowest of any cluster, but amount of slope is second highest, second to cluster 3. The sites are not in the floodplain, nor are they near slopes or upland particularly. In other words, like cluster 3 sites, those in cluster 5 are at the base of the slopes. The absence of terrace then also correlates with the rank of the watersources. Since there is no intervening terrace, the sites in the low-on-the-slope position are placed next to the river itself, rather than on a tributary. Thus, as a distance of three miles from the site is reached, the rank of the largest watersource does not increase since the site is already on the largest ranked watersource in the area. It is also the absence of terrace that leads to the cluster's position on the third dimension. Because of the absence of terrace, and therefore also of bottomland prairie, the site's position low on a forested slope means the sites have access to rather little prairie of any kind within three miles. Thus, they score high on the third dimension.

Of the nine sites in cluster 5, seven (Sg^v199, Sg^v220, Sg^v221, Sg^v222, Sg^v232, Cn^v35, Cn^v84) are ceramic sites, one (Sg^v192) has a Middle Woodland point and ceramics that are not known to be Middle Woodland, and one Sg^v160) is classified as Middle Woodland solely on the basis of projectile point evidence. The latter two sites are somewhat separate from the other seven and move toward the negative end of the dimension. Both are in the area of the confluence of the Sangamon River, South Fork of the Sangamon River, and Sugar Creek, in the middle of Sangamon Country. The floodplain in this area is somewhat broader than immediately upriver or downriver and has a broader strip of floodplain forest bordering the streams.

Functionally, then, cluster 5 appears to be largely the equivalent of cluster 3. It is only because of the difference in structuring of the natural environment that the sites differ in their location from those in cluster 3. In the previous study, this was summed up as follows:

> A feature common to the Sangamon (lower end [Division 5a]) as well as those other river valleys is that topographic zones are broad, linear, and parallel to one another and to the river. Change this structuring by the removal of the linear terrace, let the river meander back and forth from valley wall to valley wall, and the result is represented by [cluster 5]. These sites too are located primarily at bluff-base or on the slope; but because the river meanders back and forth to the base of the slopes, the sites are near the river itself rather than being constrained to situations where a tributary enters the valley (Roper, 1974: p. 9).

In sum, cluster 5 sites occupy a portion of the Sangamon River Valley physiographically transitional from that of the Illinois Valley and, accordingly, the pattern of location of Middle Woodland habitation sites differs. In general, these sites are also at the edge of the forest, are low on a slope, and away from the upland prairie. However, since the bottomland prairie covered terrace is missing in the area, the sites shift their position on both the first and third dimensions of the multidimensional scaling analysis. The sites are on the main stream rather than on a tributary.

Sites located by the third strategy listed above are probably those represented in the present analysis by both clusters 1 and 2. These sites are in the bottomlands, on either a terrace or the floodplain itself, where they have access, even within three miles, to little upland forest or upland prairie, although there is a large amount of variation within both clusters. Sites of cluster 1 are more within the bottomlands than are those of cluster 2, which are toward more upland, i.e., valley slope and uplands with associated upland forest and upland prairie. As should be expected then, cluster 2 sites score somewhat higher on dimension II than do the sites in cluster 1 because of the greater amounts of valley slope and associated upland forest surrounding the site. The rank of closest watersource is low for sites of both clusters since the sites are mostly on closed bodies of water, scored here as drainage rank = 0. As a distance of three miles from the site is attained, the value increases since the sites are not usually over three miles from the seventh order Sangamon River. These sites similarly range from a low position on the third dimension for those sites on the terrace surrounded by large areas of terrace and associated bottomland prairie, to those somewhat higher on the dimension, closer to valley slope, and therefore upland forest, and with less access to prairies of either type.

All sites in these two clusters are ceramic sites of one type or the other. Of the cluster 1 sites, four (Mn^V40, Cs^V19, Cs^V56, Cs^V83) are in Natural Division 5a, the Illinois River Section of the Upper Mississippi and Illinois River Bottomlands Division. The other four (Mn^V75, Mn^V82, Mn^V92, Mn^V94) are in Natural Division 6a, the Illinois River Section of the Illinois River and Mississippi River Sand Areas Division. In cluster 2, one site (Me^V25) is in Natural Division 4b, the Grand Prairie, one (Me^V66) is in Division 5a, and the other seven (Mn^V46), Mn^V49, Mn^V112, Mn^V117, Mn^V118, Mn^V119, Mn^V120) are in Division 6a. Most of the Weaver sites included in the analysis are in these clusters. In fact, only one Weaver component, that at Cs^V20, is not in one of these two clusters.

In sum, sites in clusters 1 and 2 occupy a physiographic position much more oriented to bottomland than those in clusters 3 and 5. Like those clusters, however, the sites are predominantly ceramic sites, although, unlike those sites, Weaver sites are well represented. The sites are located on a closed body of water, and are rather far from upland forest and upland prairie.

Cluster 4 is by far the largest cluster and is divided into three subclusters. Its position on the first dimension is from the middle to the upper end, and indeed, there is limited overlap with the sites of the third and fifth clusters. This overlap is primarily with subcluster 4a. In other words, most of the sites are farther into uplands and nearer to greater quantities of upland resources than are the sites of any cluster but 6. Amounts of upland prairie are greater than for sites in all but the sixth cluster, and the combination of upland forest and upland prairie is higher than that of sites in most other clusters. Obviously, the sites are closer to an upland forest–upland prairie edge. Additionally, sites in subclusters 4b and 4c are on the finest soils of any in the analysis.

Given the position of the sites within or near the uplands, it is perhaps somewhat surprising to find them spread along the second dimension, i.e., toward the middle to bottomland end of the dimension. Many of them are in the middle portions of the Sangamon drainage however, and all the land surrounding a site that is not slope or upland is floodplain. Furthermore, some of them are in areas of such little relief that there is not much valley slope, and therefore, unless the site is far in the uplands, the site has a fair amount of bottomland, and thus of floodplain, present within three miles. Subcluster 4a in particular has an amount of bottomland resources equivalent to clusters 3 and 5. The other two, not too surprisingly given their upland orientation, are low in amount of bottomland resources.

As with the other clusters so far discussed, the fourth cluster does not particularly differ from the others on the third dimension. Again, this indicates that there is no particular placement of the sites away from the prairies. In this case, however, it is apparent that most of the sites are in places where there is some amount of upland prairie, and indicates, in contrast to cluster 3, that the sites are far from the bottomland prairie. This observation is borne out by the fact that these sites seem to have small amounts of bottomland prairie surrounding the site, particularly sites in subclusters 4b and 4c, while being surrounded by large expanses of upland prairie. The only way for a site to not have a low score on the third dimension is to have a large amount of prairie surrounding most of the site and, since there is little bottomland surrounding most of the sites, it is upland that is primarily influencing the cluster's position on the third dimension. Again, this is interpreted to indicate location of the sites toward the uplands.

Distribution of material evidence types within the clusters is as follows: in subcluster 4a, Me^{v}11, Me^{v}27, Lo^{v}55, Lo^{v}76, and Lo^{v}78 all have ceramics, some of them diagnostic, some not; Me^{v}24, Me^{v}28, and Cn^{v}16 are identified as Middle Woodland solely on the presence of projectile points; in subcluster 4b, Sg^{v}186, Sg^{v}178, and Lo^{v}4 all have ceramics, Lo^{v}32, Lo^{v}50, Lo^{v}53, Lo^{v}65, Lo^{v}67, Lo^{v}98, and Lo^{v}101 have only projectile points; in subcluster 4c, Cn^{v}46, Sg^{v}208, and Lo^{v}108 have ceramics, while Cn^{v}57, Lo^{v}23, Lo^{v}61, Lo^{v}111, and Lo^{v}112 have only projectile points. All sites are in Natural Division 4b, the Springfield Section of the Grand Prairie Division.

In summary, cluster 4 sites are characterized by a position oriented more toward the uplands than most sites in the analysis, particularly in terms of upland prairie. The upland forest surrounding these sites is narrowing and, of course, upland prairie is present in greater abundance. Ceramic sites are present, but projectile point sites, possibly indicative of hunting camps, are present in greater quantities here than anywhere else.

Cluster 6 is formed of only two sites, both of which not only join with each other late in the cluster analysis (Fig. 17) but also join late with the rest of the analysis. In other words, they are two sites that really are quite differently located than the other sites in the analysis. As such, it may be slightly misleading to talk of their combined properties but, in general, they do differ from the other sites. In the first place, they are the highest on the first dimension, indicating a position in the uplands. Further, the amount of upland prairie and upland forest combined is higher for these two sites than any other. It might also be noted that this is the only cluster with much horizontal distance to water. Me^v16 is 0.9 m from the closest watersource.

Both sites, but particularly Lo^v10, are toward the lower end of the second dimension. Again, as with cluster 5, most of the land surrounding the site that is not upland or slope is floodplain.

On the third dimension, these sites attain the lowest scores. They have more prairie surrounding them than any other cluster of sites which might be expected since they have more upland than any other cluster.

Of the two sites, one is recognized on the basis of projectile points only, but undiagnostic ceramics are present; the other is a site recognized entirely on the basis of projectile points. Both are in Natural Division 4b.

Analysis of Late Woodland Sites

Cluster Analysis

Identical procedures of analysis were employed for the 57 Late Woodland components included in the analysis. A Euclidean distance matrix was computed, and clustered using three clustering techniques. The cophenetic correlation coefficients for these solutions are given in Table 14. The unweighted pair-group method gives the highest cophenetic correlation and accordingly is the solution discussed here. The dendrogram for this solution is presented in Fig. 20. Six clusters, formed at a distance level of 6.0 or lower, are interpreted. Two of these clusters are subdivided, as indicated in the dendrogram.

TABLE 14
Cophenetic Correlations, Late Woodland

Clustering Technique	Correlation
Unweighted pair-group	.83
Weighted pair-group	.81
Complete linkage	.80

As with the Middle Woodland sites, a three-way crosstabulation of the

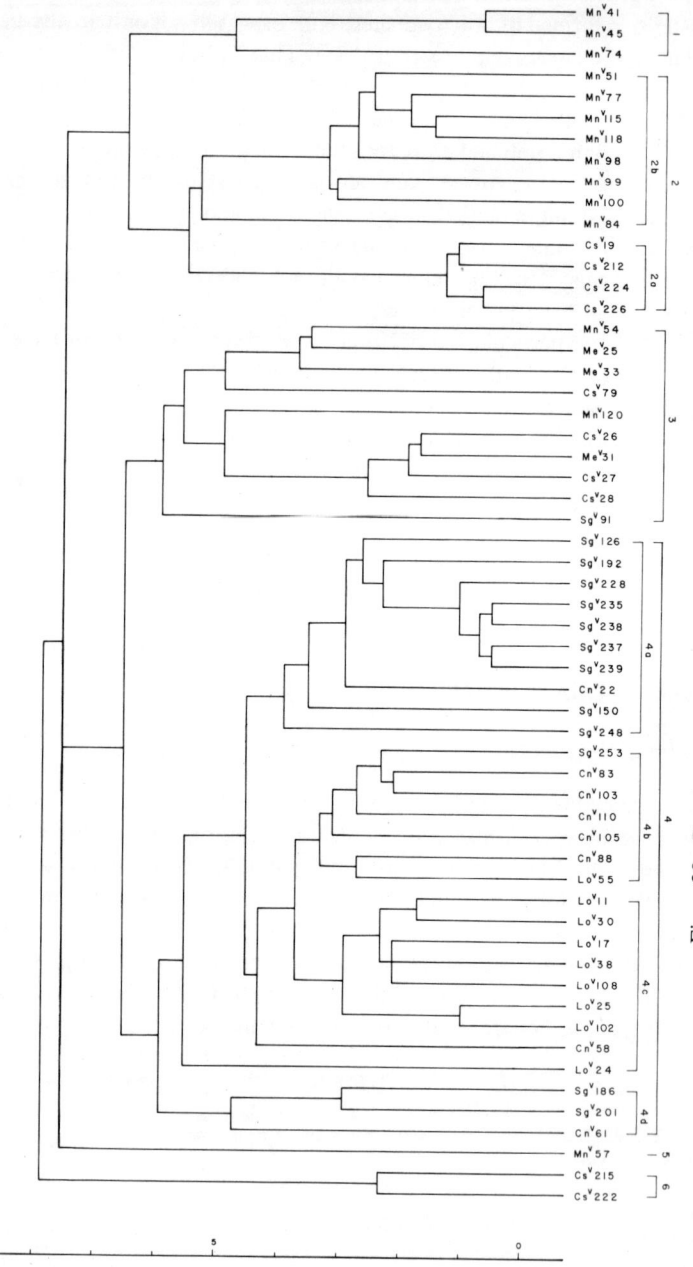

Fig. 20. Dendrogram of Cluster Analysis, Late Woodland.

distribution of the clusters, material evidence types, and natural divisions is given (Table 15). Note that the single site cluster (#5) is omitted from the table.

TABLE 15

Three-Way Contingency Table, Cluster, Natural Division, Material Evidence Type, (Late Woodland Sites)

Material Evidence Type	Natural Division	Cluster 1	2	6	3	4	Row Total
Ceramic Sites	4b–Grand Prairie	0	0	0	1	8	
	5a–Bottomlands	2	2	0	3	0	19
	6a–Sand Areas	0	2	0	1	0	
Undiagnostic Ceramics with diagnostic Projectile Points Sites	4b–Grand Prairie	0	0	0	1	11	
	5a–Bottomlands	0	0	1	3	0	20
	6a–Sand Areas	0	4	0	0	0	
Projectile Points Sites	4b–Grand Prairie	0	0	0	1	10	
	5a–Bottomlands	0	2	1	0	0	17
	6a–Sand Areas	1	2	0	0	0	
Column Total		3	12	2	10	29	56
Block Totals	$ND_1 = 31$	$ND_2 = 14$				$ND_3 = 10$	

Several things are notable from the distribution of the sites in the table. The first is the distribution of the clusters within the natural divisions. All cluster 1, 2, and 6 sites are in Natural Divisions 5a and 6a, i.e., the divisions at the lower end of the Sangamon River, as are most of the cluster 3 sites. All cluster 4 sites are, however, in Natural Division 4b, in the middle of the drainage, as is the single site that is regarded as cluster 5.

Second, the distribution of the material evidence types within the natural divisions is also apparent. Ceramic sites occur in all natural divisions. There seem to be fewer in division 6a than in the other divisions, but this may be merely a function of fewer sites in the analysis in division 6a. Projectile point sites, however, are in all natural divisions within the drainage.

Third, however, there appears to be less of a choice of type of situation for the different types of sites than there was in Middle Woodland. This may occur for several reasons: (1) subsistence practices may have shifted sufficiently that the variables examined in this study are not sufficient to account for Late Woodland site location (for example, a greater dependence on horticultural products might lead to more of a selectivity of soil conditions than vegetation), (2) the structure of the settlement pattern itself may have changed, and (3) sampling error is, as always, a possibility.

Multidimensional Scaling

The cophenetic correlation coefficient of 0.83 indicates that not only is the dendrogram a fairly accurate portrayal of the structure of the data matrix, but also that a hierarchical structure may well exist within the data. Even so a scaling of the data will help provide a complementary interpretation, place the clusters in perspective, and help provide a basis for inference of Late Woodland settlement patterns. The fairly distinct clustering structure will, however, make discussion of the multidimensional scaling results in these terms easier and more meaningful.

As before, the distance matrix was input to the MDSCAL program for multidimensional scaling. Stress values and cophenetic correlations were computed for all solutions from 9 down through 2 dimensions. The stress values and correlation curve for the total problem is presented in Fig. 21. No distinct break is present in the stress curve, but a break is suggested after three dimensions in the correlation curve. In view of the high correlations between the original and reconstructed distances, as well as visualizability and interpretability of the solution and the fact that this matches the number of dimensions interpreted for Middle Woodland, the three dimensional solution for the Late Woodland sites problem is interpreted and presented here. The varimax rotated configuration is given in Table 16, the plots in Fig. 22a-c. The matrix of correlations between the original two sets of variables (original data, and multidimensional scaling configuration) and canonical variables is given in Table 17.

Dimension I shows high positive correlations with upland forest, as well as with the valley slope and upland combination, and has a negative correlation with bottomland prairie and floodplain forest, particularly floodplain forest within three miles. It also has a somewhat weak, but noticeable correlation with soil texture. Watersource correlates positively with this dimension, as does vertical distance to water. There is some suggestion in the second canonical root of a negative correlation between largest watersource within two and three miles and this dimension.

Dimension II has positive correlations with floodplain forest and floodplain, and with upland prairie, and negative correlations with bottomland prairie, terrace, and soil. Watersources within two and three miles also correlate with the dimension. Reasons for these correlations will be made clear when the composition of the individual clusters and sites and their positions on the dimensions are discussed.

Dimension III has a negative correlation with upland prairie and a positive correlation with bottomland prairie and with soil; also a positive correlation with upland forest and a negative correlation with bottomland in general. It is suggested that this dimension is very similar to the first dimension of the Middle Woodland analysis.

Clusters 1, 2, and 6 all are quite similar on the first and third dimensions, and actually are only separated by their widely disparate positions on the second dimension. All three clusters are well toward the negative end of the dimension. It will be recalled that this dimension has a negative correlation with bottomland prairie in particular, and with floodplain and terrace. The indications are that these sites are placed, for the most part, at the floodplain edge of a broad terrace. It is only in this, or a similar manner, that the sites could have no valley slope or uplands within one mile of a site and could also be about evenly divided

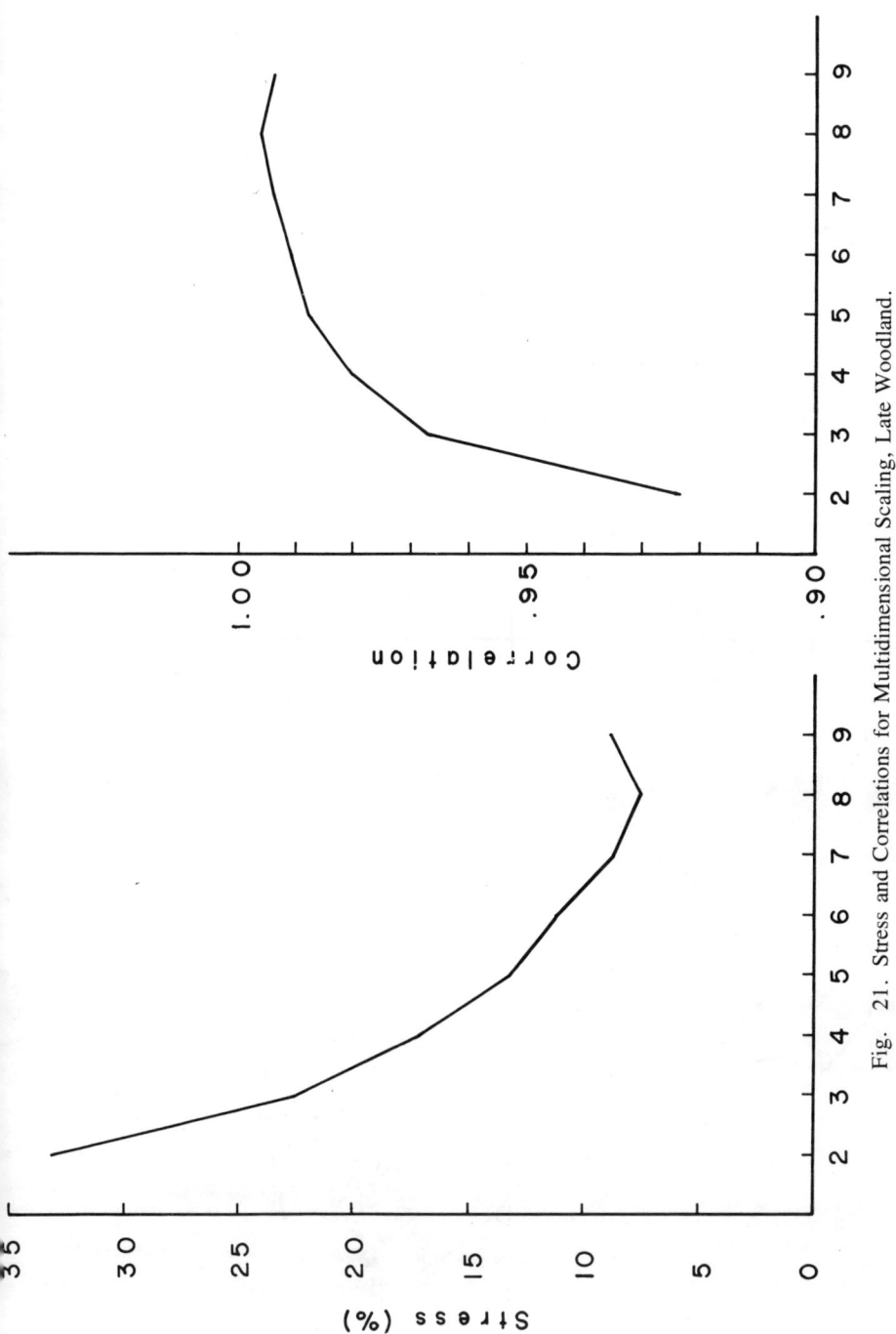

Fig. 21. Stress and Correlations for Multidimensional Scaling, Late Woodland.

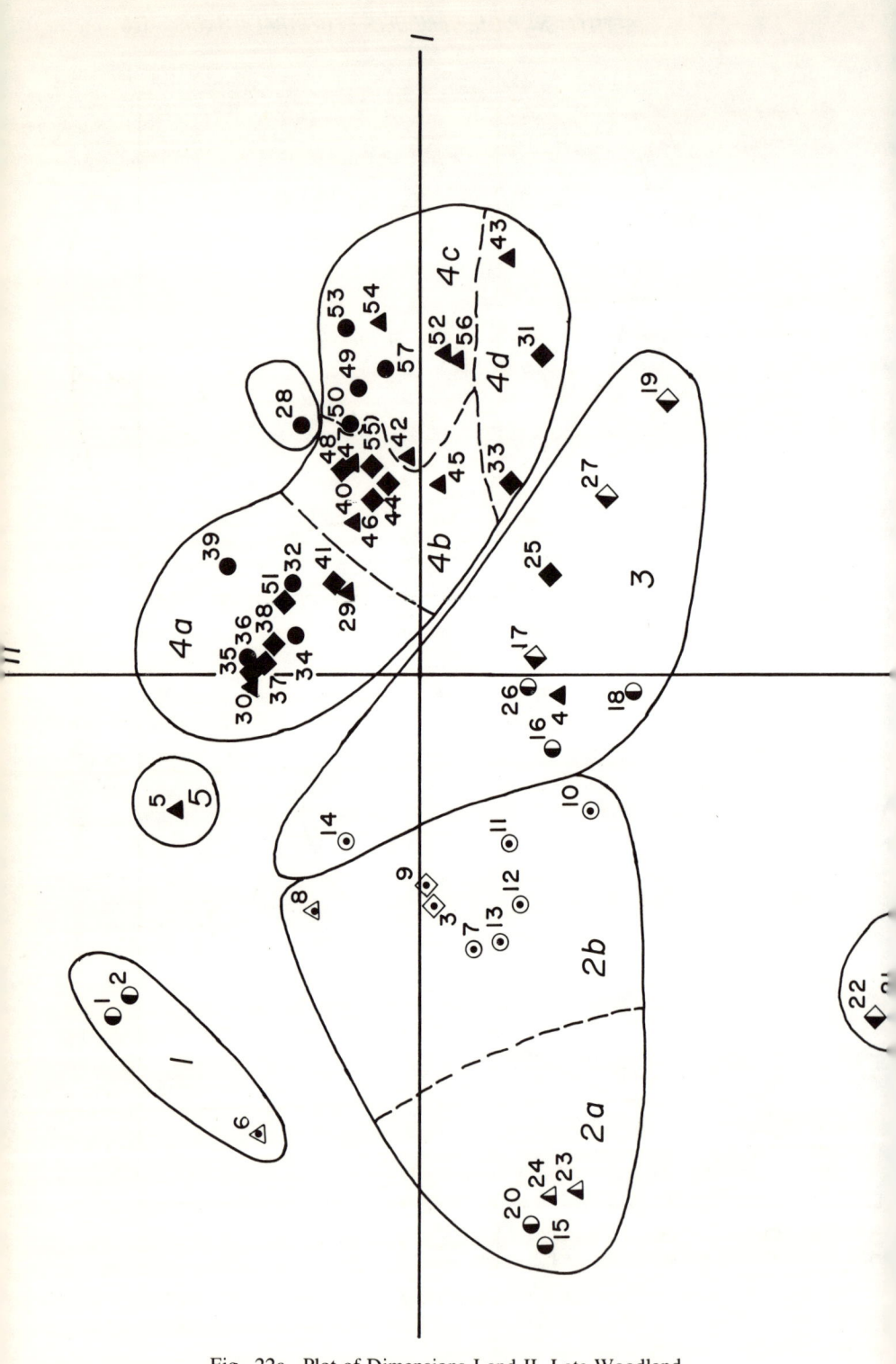

Fig. 22a. Plot of Dimensions I and II, Late Woodland.

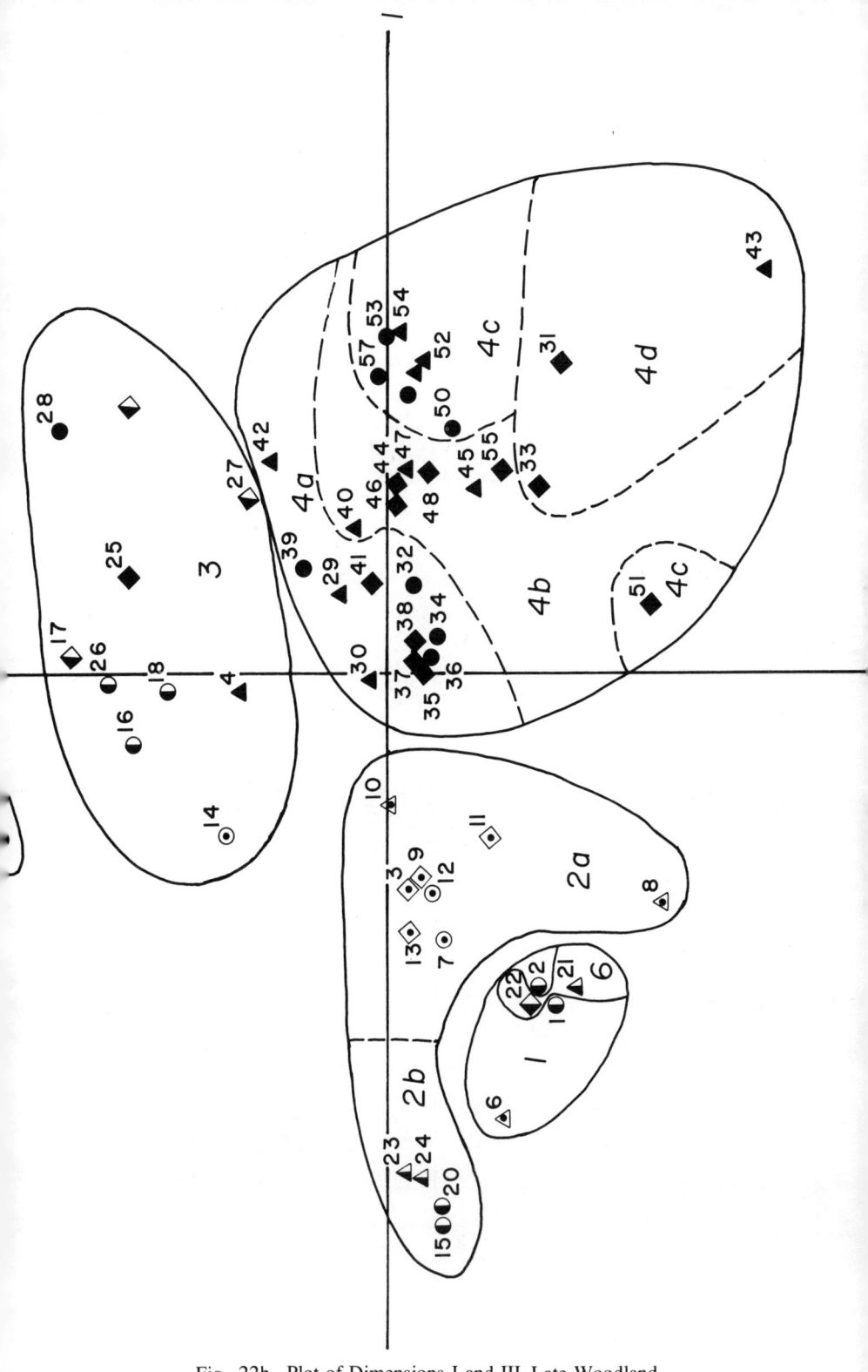

Fig. 22b. Plot of Dimensions I and III, Late Woodland.

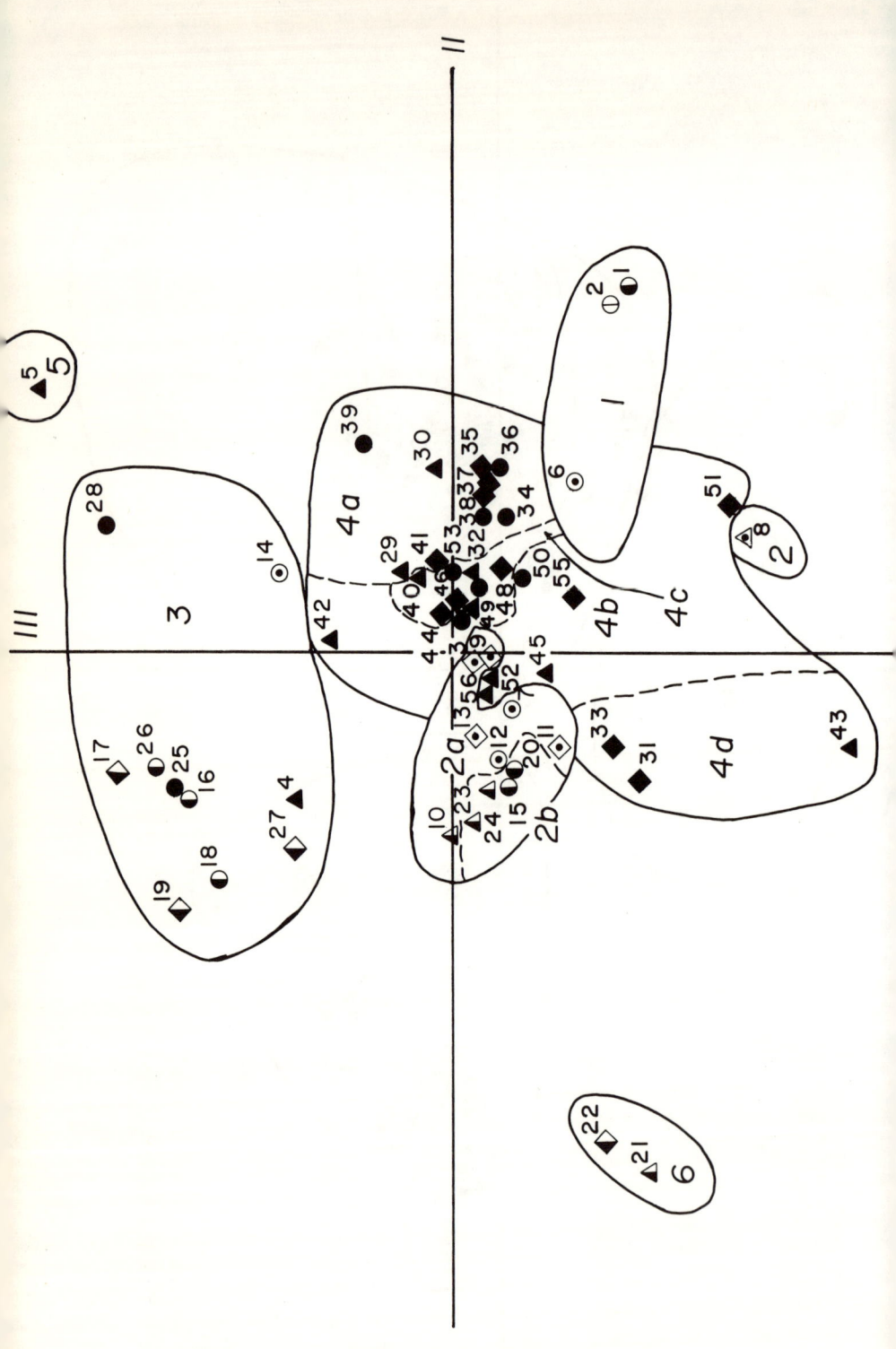

Fig. 22c. Plot of Dimensions II and III, Late Woodland.

TABLE 16
Varimax Rotated Muiltidimensional Scaling Configuration, Late Woodland

Site No.	I	II	III
Mn^{v}41	−0.977	1.030	−0.520
Mn^{v}45	−0.922	0.979	−0.468
Mn^{v}51	−0.636	−0.026	−0.064
Mn^{v}54	−0.051	−0.413	0.459
Mn^{v}57	−0.387	0.739	1.216
Mn^{v}74	−1.317	0.487	−0.367
Mn^{v}77	−0.785	−0.157	−0.175
Mn^{v}84	−0.678	0.324	−0.857
Mn^{v}98	−0.607	−0.008	−0.097
Mn^{v}99	−0.383	−0.510	−0.001
Mn^{v}100	−0.482	−0.266	−0.317
Mn^{v}115	−0.651	−0.300	−0.137
Mn^{v}118	−0.763	−0.237	−0.069
Mn^{v}120	−0.475	0.225	0.509
Cs^{v}19	−1.631	−0.379	−0.167
Cs^{v}26	−0.208	−0.401	0.792
Cs^{v}27	0.055	−0.341	0.984
Cs^{v}28	−0.042	−0.640	0.689
Cs^{v}79	0.796	−0.735	0.802
Cs^{v}212	−1.573	−0.335	−0.169
Cs^{v}215	−0.923	−1.460	−0.587
Cs^{v}222	−0.976	−1.377	−0.448
Cs^{v}224	−1.479	−0.478	−0.062
Cs^{v}226	−1.492	−0.389	−0.106
Me^{v}25	0.289	−0.385	0.809
Me^{v}31	−0.028	−0.322	0.869
Me^{v}33	0.521	−0.558	0.466
Sg^{v}91	0.724	0.365	1.019
Sg^{v}126	0.243	0.228	0.146
Sg^{v}150	−0.016	0.517	0.051
Sg^{v}186	0.925	−0.360	−0.546
Sg^{v}192	0.267	0.390	−0.084
Sg^{v}201	0.556	−0.268	−0.471
Sg^{v}228	0.113	0.382	−0.158
Sg^{v}235	0.027	0.510	−0.112
Sg^{v}237	0.044	0.515	−0.119
Sg^{v}238	0.035	0.470	−0.101
Sg^{v}239	0.091	0.441	−0.089
Sg^{v}248	0.318	0.584	0.260
Sg^{v}253	0.443	0.208	0.100
Cn^{v}22	0.270	0.264	0.046
Cn^{v}58	0.632	0.039	0.361
Cn^{v}61	1.200	−0.261	−1.178
Cn^{v}83	0.556	0.104	0.036
Cn^{v}88	0.550	−0.055	−0.279
Cn^{v}103	0.508	0.144	−0.015
Cn^{v}105	0.611	0.214	−0.061
Cn^{v}110	0.598	0.233	−0.132
Lo^{v}11	0.830	0.190	−0.066
Lo^{v}17	0.727	0.213	−0.204
Lo^{v}24	0.210	0.414	−0.818
Lo^{v}25	0.923	−0.071	−0.112
Lo^{v}30	1.001	0.229	0.000
Lo^{v}38	1.017	0.131	−0.031
Lo^{v}55	0.605	0.154	−0.354
Lo^{v}102	0.915	−0.102	−0.101
Lo^{v}108	0.887	0.108	0.027

TABLE 17
Correlations of Original and Canonical Variables, Late Woodland

Variable	I	II	III
Original:			
1–Bottomland Prairie–1 mi (BP1)	−.71	.12	−.53
2–Upland Prairie–1 mi (UP1)	.08	−.52	.42
3–Floodplain Forest–1 mi (FF1)	−.08	.53	.52
4–Upland Forest–1 mi (UF1)	.79	−.22	−.22
5–Bottomland Prairie–2 mi (BP2)	−.67	.07	−.69
6–Upland Prairie–2 mi (UP2)	.29	−.56	.59
7–Floodplain Forest–2 mi (FF2)	−.46	.61	.32
8–Upland Forest–2 mi (UF2)	.88	−.14	−.06
9–Bottomland Prairie–3 mi (BP3)	−.58	.15	−.63
10–Upland Prairie–3 mi (UP3)	.49	−.43	.62
11–Floodplain Forest–3 mi (FF3)	−.66	.53	.19
12–Upland Forest–3 mi (UF3)	.85	−.07	−.17
13–Floodplain (FP)	−.54	.60	.36
14–Terrace (T)	−.66	−.05	−.53
15–Valley Slope (VS)	.63	−.04	−.36
16–Upland (U)	.64	−.46	.42
17–Closest Water Source (W)	.63	.15	.14
18–Horizontal Distance (H)	.20	.20	−.24
19–Vertical Distance (V)	.53	−.07	−.35
20–Largest Water Source–1 mi (W1)	.45	.35	.44
21–Largest Water Source–2 mi (W2)	−.28	.66	−.14
22–Largest Water Source–3 mi (W3)	−.20	.60	−.35
23–Soil Texture (S)	−.51	.02	−.50
Dimension:			
1	.88	−.48	.28
2	.34	.66	.65
3	.52	.34	−.75

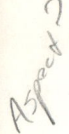
Aspect?

between floodplain and terrace. Further, these sites, especially those in cluster 1, have more floodplain forest within three miles and less upland forest and upland in general than sites in other clusters. This is particularly true of sites in clusters 1, 2a, and 6. Cluster 2b is separate from the rest of the sites beĉause of the uplands in Mason County, and it is indeed this dimension that separates clusters 2a and 2b (2b sites are closer to the back edge of the terrace).

Since the first dimension also has a positive correlation with closest watersource, the sites at the negative end may be suspected to be on a watersource of low rank, and indeed they are. Most are on lakes or sloughs, scored as zero. The first dimension is also correlated with vertical distance to water, and again, the position of these sites at the negative end of the dimension might suggest that the sites have a low elevation above their watersource. Again, this is true. Most of the lakes and sloughs at the lower end of the river are within the 420–440' contour interval; most of the sites are along the 440' contour line (Fig. 23), on portions or remnants of the Beardstown Terrace.

On the third dimension, sites in all three of these clusters are at the middle to lower end of the dimension. It may seem strange for these bottomland sites to

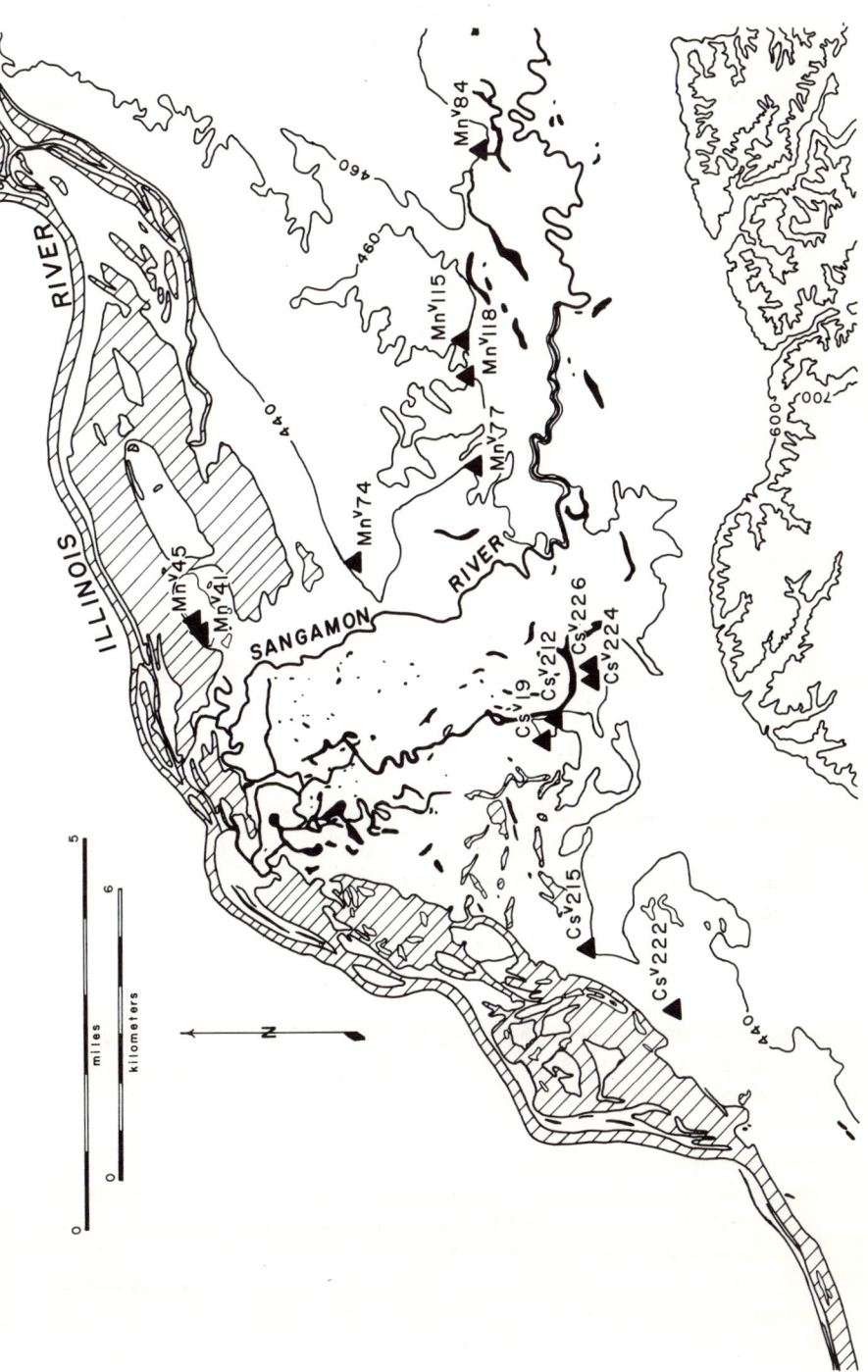

Fig. 23. Late Woodland Sites at Lower End of Sangamon River.

appear to correlate highly with the end of the dimension that has a negative correlation with bottomland in general, but this is probably because the area within three miles of the sites includes much water in the form of backwater lakes and sloughs. Certainly, however, there is no upland prairie within three miles of these sites. The explanation for the apparent correlation of the floodplain forest and the upland prairie is the previously noted proximity of the two zones in the lower reaches of the Sangamon on the Mason County sand terraces.

It is the second dimension that really separates clusters 1, 2, and 6 (see plots, Fig. 22a,c). The first cluster is near the positive end of the dimension. This dimension correlates with floodplain and floodplain forest, and with upland at the positive end, and has a negative correlation with bottomland prairie, terrace, and soil. Cluster 1 sites could then be expected to be in the floodplain and floodplain forest. Large amounts of water surrounding the sites perhaps partly influence these results, as does the proximity of the upland prairie to the floodplain forest in Mason County. Indeed, two of the sites are on a former island in the Illinois River floodplain, while the other is on a terrace promontory extending out into the floodplain. The area near the two sites is thus surrounded by large quantities of floodplain forest and water.

Sites in cluster 6 are at the extreme negative end of the dimension, correlated with bottomland prairie, terrace, and soil. These sites are on a terrace, with large amounts of terrace and water surrounding the site, undoubtedly causing the move toward the negative end of the dimension. Soils of the terrace are frequently coarse due to their derivation from glacial outwash. Most of these sites are also on the sand terrace system of the Sangamon and Illinois valleys. These sites are, therefore, in close proximity to large amounts of upland prairie and floodplain forest, as well as to bottomland prairie. With this accessibility to large quantities of those resources that correlate with both ends of the dimension, the sites occupy an intermediate position on the dimension, between the two clusters with which it is otherwise associated.

Of the cluster 1 sites, two (Mn^v41 and Mn^v45) have Maples Mills ceramics. Both are on Knapp's Island, now joined to the mainland, on a rise on the northwest margin of the island (see Fig. 23). The other (Mn^v74) is a site identified by the presence of a projectile point only, and is near the edge of the terrace overlooking the Sangamon River-Illinois River confluence.

Cluster 2 is composed of 12 sites and is subdivided. Four sites have Maples Mills ceramics (Mn^v77, Mn^v115, Cs^v19, and Cs^v212). The two Cass County sites are, however, dominated by Mississippian ceramics with smaller proportions of Maples Mills and other grit-tempered ceramics. Four sites are recognized on the basis of projectile points, but have undiagnostic ceramics in the surface collections (Mn^v51, Mn^v118, Mn^v98, and Mn^v100).

The other four sites in the cluster (Mn^v99, Mn^v84, Cs^v224, and Cs^v226) are recognized on the basis of projectile points only. Of the cluster 6 sites, one (Cs^v222) has a Late Woodland point and undiagnostic ceramics, the other (Cs^v215) has only a projectile point.

Late Woodland cluster 3 sites occupy a position on the first dimension that is intermediate but ranges from just higher than the cluster 1, 2, and 6 sites, to a point near the positive end of the dimension. In this position, it overlaps with cluster 4. This first dimension has a positive correlation with valley slope, uplands, upland forest, and watersource, a negative correlation with bottomland prairie, floodplain, terrace, and a weak negative correlation with floodplain forest. The intermediate position of the sites of these two clusters on the dimension might well indicate a position midway between the bottomland and the upland—at the transition from floodplain or terrace (i.e., bottomlands in general) to slope, near the bottomland edge of the forest. The scattering of cases along the dimension, however, indicates a scattering of the sites over the terrace and slopes, some of the sites being near the uplands.

Division of cluster 4 into four subclusters helps to interpret this situation. Subcluster 4a sites are near the middle of the first dimension. Compared with the remainder of the subclusters, these are definitely bottomland oriented sites. Terrace is absent or nearly absent, but the amount of floodplain surrounding the sites is as high as that of sites in cluster 2 and higher than that of sites in cluster 6. Amount of floodplain forest, as well as the combination of bottomland resources, is higher than for cluster 3 sites or sites in the remaining subclusters of cluster 4. In other words, subcluster 4a sites manifest some similarities to sites in clusters 1, 2 and 6, but show a variation due to spatial variation in structure of the biophysical environment. Most of the subcluster 4a sites are in a bottomland area near the confluence of the Sangamon River, South Fork, and Sugar Creek. Here the valley broadens to low floodplain with backwater lakes situation similar to that near the Sangamon-Illinois confluence, but in a narrower valley setting. Rank of nearest watersource is higher since the sites are either on a fifth (all 3 streams are fifth order before their confluence) or sixth (after confluence) order stream. Because the sites are in the floodplain rather than on a terrace, soils are somewhat finer than the cluster 2 and 6 sites (but not cluster 1). Since the valley is narrower than at the Sangamon-Illinois confluence, a three-mile radius around upriver sites includes slope and upland resources. For this reason, these sites move to a higher position on dimension I than do the cluster 1, 2, or 6 sites.

The remainder of the subclusters in cluster 4 are in a higher position on the first dimension, indicating less of a placement in the uplands, i.e., the slope and uplands. The combinations of valley slope and uplands, and of upland forest and prairie are far higher for these 3 subclusters than any other set of sites. The nearest watersource variable as compared with largest ranked source within one, two, or three miles indicates that the sites are not on the highest ranked watersource in the area but rather are frequently on a lower rank tributary stream.

As with the first dimension, the second dimension does not separate these sites in the cluster 3 and 4 sites either. In fact, the overlap is even closer to total. The two clusters also overlap with cluster 2. It will be remembered that it was dimension II that separated clusters 1, 2, and 6 from one another. The position of cluster 2 was explained by its correlation with resources that correlate with both ends of the dimension, i.e., both upland prairie and floodplain forest versus bottomland prairie, and the same explanation can be applied here. Although there is a total overlap of the two clusters on this dimension, it is obvious from the plot (Fig. 22) that the bulk of the cluster 3 sites are toward the negative end of the dimension, while a large proportion of the cluster 4 sites move toward the upper end of the dimension. This is particularly true for subcluster 4a, which, as already noted, is farthest toward the floodplains in Natural Division 4b. Subcluster 4d scores the lowest on this dimension—with less access to floodplain resources than any but the cluster 3 sites. Since a terrace is absent, the only way for this to happen is for the sites to be well back from the floodplain and to be near a rather narrow strip of floodplain. The lower end of the dimension correlates with bottomland prairie, terrace, and soil. Six of the sites in cluster 3 are in Natural Division 5a, the Illinois River Section of the Upper Mississippi River and Illinois River Bottomlands Division, which has already been characterized as having linear parallel microenvironments, including a broad terrace. Three of the sites are in division 4b, the Springfield Section of the Grand Prairie Division, but 2 of them are close enough to Division 5a to have portions of the resources of Division 5a included in their three-mile radii. The same is true of the single site of this cluster that is in Division 6a, the Illinois River Section of the Illinois River and Mississippi River Sand Areas Division. This latter site is farthest toward the positive end of the dimension, correlating most highly with floodplain forest and upland prairie, a correlation explained in the discussion of the previous group of clusters. All sites in cluster 4 are in Natural Division 4b, characterized by a less rigid structure than Natural Division 5a, and by increasingly less relief and narrower strips of stream-skirting forest.

It is the third dimension, however, that separates clusters 3 and 4 into mutually exclusive, non-overlapping groups. Cluster 3 sites are at the top of the dimension. Only the single site cluster 5 is higher. The positive correlation is with bottomland prairie and upland forest. The combination of these two resources is the highest for sites in this cluster than in any other cluster. In reporting the correlations of this dimension with the original variables, it was suggested that this dimension is similar to the first dimension of the Middle Woodland analysis. It is further suggested that these sites are similar to the sites in Middle Woodland cluster 3. Indeed, the reader who has been scrutinizing the tables carefully will already have discovered that four of the sites in Late Woodland cluster 3 are multicomponent Middle Woodland/Late Woodland sites. Although these sites are not as predictably placed as the Middle Woodland sites, they are generally on the slopes or bluff base or near the back edge of the terrace, more or less in a forest edge position.

The Late Woodland cluster 4 sites correlate less highly with the third dimension, and indeed, include some of the lowest sites on the dimension. The negative end of this dimension correlates with upland prairie and with bottomland. The forest is apparently narrowing sufficiently for the sites to have either bottomland resources or upland prairie. Subcluster 4a sites thus have a greater amount of floodplain and/or bottomland resources, while 4a sites have larger amounts of upland prairie. They are separated from the cluster 3 sites, however, because of the smaller amounts of the combination of bottomland prairie and upland forest.

The single site regarded as cluster 5 is in many ways not too dissimilar to cluster 3, but is definitely separated from the sites in that cluster. It occupies roughly the same position on the first dimension as the upper end of cluster 2 and the lower end of cluster 3. The site is surrounded by an amount of bottomland prairie that is less than the average for cluster 2 sites, but more than the average for cluster 3 sites. It is, however, on a watersource of high rank. On the second dimension, the site occupies a position similar to cluster 1. On the third dimension, it is higher than any of the cluster 3 sites. This "cluster" is second only to cluster 3 in the amount of the combination of bottomland prairie and upland forest surrounding the site.

Of the ten sites in cluster 3, five (Mn^v120, Cs^v26, Me^v31, Cs^v28, and Sg^v91) are ceramic sites, all with Maples Mills ceramics. Only Me^v31 has Mississippian ceramics in association with the Maples Mills, and none of the sites have Albee ceramics. Four of these sites (Me^v25, Me^v33, Cs^v79, and Cs^v27) have Late Woodland projectile points and ceramics that are either not diagnostic or include ceramics diagnostic of the Middle Woodland period. Mn^v54, the tenth site, is identified by projectile points only.

Of the 29 sites in cluster 4, 8 (Sg^v192, Sg^v228, Sg^v237, Sg^v248, Lo^v11, Lo^v30, Lo^v17, and Lo^v108) have Maples Mills ceramics. Additionally, Sg^v248 has some Mississippian ceramics, and Lo^v11 and Lo^v108 have Albee ceramics. Eleven of the sites (Sg^v235, Sg^v238, Sg^v239, Cn^v22, Cn^v83, Cn^v103, Cn^v110, Lo^v55, Lo^v24, Sg^v186, and Sg^v201) have undiagnostic ceramics but are assigned to the Late Woodland period on the basis of projectile points. The other ten sites (Sg^v126, Sg^v150, Sg^v253, Cn^v105, Cn^v88, Lo^v38, Lo^v25, Lo^v102, Cn^v58, and Cn^v61) have only Late Woodland points and no pottery at all. The cluster 5 site (Mn^v57) has only Late Woodland projectile points and no pottery at all.

Two of the 8 ceramic sites in cluster 4 also have Middle Woodland components although, in both cases, these Middle Woodland components are identified only from points. Two of the sites with non-Late Woodland or unrecognized pottery have Havana ceramics in addition to the Late Woodland points. None of the Late Woodland only sites have any Middle Woodland material. In other words, among these sites, all of which are in Natural Division 4b (Grand Prairie) there is less mixing of the Middle and Late Woodland material.

Summary

This chapter has presented a discussion of the statistical analysis of the Sangamon Woodland sites data. The analysis was directed toward the solution of seven research questions outlined in the introduction to the chapter. Middle and Late Woodland sites were separately analyzed.

Twenty-three environmental variables were input to two types of multivariate analysis: cluster analysis and multidimensional scaling. Three-way crosstabulations of material evidence type, Natural Division of Illinois, and cluster were presented. The multidimensional scaling analysis complemented the cluster analysis by providing insight into the question of how the clusters of sites differed. In both the Middle and Late Woodland analysis, three dimensions were extracted and interpreted. Canonical correlations between the original variables and the multidimensional scaling configuration assisted in interpretation of the dimensions.

VI. MODELS OF WOODLAND SETTLEMENT PATTERNS IN THE SANGAMON RIVER VALLEY

The analyses of Middle and Late Woodland sites in the preceding chapter can be interpreted to show a shifting settlement pattern. Although at the present time we are unable to completely account for the shift, it is possible to document the different configurations of settlement. Such documentation will make use of several lines of evidence: (1) the cluster analysis and multidimensional scaling, (2) the distribution of material evidence types, (3) other evidence of site function from either survey or excavation, and (4) comparison of the Sangamon River Valley with other river valleys in central Illinois.

Middle Woodland

The crosstabulation of clusters, natural divisions, and material evidence types in Chapter V suggested several preliminary conclusions: (1) Middle Woodland peoples selected particular types of situations for locating functionally distinct sites, (2) placement of functionally equivalent sites varies with the structure of the natural environment, and (3) different portions of the Sangamon River drainage were differentially used. On the basis of the multidimensional scaling analysis, the preliminary conclusions may now be expanded, refined, and discussed in greater detail.

Ceramic sites are positioned so as to have access to large quantities of either bottomland resources or upland forest or both. Projectile point sites, however, are in situations where either by apparent choice, or by the fact that narrowing of environmental zones occurs, have less bottomland and a greater amount of upland prairie within a three mile catchment area.

Ceramic sites in particular show variation in their catchment areas. Part of this may be seen as due to spatial variation, and part as due to apparent cultural choice of situation. Accordingly, two types of ceramic sites, one of which shows clear spatial variation, may be discerned in the Sangamon River Valley.

Ceramic Type I Sites

Ceramic sites in clusters 3, 5, and 4 (particularly 4a) vary among each other in one major respect, viz., the natural division in which they are found. The locations of these sites are quite similar in their relationship to the valley slope, uplands, bottomlands, and associated vegetation zones. These sites are generally at the base of a slope or at the back edge of a terrace, and near the valley edge of the upland forest. They are several miles from the upland prairie, although the effects of spatial variation are evident. As one proceeds upstream, however, the stream–skirting forest narrows and eventually becomes discontinuous as relief decreases. The sites do not differ greatly from one cluster to another in the amounts of uplands versus bottomlands, particularly within one mile of the site. At a distance of two miles, and even more at three, the narrowing of the forest begins to separate the sites. The presence of terrace distinguishes cluster 3 from clusters 5 and 4a because of the greater amount of bottomland prairie. Cluster 5, on the other hand, is differentiated from clusters 3 and 4a because of the very small amount of prairie of either type to which it has access. Clusters 3 and 4a appear similar on Dimension III but differ in that the prairie available to cluster 3 sites is bottomland prairie, while that available to cluster 4a sites is upland prairie. The terrace also correlates with choice of closest watersource, cluster 3 sites being on a low order side stream, while clusters 4a and 5 sites are on the main stream. All sites are high enough above the river level to escape flooding. Further, the soil on which the sites are located is generally coarse enough to provide reasonable drainage and thus promote some degree of dryness and comfort for occupation. The perspective drawing (Fig. 24) summarizes these ideal types of site locations. The drawing is a schematized composite representation of different portions of the valley. The two sides of the "river" in the figure, however, will serve to illustrate the kinds of situations described by clusters 3 and 5.

Cluster 3 sites must be considered similar in location to the classic description of the Middle Woodland Havana sites in Illinois. It was probably Griffin (1956: p. 68) who first pointed out certain general regularities in the placement of Middle Woodland sites in the Illinois River Valley:"The majority of the Hopewellian village sites are located in the main valley floor or adjacent tributary valley . . . ."McGregor's (1957) description of the location of "Early Hopewell" sites in the Illinois River Valley is more explicit: "42% of these villages are located on side streams, just within the edge of the bluffs, and just

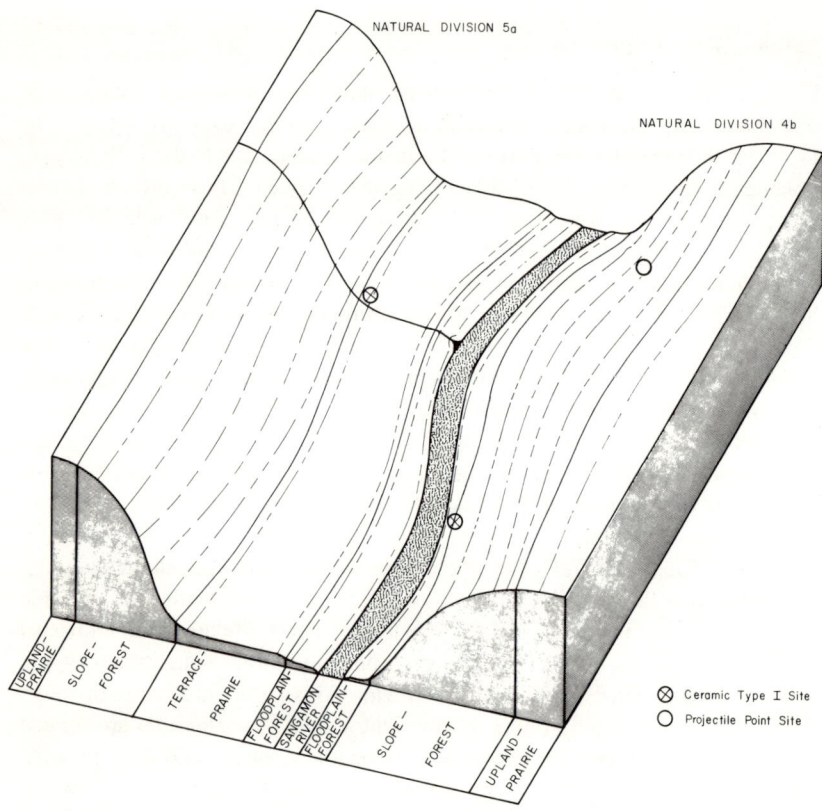

Fig. 24. Three-Dimensional Contrast of Situations in Different Natural Divisions and Ideal Site Locations in these Divisions, Middle Woodland.

above the level of the floodplains, 27% are at, or near, the river level . . . some 20% are located in river valleys far from the Illinois." His description of "Late Hopewell" (roughly equivalent to the Steuben or Pike phases) is similar: "59% of the sites are located on the slopes of the bluffs, where a side stream comes into the valley or near a lake. 24% are at river level . . . ." (McGregor, 1957: p. 276).

Wilson (1961: p. 36), using McGregor's study as a background, described a similar placement of sites in the upper central Spoon River Valley:

> The preferential location of Hopewellian villages thus seems to have been on a second bottom or other raised ground, on or near a secondary stream which entered the Spoon River within a few hundred yards to several miles. None of the villages were right on the river itself, . . .

Struever notes that Middle Woodland sites are found "at the base of the steep bluffs" and "at the junction of a secondary stream with the Illinois Valley"(1968c: p. 295),while Harn (1971: p. 26) citing Struever, notes: "The settlement pattern in the north-central Mississippi Valley,as far as is known,is reminiscent of the pattern commonly associated with Middle Woodland sites in the lower Illinois Valley."

A similar location strategy was employed by Havana Tradition people in the Wisconsin River Valley in Wisconsin:

> The other Middle Woodland sites excavated in the Wisconsin River Valley . . . like Millville, are located on the base of the first terrace of the Wisconsin River, at the base of a hollow through which flows a small stream tributary to the Wisconsin. . . .(Freeman, 1969: p. 85).

Similarly, in Henderson County, Illinois, Gregg recently reported three Havana sites, two of which "are situated in bluff-base locales where tributary streams enter the Mississippi River floodplain" (Gregg, 1974: p. 233).

Unfortunately, all the cited works consider primarily topographic and hydrographic rather than biotic variables. Wilson (1961: p. 38) mentions that "the chosen habitation sites were close to or within the forests where such game [deer] lived." Harn (1971: p. 26) notes that "all microhabitat zones in the bottomlands and uplands were easily accessible." Only Gregg (1974) has really examined biotic context in more than a passing mention. Gregg (1974: p. 240) found that his two bluff-base sites were on silt loams originally covered with prairie grasses, but were "no more than a mile from the oak-forest regions."

The situation represented by the fifth cluster has not been explicitly noted elsewhere in the Illinois Woodland literature. This may be because observed patterns do not fit the previously published descriptions of Illinois Middle Woodland settlement patterns and are thus are not reported. The Sangamon

Valley is in a unique position in Illinois in that it is a tributary of the Illinois River with sufficient length to include much diversity of biophysical environment, and shows a continuum of change from a situation similar to that of the Illinois, to a situation very different from the Illinois. Thus, it is possible to define the transition in site location patterns and to explain the difference in terms of the difference in the structuring of the biophysical environment.

Looking at the literature of other river valleys, a pattern similar to that found in the upper portion of the Sangamon for Middle Woodland ceramic sites is recognizable. On the Wood River Terrace, Munson (1971: p. 7) found Havana villages in two physiographic zones: "talus slope-terrace and natural levee, both near large permanent bodies of water." It appears that 8 out of 9 of Farnsworth's (1973: p. 20) sites in the Macoupin Valley are in close proximity to Macoupin Creek itself rather than where a tributary enters the Macoupin Valley. (This, however, is an inference based on negative evidence since Farnsworth does not specifically mention it, and upon a rather small scale map in his report.) Similarly, Gardner's sites in the Kaskaskia valley would appear to fit the description of the Havana sites in the middle to upper portions of the Sangamon Valley (Springfield Section of the Grand Prairie Division):

1. Settlements are located in an area where two major streams, the West Okaw and Kaskaskia Rivers, join and where there is a considerable expanse of floodplain.
2. Sites are always on unflooded ground as close to the river as was possible and still maintain flood-free conditions. (Gardner, 1969: p. 160)

Neither Farnsworth nor Gardner discusses biotic context, except that Farnsworth (1973: p. 19) notes that Middle Woodland habitation sites occur only in his Floodplain Forest and Upland Forest zones.

When sites similar to the ceramic type I sites have been excavated, they have given evidence that their excavators have inferred to be representative of a habitation site inhabited during all or much of the year and over a period of a number of years. The Pool site in the Illinois River Valley (McGregor 1958), the Apple Creek site in the same valley (Struever 1968b, c; Parmalee, Paloumpis, and Wilson 1972), and the Jasper Newman site in the Kaskaskia Valley (Gardner 1969) all produced evidence of structures, numerous features, high densities of ceramics, and chipped stone tools of a variety of classes representing a variety of domestic and related activities. Floral and faunal remains have been interpreted to indicate an occupation during a large part of the year (e.g., Parmalee, Paloumpis, and Wilson, 1972: p. 58).

Two general lines of evidence from the Sangamon River area may be used to support an hypothesis of similar function of sites in the present analysis: (1) features noted in the survey of some of these sites, and (2) limited test excavations on one site.

The surfaces of several sites in the Sangamon River Valley have yielded high densities of ceramics, chipped stone tools, and debitage, bone, shell, and fire-cracked rock. In addition, several have suggestions of spatial variability across the site. For example, Me^{v}31, the Clary Creek site, upon survey done under ideal conditions, revealed 6 very distinct areas of organic staining each with very high debris densities, and with virtually no scatter between them. Probing with a 2 cm soil corer indicated a depth of at least 75 cm in all 6 stains. Chipped stone debris included projectile points, drills, scrapers, preforms, one "hoe," miscellaneous bifacially worked fragments, utilized flakes, cores, and unmodified debitage. Clary Creek is not the only site on which such a wide range of tools has been recovered in addition to high densities of sherds, fire-cracked rock, etc., nor is it unique in its apparent depth. In general, the surface descriptions of a number of sites widely scattered through the valley that have been examined under good survey conditions conform quite closely to the description given by Struever (1968c: p. 297) for similarly located sites in the Lower Illinois River Valley:

> Middle Woodland bluff-base sites reveal a heavy scatter of debris; sharp increases are noted over Early Woodland in the density of all stone artifact types relating to exploitative and maintenance tasks, and in the density of sherds, faunal debris, and hearth stone. The soil within the site area is usually dark-stained, reflecting its high organic content. The site limits are sharply defined by the color differences between the organically stained habitation area and the unstained soil around it.

One Sangamon River site, 11 Cs^{v}20, the Eilers site, was tested in the summer of 1972. The site is on a slope facing the Sangamon Valley, where Miller Creek enters the Sangamon Valley (a cluster 3 site). Five 3-meter-square test units were dug in 10 cm levels to sterile soil. All soil was passed through ¼" mesh screen, additionally a 20-liter sample from each level was waterscreened through $^1/_{16}$" mesh screen for recovery of small-scale faunal and floral remains. In the major part of the site, debris extended vertically to a depth of about 80 cm. Ceramics, lithic debris including both artifacts and unmodified debitage, bone, floral remains, and mussel shells were recovered in great quantities.

Ceramics are abundant. Pottery represents Havana, Hopewell, and Weaver wares. In general, the Havana-Hopewell and Weaver ceramics are spatially separated in the excavations. A number of vessel sections are liberally coated with carbonized material on the interior, probably indicative of food preparation activities. Chipped stone debris includes projectile points, knives, drills, scrapers, one "hoe," other bifacially worked items, retouched flakes, and unmodified debitage. Awls and flakers are made of bone; a section of long bone of a large mammal is cut and worked into the shape of a bear canine. The large quantities of mussel shell include a number of valves modified by cutting a hole through one side.

Floral remains, identified by F. B. King, have been reported elsewhere (King and Roper 1976). In general, the Havana component is dominated by hazelnuts, with smaller quantities of hickory, black walnut, persimmon, and hackberry. The Weaver component is dominated by hickory nut shells and hackberry seeds, with smaller quantities of hazel, black walnut, and wild plum. Other seeds are present in small quantities in both components (King and Roper, 1976: p. 145).

Faunal remains are in a much less complete state of analysis. Species so far identified are listed in Table 18.

TABLE 18

Faunal Remains Identified at the Eilers Site

MAMMALS	REPTILES
Racoon	Mud Turtle
River otter	Box Turtle
Canis sp.	Painted Turtle
Squirrel (*Sciurus* sp.)	Red-ear Turtle
Beaver	Soft-shell Turtle
Muskrat	
Cottontail Rabbit	
White-tailed Deer	FISH
Man	
	Catfish
	Drumfish
BIRDS	Bowfin
	Buffalo
Turkey	
Prairie Chicken	
Duck (*Anas* sp.)	MUSSELS

The nature of the assemblage indicates a use over several seasons, and the use of a number of different resource zones. All of the floral elements are of species that occur in upland forest or open woodlands, although some of them are also found in other zones. All are late summer through early fall products (King and Roper, 1976: p. 147). The animals taken also represent a variety of habitats—bottomlands and aquatic habitats, woods, forest edge, and prairie. Less seasonal constraint is implied. Several species are less active in winter, or else hibernate, or are limited in the period of the year during which they are available (for example, the ducks) but the remainder are available at any time. Mussels are probably best collected when water levels are low, as would be expected in the late summer.

In summary, the Eilers site, the only one of the cluster 3, 4, or 5 sites in the Sangamon Valley so far tested, has many of the characteristics described for bluff-base Middle Woodland sites elsewhere in Illinois. The excavations were not extensive, but the quantity of ceramics, stone tools, and fire-cracked rock indicate an intense occupation.

Ceramic Type II Sites

Ceramic type II sites are those in clusters 1 and 2, i.e., at the lower end of the

Sangamon River, in Natural Division 6a and the floodplain portion of 5a. The differences between the two clusters have already been described.

Comparative literature for cluster 1 and 2 sites is hard to obtain. Havana sites are not unknown on the terraces and floodplains of the major rivers. In fact, Struever postulates two types of sites on the floodplain, one a "regional exchange center" (1968c: p. 308) at which groups congregated periodically to trade and carry out ritual activity, and another type for which he notes that "because none have been excavated, the Middle Woodland sites located on the sand ridges in the floodplain—sometimes three or more miles from the nearest bluff-base site—remain a mystery" (Struever, 1968c: p. 304). He has further noted that:

> We might also predict that seasonality analysis would disclose that these floodplain sites were occupied during a specific time of the year in contrast to long term, if not year-round, occupation of the settlements on the talus slopes at the valley margins.(Struever and Houart, 1972: p. 63)

Thus, in spite of his speculation that these might be "Summer Agricultural Camps" (Struever 1968c: p. 307), the function of the sites is unknown in the Illinois River Valley.

In working with a similar dichotomy of upland or "bluff-crest" and "valley floodplain" sites, Farnsworth (1973: p. 33) found no difference at all in the area of scatter, cobble count, and sherd density measurements for the two groups of sites. He concluded that either his site types were meaningless, or the survey data were so inaccurate as to be meaningless.

Gregg, however, did find an apparent difference in the activities represented at sites in the Mississippi River floodplain in Henderson County. In comparing a site in the floodplain with the two at bluff base, he found that the flakes from the floodplain site were much less heavily utilized, indicating to him a lack of concern for economy of resource material (Gregg, 1974: p. 241). He concluded that the floodplain site's occupation was of a generalized nature. This site, it should be noted, is on a sandy soil, formed under a native vegetation of forest, but is less than a mile from bottomland prairie. The Henderson County area along the Mississippi River appears to have some similarities to the lower end of the Sangamon, i.e., a fairly broad floodplain, with extensive sandy areas.

Certainly other major Middle Woodland sites in central Illinois are in similar topographic positions in the sand areas of the Illinois River, the two major examples being the Havana (McGregor 1952) and Clear Lake (Fowler 1952) sites, both in northern Mason County on the Illinois River. The functions of these sites, and their role in the Middle Woodland settlement pattern are, however, totally unclear. Both were investigated before settlement patterns were a focus of study. The reports are inadequate for comparison with reports of recently excavated sites.

Many floodplain sites are adjacent to mound groups. Havana and Clear Lake are but two examples of such sites. The bottomland sites in the Sangamon River

Valley are sometimes adjacent to mound groups. Knapp's Island (Mn^{v}40) reportedly has a mound group, although we were unable to locate it in July 1971. A number of mounds were observed near 11Mn^{v}46.

Clusters 1 and 2 contain most of the Weaver components in this study. Unfortunately, very little is known of Weaver settlement patterns in central Illinois. For one thing, as was noted in Chapter III, even the distribution of Weaver is not well known, and for another, where it is known, its settlement pattern is poorly reported. Generally a useful source of comparative information, McGregor (1957) notes only that Weaver sites are "variable in location, from the top of the bluffs to the bottom of the main river and the bottom of the Spoon River" (McGregor, 1957: p. 276). The most useful statement on Weaver phase settlement is that by Munson, Parmalee, and Yarnell in comparing the Scovill site to other Weaver sites in the Spoon River Valley:

> Five other Weaver focus villages are known for the lower 10 mi of the Spoon River Valley, . . . Each is situated on the margin of the first terrace above the floodplain of the Spoon. Size ranges from about one-half to one acre . . . Each site is situated adjacent to a tributary stream. None is more than one-fourth mile from the base of the bluff nor more than 200 yards from the channel of the Spoon River or a navigable tributary (Munson, Parmalee, and Yarnell 1971: p. 429).

But large Weaver components are also found in exactly the same locations as major Havana components in central Illinois. The Weaver site itself has both Havana and Weaver components (Wray and MacNeish 1961), as does the Clear Lake site (Fowler 1952). The Eilers site (11Cs^{v}20) has both a Havana and a Weaver component, and a few Weaver sites located in Menard County while this study was in preparation are definitely not in the bottomland situation as are the Weaver sites in clusters 1 and 2.

In the Sangamon River Valley, test excavations were conducted by the Illinois State Museum in the spring of 1972 on the Griffie site (Mn^{v}94), one of the cluster 2 Weaver sites. Although the faunal remains have not yet been analyzed, it is evident that fish remains are abundant, and other aquatic species well represented. Charred floral remains identified by F. B. King are reported elsewhere (King and Roper, 1976: p. 145). As with the Weaver component at the Eilers site, hickory is the dominant species. Habitats represented by the Griffie site flora are virtually the same as those represented by the Eilers flora.

Occupation of ceramic type II sites during the same seasons and for the same purposes as the ceramic type I sites might be uneconomical. In the first place, occupation of a number of the cluster 1 sites would carry with it a fairly high risk of flooding, particularly in the spring (see Table 9). Second, the diversity of accessible resource zones is not as high and is oriented toward the bottomland zones, which do not contain the species diversity of the upland forest and open woodland zones. Unfortunately, however, the data from the Eilers and Griffie sites are not yet in a sufficiently advanced stage of analysis to permit a more rigorous comparison of exploitative practices at the two sites. Because no other Middle Woodland sites in the Sangamon Valley have been excavated, no further comparative statements can be ventured.

An alternative explanation, of course, is that the two types of sites are temporally distinct. King and Roper (1976) have suggested that the shift in observed floral remains at the Eilers and Griffie sites may be due to a slight shift in climate, with a concomitant shift in prairie-forest borders. Such a shift would affect the bottomlands far less than the uplands, and could account for the shift in site location strategy. King and Roper (1976: p. 149) conclude: "It seems possible to us that a warmer and/or drier period around A.D. 300 could have discouraged settlement (and/or exploitation) and placed increased emphasis on the utilization of bottomland resources."

Fig. 25a contrasts the location of ceramic type II sites with the sites of the lower Sangamon Valley variant of ceramic type I in a somewhat idealized cross-section of the valley. The accompanying circle diagrams (Fig. 25b-c) are, however, of real sites used in the analysis and serve to illustrate the differences in resource availability among sites in various groups.

Projectile Point Sites

The final type of Middle Woodland site is the type identified solely by the presence of projectile points. We have already noted the clustering of projectile point sites in clusters 4b, 4c, and 6, and the near exclusive distribution of these sites in the Springfield Section of the Grand Prairie Division. It was earlier suggested that different portions of the Sangamon River drainage were differently utilized. The ceramic type II sites are found in a riverine-floodplain situation, while the projectile point sites are in the upland forest-upland prairie context. The major characteristics of the locations of these sites have already been described. Their upriver location may not be surprising. McGregor (1959: p. 21) notes: "What appear to have been temporary campsites are widely scattered throughout headwater drainages. These may have been hunting camps, seasonally occupied." The locations of these temporary "limited-activity" sites would be such that the readily available resource diversity would not be great, but quantitative availability of selected species, such as deer, rabbit, and other forest-edge dwellers would be high.

There is only a small amount of comparative literature for the projectile point sites recognized here. Both Munson (1971) and Harn (1971) identified small Havana camps in the vicinity of present day East St. Louis and noted that they were scattered through a wider number of physiographic zones than the Havana "villages." More directly, Farnsworth (1973: p. 34) has described two nonceramic Middle Woodland site types in the Macoupin Creek Valley. They are characterized by localized chipping scatters, are small, and yield points of the Snyders group. Farnsworth (1973: p. 34) concludes:

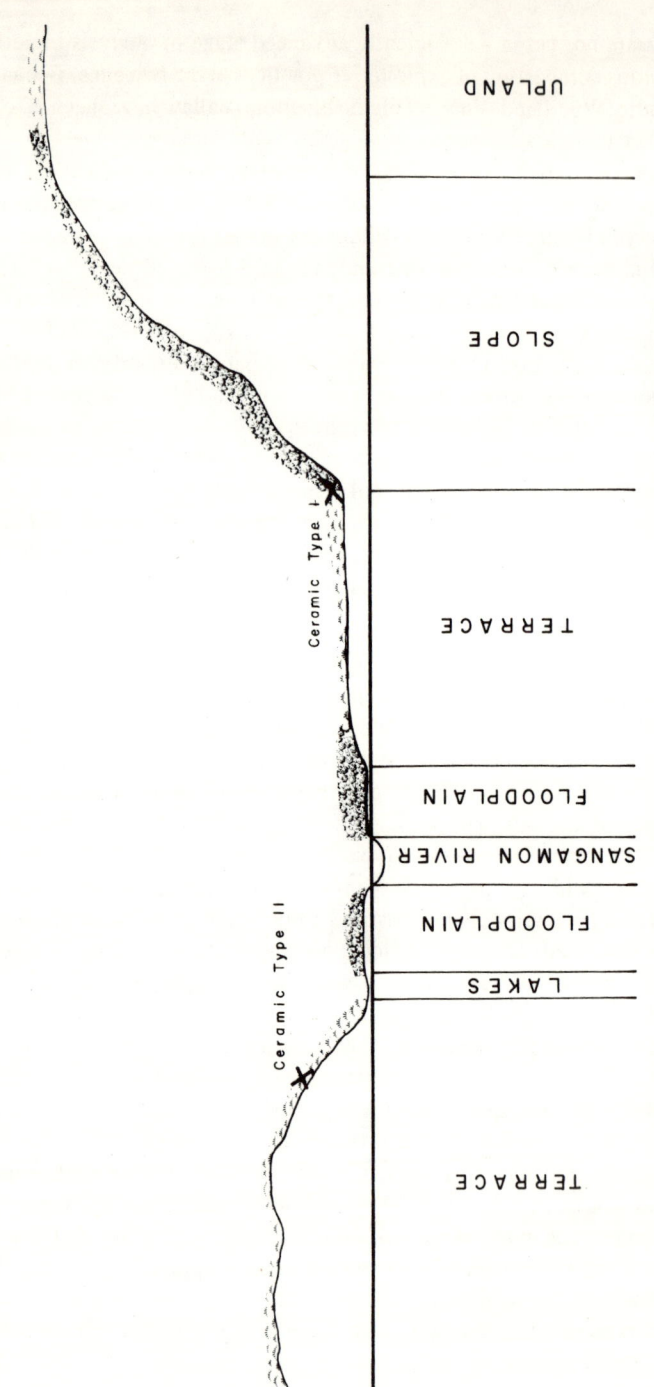

Fig. 25a. Idealized Cross-Section of Lower Sangamon with Idealized Middle Woodland Site Locations.

SETTLEMENT PATTERN MODELS IN CENTRAL ILLINOIS **125**

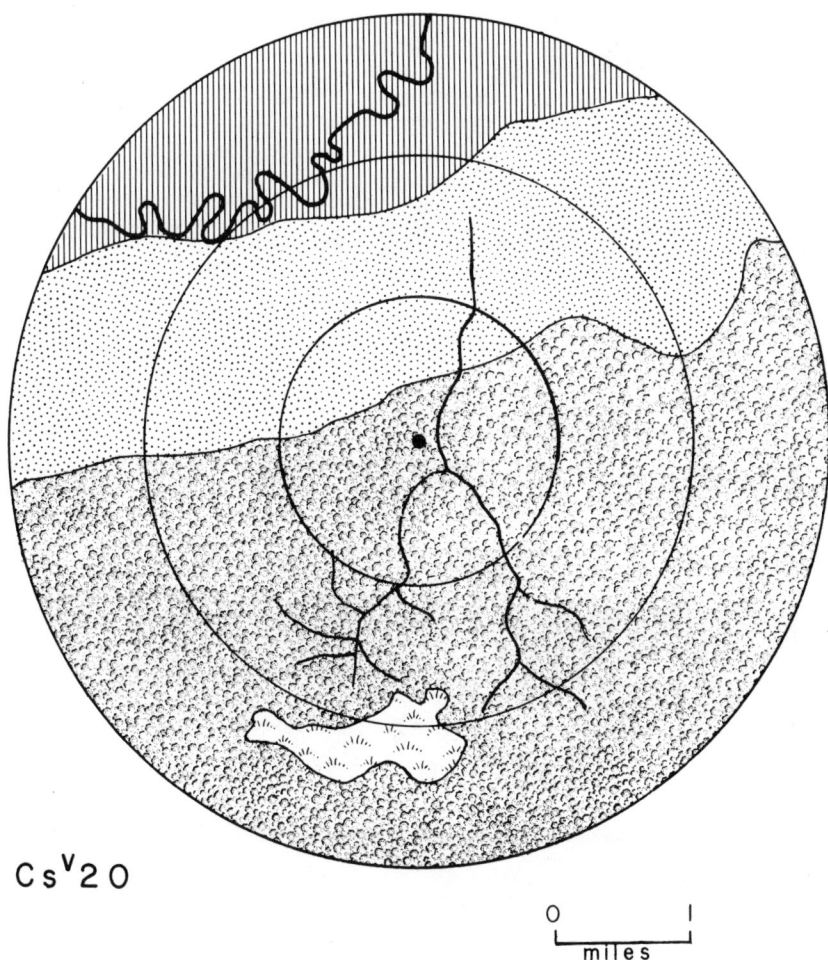

Fig. 25b. Site Catchment Drawing of Selected Middle Woodland Site (Ceramic Type I, Natural Division 5a).

126 *Donna C. Roper*

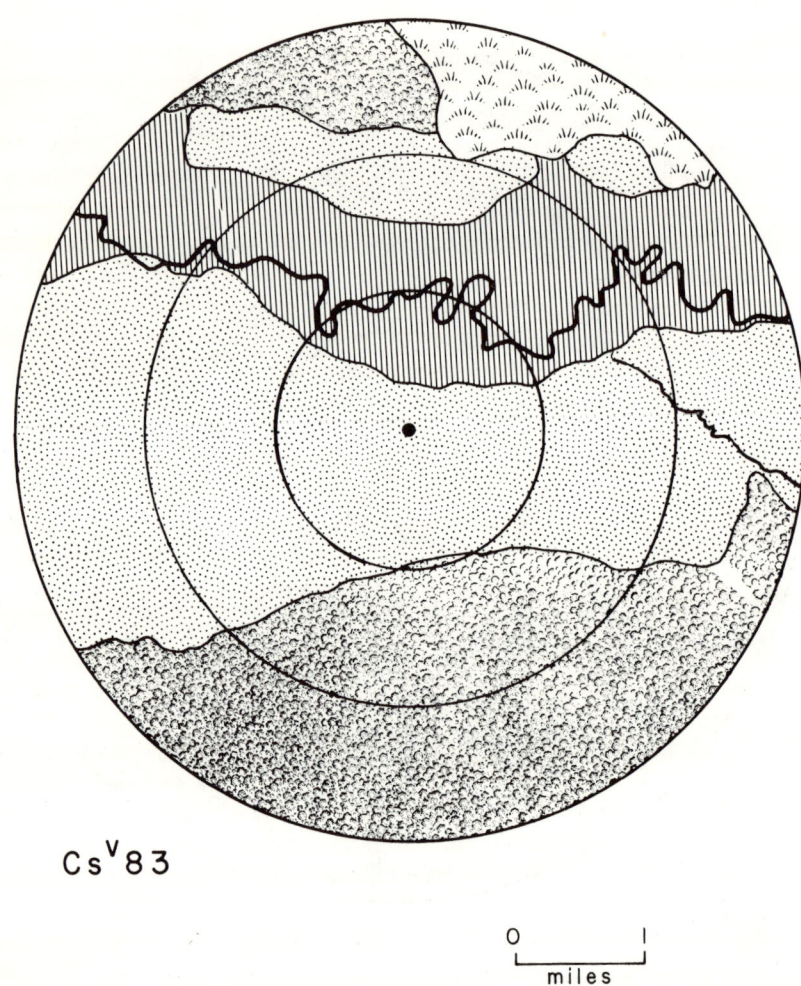

Cs^v83

Fig. 25c. Site Catchment Drawing of Selected Middle Woodland Site (Ceramic Type II, Natural Division 5a).

If the two [non-ceramic] settlement types are verified by future surveys, they constitute an important amendment to our present concepts of Middle Woodland subsistence-settlement. Since ceramics are indicative of culinary and food-storage activities, the absence of pottery at both these putative settlement types suggests that they represent the temporary hunting camps of Middle Woodland groups whose base camps are the Valley Floodplain and BluffCrest sites in the Macoupin Valley itself.

Similarly, Gardner (1969: p. 160) recognizes the presence of Middle Woodland points in the uplands, and Munson, Parmalee, and Yarnell find that Steuben Expanding Stemmed points, possibly related to Weaver, "show up in surface collections made in the upland prairie regions, often many miles from the valleys of the Illinois River and its major tributaries" (1971: p. 429).

Excavations at the Airport Site, in Sangamon County just north of Springfield, almost certainly revealed a late Middle-early Late Woodland component (Roper 1978). Although Archaic components were also present at Airport, it is clear that the Woodland occupation contained only a very limited range of debris types. This component was not identified until after the original version of this study was completed and was therefore not included in the analysis. The site's location would almost certainly correspond to that characteristic of cluster 4b or 4c, however.

Fig. 26a contrasts the location of this type of site with the location of the ceramic type I sites in the middle to upper portions of the valley using an idealized cross section of the valley. The accompanying concentric circle diagrams (Fig. 26*b-c*) are, however, from actual sites included in the analysis, and serve to illustrate the differences in resource availability.

In general, the Middle Woodland settlement system seems to include (1) base camps, probably occupied for much of the year and over a period of years, (2) bottomland camps, probably occupied seasonally, perhaps in the late summer or winter when flood risk is low and aquatic resources are abundant, and (3) hunting camps, in the uplands perhaps miles from the base camp, probably occupied only by a portion of the male population for short periods of time. If this system model were to be validated, it would appear that general purpose sites (i.e., base camps) were located to maximize *diversity* of resources, while more specialized camps were located to maximize *quantities* of selected resources.

The observed distribution of sites in the Sangamon River Valley, coupled with the knowledge of the environmental situation of these sites provides some further insights into the Middle Woodland use of the Sangamon River Valley. It has been argued elsewhere (Roper n.d.) that the area immediately surrounding a site (i.e., the territory—cf. Higgs et al., 1975: p. ix)—in this study, the 3-mile radii—should not be considered to be the actual catchment of the site, but instead as an analytical device. A catchment is correctly viewed as a behavioral unit, and is inferred from comparative knowledge of site territories (used as above), resource distribution, site contents, and settlement system morphology. Thus, although a site catchment analysis will typically begin with an

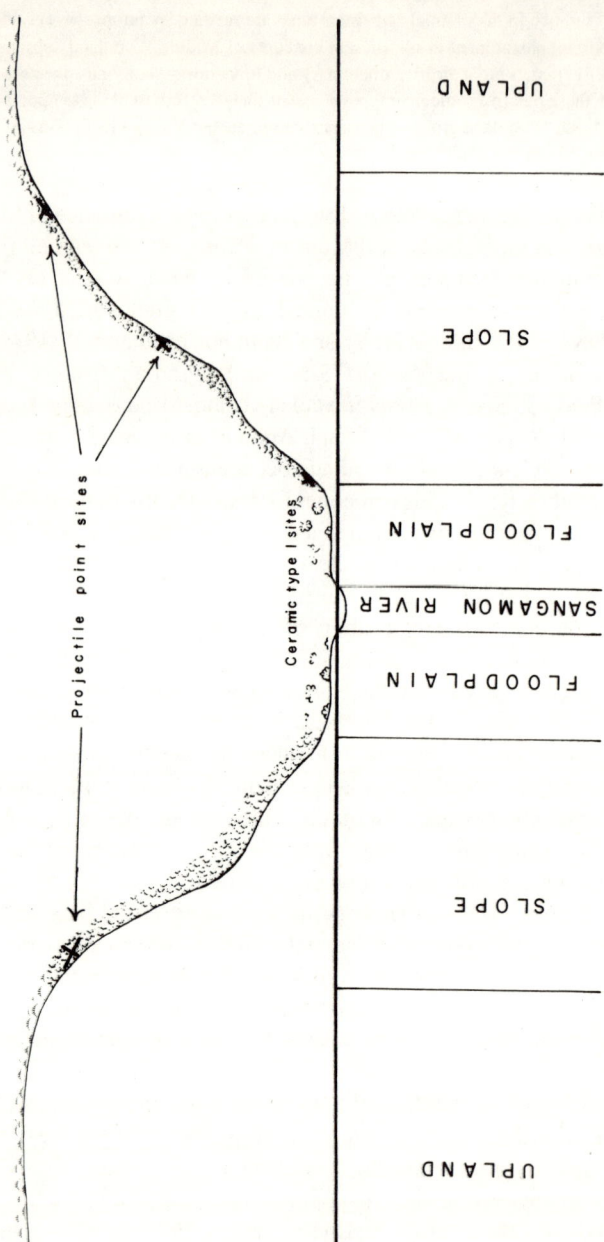

Fig. 26a. Idealized Cross-Section of Middle Sangamon with Idealized Middle Woodland Site Locations.

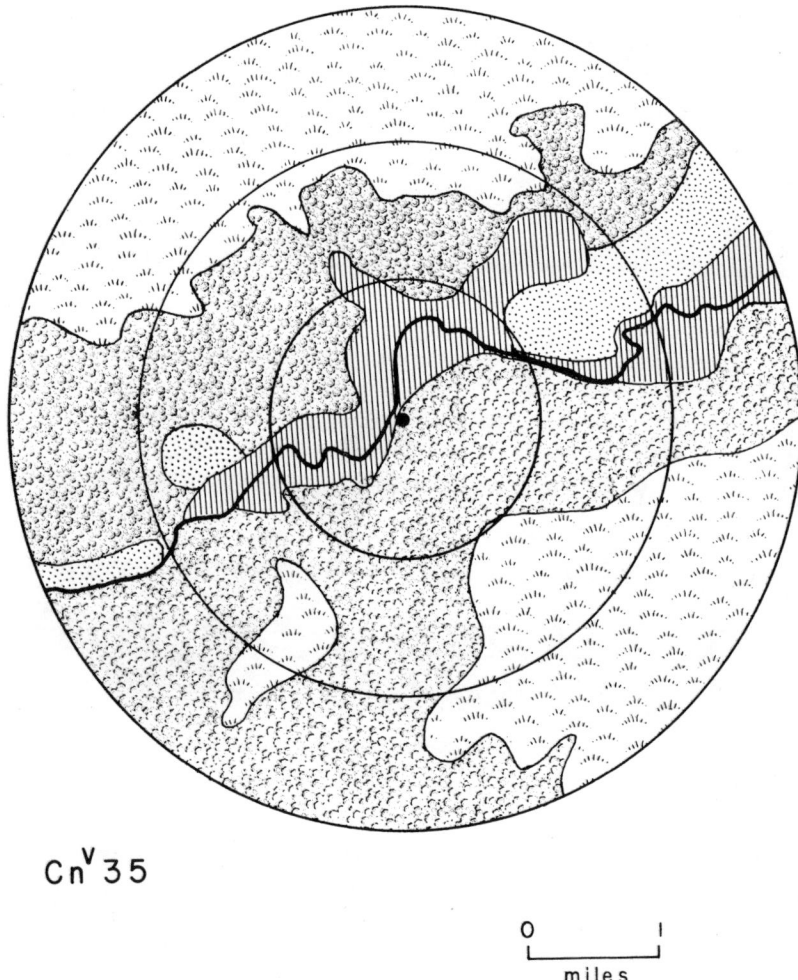

Fig. 26b. Site Catchment Drawing of Selected Middle Woodland Site (Ceramic Type I, Natural Division 4b).

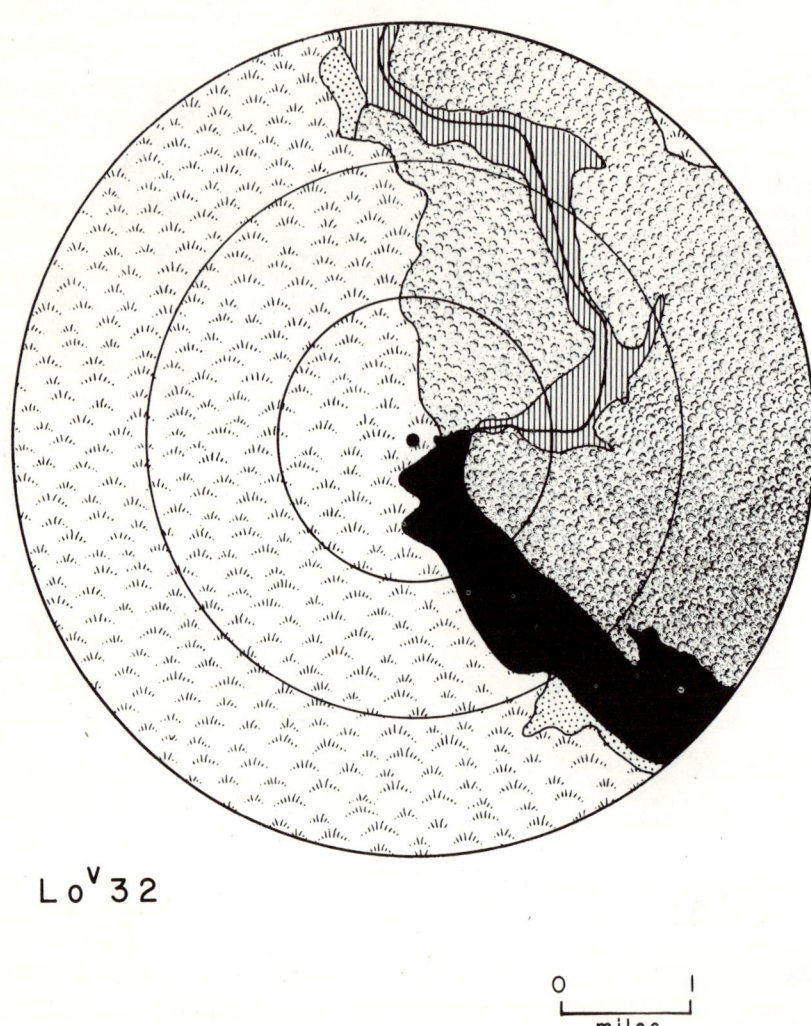

Fig. 26c. Site Catchment Drawing of Selected Middle Woodland Site (Projectile Point Type, Natural Division 4b).

examination of the resources contained within some given time or distance contour of the site(s) under examination, this should not be the end product of the analysis. More of an ideal goal is the analysis such as done by Flannery (1976) for Mesoamerican Formative villages in Oaxaca and Tehuacán in which he asked the question: from how far away must the resources represented at the sites have come (Flannery, 1976: p. 103)? Data are not yet available to fully answer this sort of question for Middle Woodland communities in Illinois; nevertheless, available data suggest the catchment and use of space may be somewhat as follows.

Base camps were located so as to minimize the amount of effort necessary to acquire requisite quantities of staple resources, such as nuts and other vegetal foods. These base camps were located at the base of the bluff or back edge of the terrace, within the edge of the broad upland forest, and near a permanent source of water. Although such sites were located throughout the valley, the bulk were at the lower end of the Sangamon River Valley. The location chosen, however, not only provided for acquiring these resources from within a few miles, but also provided a degree of comfort and protection from flood and standing water. However, the immediate vicinity of the site was not adequate for providing sufficient quantities of all resources, nor was the quantity of certain seasonally abundant resources maximized from such a location. Accordingly, the other two types of sites were used. The bottomland sites were possibly for procurement of aquatic resources. These sites too are largely concentrated in the lower portion of the Sangamon River Valley. Procurement of other resources, such as deer, probably required even longer forays from the main villages. Examination of the distribution of projectile point sites suggests that much hunting occurred in the uplands of the middle reaches of the Sangamon River Valley. In total, therefore, the Middle Woodland catchment area included the whole of the Sangamon River Valley and undoubtedly beyond.

Late Woodland

The results of the analysis of Late Woodland material evidence types, clusters, and natural divisions gave far different results than a similar analysis of the Middle Woodland sites. Clusters, as expected, were not randomly distributed within natural divisions, but the material evidence types were more nearly randomly distributed within clusters and natural divisions than they were with the Middle Woodland sites. The implication is clear that there has been a structural change within the settlement pattern. No longer are different portions of the Sangamon Valley differently utilized. Projectile point sites and ceramic sites both occur throughout all natural divisions, and different types of situations are no longer used for different purposes. Two types of sites are defined.

Type I sites are represented by clusters 3, 4b, and 4c. A variant is represented by cluster 4d. These sites are on the slopes and in the forest, but they vary considerably in their location on the slope. Some of them, most dramatically those in cluster 3, are in positions very similar to some of the Middle Woodland ceramic type I sites in the lower Sangamon Valley (Natural Division 5a).

The major difference between cluster 3 and 4 sites is the difference between the natural divisions in which the sites occur. Most cluster 3 sites are in Natural Division 5a, while cluster 4 sites are in Natural Division 4b. The presence or absence of terrace and associated bottomland prairie is the major difference between the two groups of sites. Within cluster 4, the difference between subclusters 4b, 4c, and 4d is the amount of upland forest surrounding the site, reflective probably of a narrowing of forest as one moves upstream.

Type II sites are represented by clusters 1, 2, and 6, and subcluster 4a. These are bottomland oriented sites. They are on a floodplain, terrace remnant, or terrace edge, and are surrounded by much floodplain forest and bottomland prairie. The major difference between sites in the various clusters is: (1) position in the bottomlands separates clusters 1, 2, and 6 from one another, and (2) the upriver narrowing of the valley differentiates these from subcluster 4a.

These types of situations are summed up in two cross section drawings, the first (Fig. 27a) cross-cutting hypothetical situations in Divisions 5a and 6a, the other (Fig. 28a) cross-cutting the Sangamon near the confluence of the Sangamon River, the South Fork, and Sugar Creek. Both of these are accompanied by catchment area drawings (Fig. 27b-c, 28b-c) of actual sites illustrating some of the contrasts encountered.

Although Maples Mills was originally recognized by Cole and Deuel, they note that it was known to them only from mounds (1937: p. 203). Schoenbeck (1946: p. 34) reports 19 Maples Mills habitation sites in the Peoria area, but only discusses the pottery. In view of the fact that Schoenbeck had reported these sites over a decade before McGregor published his site distribution study, it is interesting that McGregor mentions only two Maples Mills sites, and thus concludes that his sample is inadequate for generalization. He (McGregor 1957: p. 277) does, however, report that one of the two sites was on a river bottom. Apparently, placement on river bottoms is characteristic of Maples Mills sites. Wilson (1961: pp. 87–89) discusses Late Woodland in general, noting the near unanimous choice of river terraces or erosional remnants for sites in the upper central Spoon Valley.

Probably the most explicit mention of Maples Mills site placement is the study of three sites in the central Illinois River Valley by Munson and Harn (1966). All three of the sites they report were on remnants of the Beardstown Terrace in the Illinois River floodplain, not too far north of the mouth of the Sangamon.

Aside from Maples Mills specifically, Late Woodland sites in other areas seem to show either a dichotomous settlement pattern similar to that detected in the Sangamon Valley, or a bottomland orientation similar to that just described in the Spoon Valley. Winters (1967: p. 60) and Stephens (1975: p. 7) both

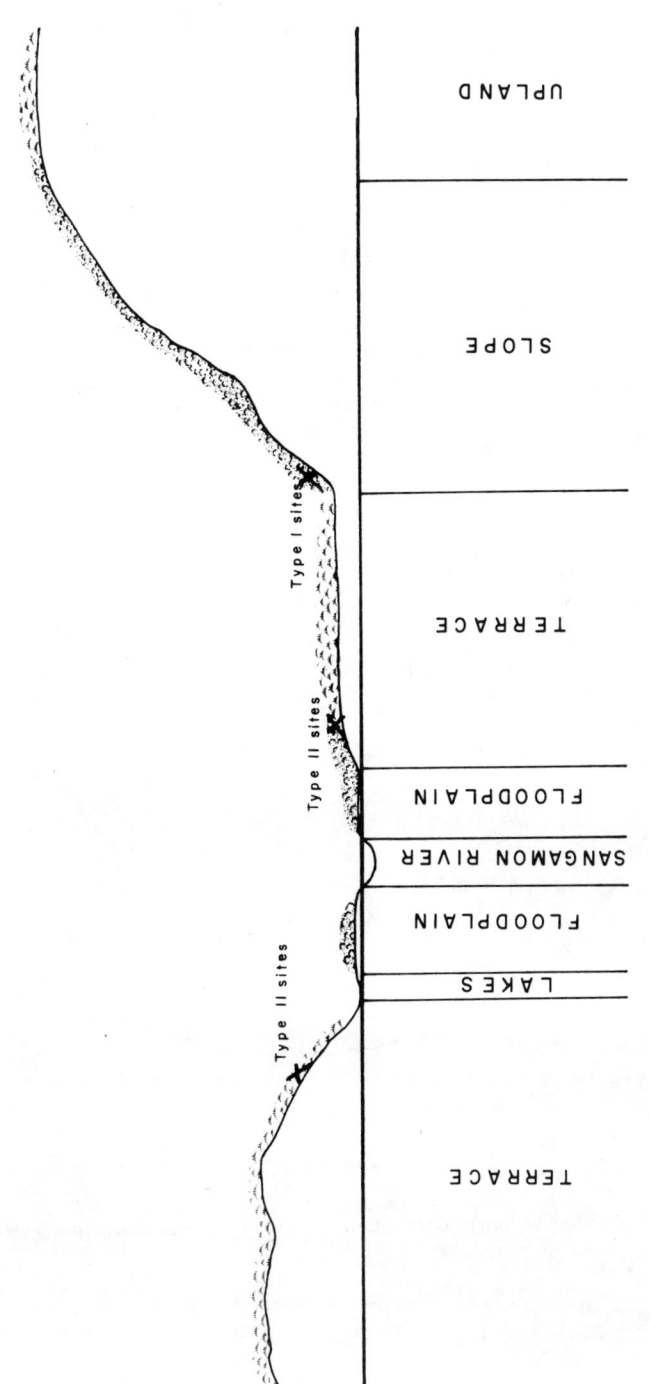

Fig. 27a. Idealized Cross-Section of Lower Sangamon with Idealized Late Woodland Site Locations.

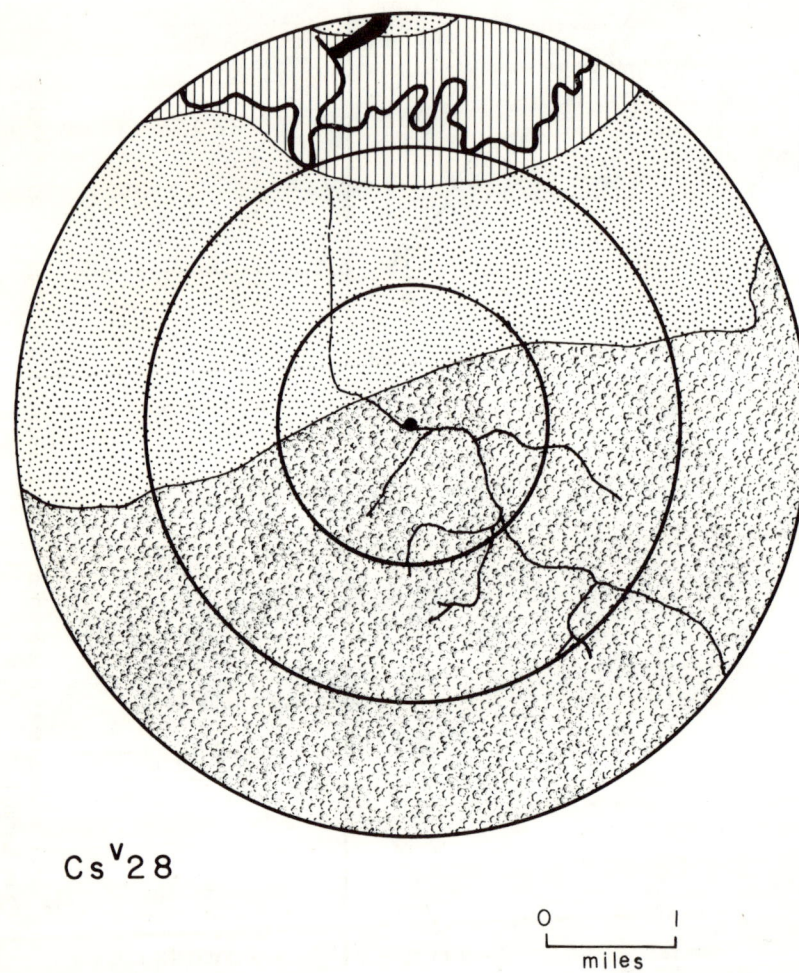

Fig. 27b. Site Catchment Drawing of Selected Late Woodland Site (Type I).

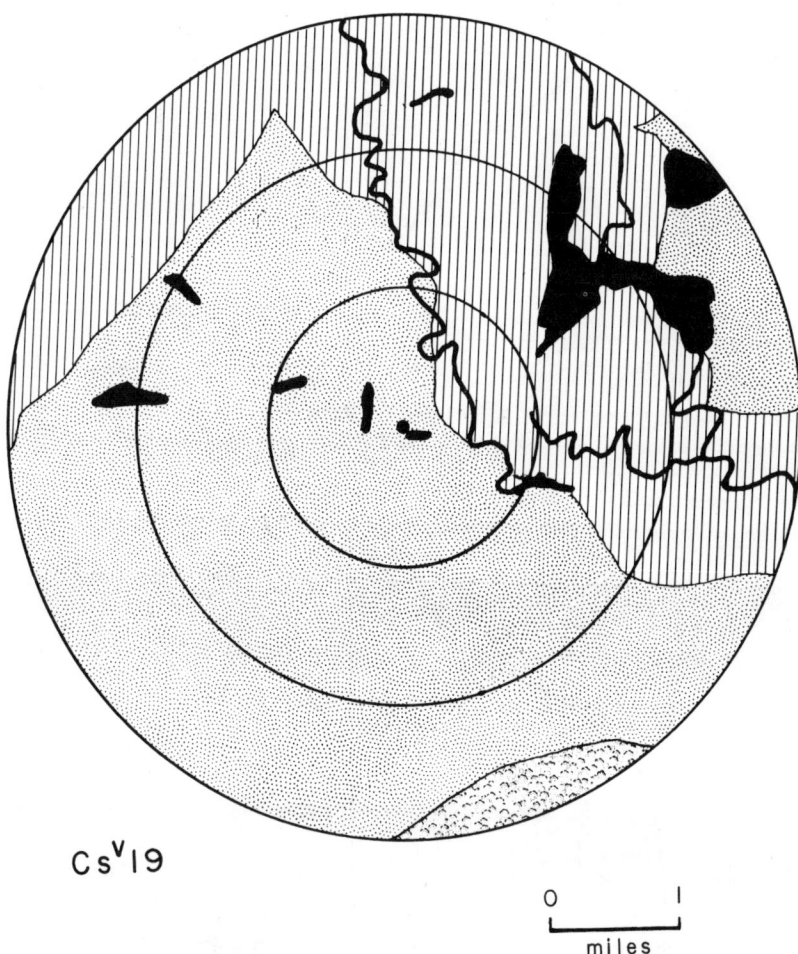

Fig. 27c. Site Catchment Drawing of Selected Late Woodland Site (Type II).

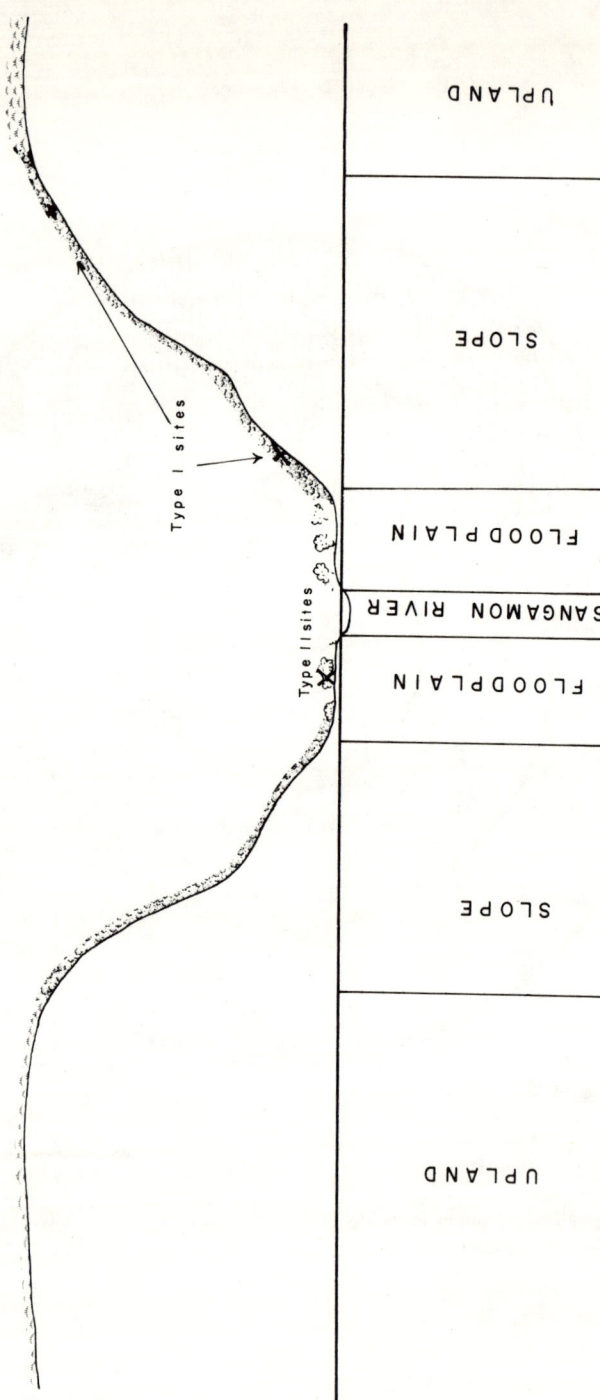

Fig. 28a. Idealized Cross-Section of Middle Sangamon with Idealized Late Woodland Site Locations.

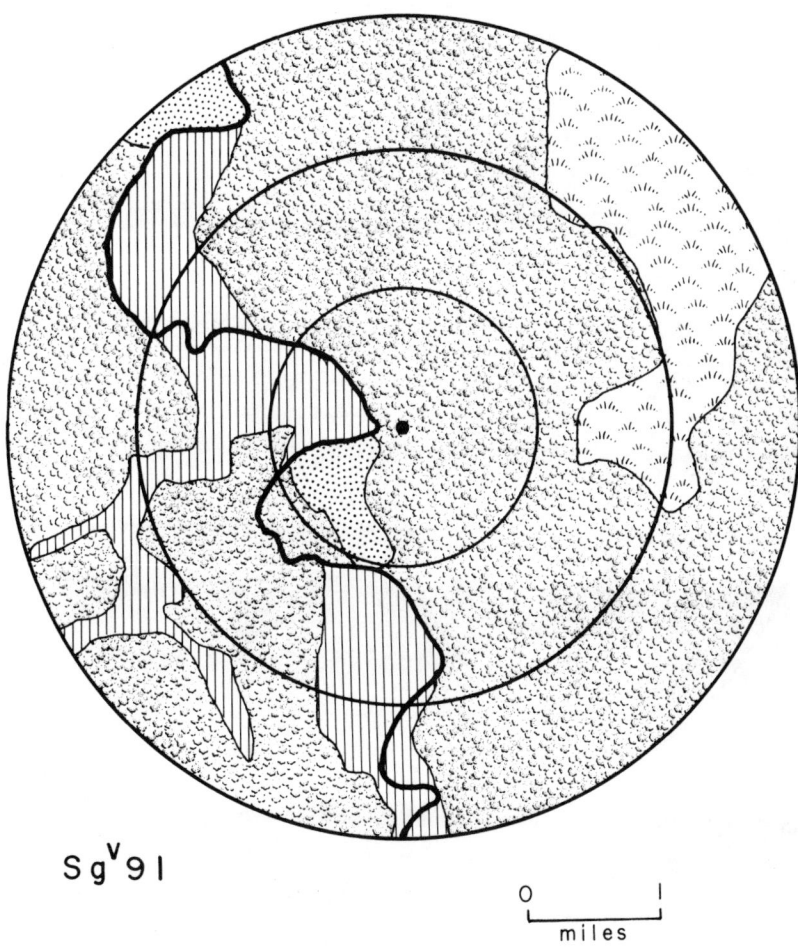

Sg^{v}91

Fig. 28b. Site Catchment Drawing of Selected Late Woodland Site (Type I).

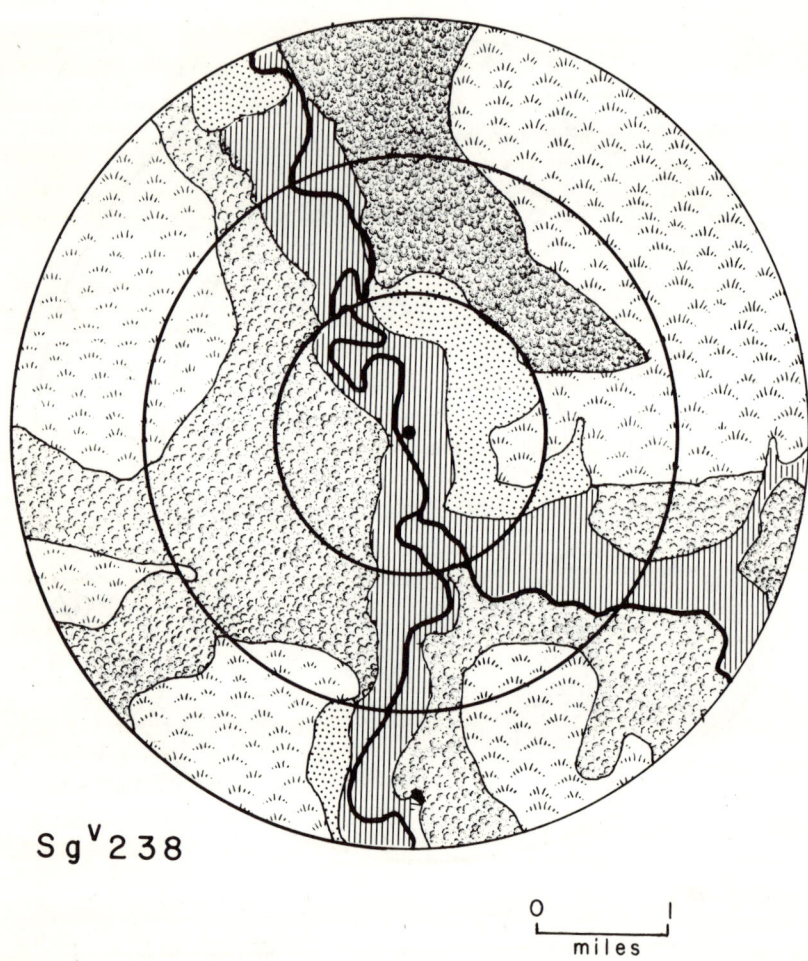

Fig. 28c. Site Catchment Drawing of Selected Late Woodland Site (Type II).

described Late Woodland sites as occurring on the T-1 of the Wabash River Valley. Munson (1971: p. 9) found 3 of 4 Early Bluff sites in the Wood River Terrace area of the Mississippi River valley to be on bluff edges, the fourth on T-1; while Late Bluff villages "occupy physiographic zones roughly comparable to those of Early Bluff, at least within the survey area, although bottomland zones are utilized to a slightly greater extent" (Munson, 1971: p. 11). Harn (1971: p. 32) found that T-1 was the predominantly used zone for Late Woodland occupations in the American Bottoms of the Mississippi River Valley.

The best comparative information is from the Kaskaskia River Valley. Sites included in Gardner's (1973) Vandalia Complex are on either the bluff-crest or a terrace edge or remnant in the bottoms. Kuttruff's (1974) analysis of Late Woodland settlement in the Lower Kaskaskia Valley considered the locations of 131 sites. Although the sites actually occurred in 5 zones, 114 (87%) were on either a terrace or sand ridge in the valley bottom or the edge of the Kaskaskia River bluff (Kuttruff, 1974: p. 178), most of the latter in bluff-edge situations where the floodplain was adjacent to the bluffs (Kuttruff, 1974: p. 180). Kuttruff (1974: p. 181) concludes:

> When this particular patterning of Late Woodland components on the bluffs and terrace edge is articulated with the two major resource zones . . . the significance of this pattern is quite clear. The regular association of Late Woodland sites with either the edge of a terrace formation, a bluff-edge or bluff-base location, where the bluff is adjacent to the floodplain, places the component on the ecotone between the two major resource zones. This maximizes the number of resources available to a given component and minimizes costs involved in exploiting the two areas. Thus, the Late Woodland populations appeared to have dispersed themselves in such a way that all the available resources of the valley and adjacent uplands would have been readily available to most of the sites.

The type II Late Woodland sites in the Sangamon River Valley are certainly analogous to the T-1 sites so universally reported in the comparative literature, while the type I sites correspond to the bluff-crest loci. The Sangamon River type I Late Woodland sites are not necessarily on the bluff-crest, but the important point is that whatever the actual site location, the *situation* is not as highly variable.

Interpretation of this pattern in terms of the settlement system is somewhat complicated. Munson and Harn (1966: p. 167) have offered what is probably an unduly complicated interpretation by noting that their Maples Mills sites "represent elements of what appears to be a rather complex settlement pattern." Kuttruff (1974: pp. 181–82), on the other hand, has probably oversimplified: ". . . it can be proposed that in terms of subsistence each component was in a position to be relatively autonomous. The various components in this scheme, therefore, were functional equivalents within the structure of the Late Woodland subsistence system." An interpretation is here offered that sees the Late Woodland settlement pattern as essentially similar to late prehistoric and early historic native settlement patterns in many parts of the Eastern United States and the Plains.

It is suggested that the presence of two distinct types of sites, equally as prominent and both well represented throughout the valley, may represent a seasonally interchangeable occupation of the two types of sites. Such a settlement pattern is common in the Eastern United States in late prehistoric and early historic times. Bushnell (1919, 1922) has extensively documented this type of settlement pattern among many groups east of the Rockies in early historic times. In essence, the pattern consists of a summer encampment in a place at which structures are erected, fields cleared and cultivated, and from which hunting in the immediate vicinity takes place. Summer camps in particular may be reoccupied from year to year, perhaps with rebuilding of structures, and construction of new storage facilities:

> Evidently the central village, often surrounded by or in the vicinity of the extensive cornfields, would be occupied during the spring, summer, and early autumn, and later in the year, after the harvest, it would be temporarily abandoned, the families removing to the forests, there to hunt during the ensuing season. . . . Such was the condition in the "country of the Illinois" and elsewhere from the Mississippi to the Atlantic (Bushnell, 1919: p. 45).

Fitting (1969; Fitting and Cleland 1969) has adduced archaeological evidence supporting this form of settlement pattern in parts of Michigan in Late Woodland times. More pertinent to the present case, however, are suggestions of seasonal occupation at several excavated Late Woodland sites in central Illinois, and implications of seasonally shifting settlement patterns in several river valleys at the same time.

Lewis (1975) in reporting the Hood site in Macon County, on the Sangamon River, but upstream from the area included within the present study, suggests that Hood was a seasonal occupation, probably during the summer and fall. His inferences are based on the nature of the floral and faunal assemblages, and the tools and features present at the site.

Perhaps somewhat more suggestive of the seasonal cycle of the Late Woodland inhabitants of central Illinois is Gardner's report (1973) on the "Vandalia complex" in the Kaskaskia Valley. Gardner first reports on the Dotray site near the bluff of the confluence of several creeks feeding the Kaskaskia. Ceramics are predominantely of the Albee cordmarked type. The Dotray site had four structures and six features. Ceramically similar sites are found "on small knolls with an elevation of no more than 4 feet above the surrounding floodplain" (Gardner, 1973: p. 221). In summarizing the settlement pattern revealed by the Vandalia material Gardner (1973: pp. 225–26) notes the following:

> On the basis of the similarities between the ceramic material from the Dotray site and the sites in the Kaskaskia River floodplain, it is assumed they equate in time and are rather closely related. The difference in environmental zones between the bluff-prairie and the river bottoms is suggestive of difference in seasonal occupation. . . .

The available evidence suggests then the Dotray site was a highly specialized seasonal encampment of groups who at other times occupied portions of the Kaskaskia River bottoms. In all likelihood, this was a fall or winter encampment which was inhabited when these people were gathering nuts from the bluff woodlands and perhaps hunting in the prairie. This type of seasonal shift is well known in the eastern United States in the ethnographic literature.

In sum, the Late Woodland settlement system in the Sangamon Valley seems to include 2 types of components: (1) upland sites on the slope, often near the bluff-crest, well within the upland forest, and (2) bottomland sites, on the floodplain or terrace, well within the floodplain forest and bottomland prairie. Rather than the suggested base camp-ancillary camp arrangement of the Middle Woodland sites, it is suggested that the Late Woodland site types are complementary to one another, perhaps on a seasonally interchangeable basis. Further, both site types are spread throughout the Sangamon Valley, suggesting (1) the catchment for a Late Woodland settlement system was far smaller than before, and (2) a major territorial reorganization occurred between the Middle and Late Woodland periods. Specifically, the Late Woodland settlement system could be confined to a smaller area, with several such units occupying the same amount of space as a single Middle Woodland unit. Areally more confined, more autonomous social units are thus suggested.

VII. SUMMARY AND CONCLUSIONS

Survey and site location analysis are receiving increased attention in archaeology. A basic contention of this study, however, is that the survey, in the Midwest at least, has not made full use of its potential. Through the influence of Binford (1964), Struever (1968a), and others, emphasis has come to be placed on sampling strategy in archaeological survey. This is, of course, not unhealthy. The problem is that in the rush to do these new things, the potential of the traditional data is frequently ignored. Stratified designs are recommended, but a research population is most efficiently stratified on the basis of some prior knowledge of the study area. This study is an example of how traditional survey information may be used to generate settlement pattern models, which may be employed in the efficient structuring of archaeological surveys.

Ceramics and projectile points were used to identify sites and place them within the Middle or Late Woodland period. For each identified site, a series of environmental variables was evaluated, in accordance with a theoretical model of how man interacts with his natural environment. The analysis of those data is best summarized as direct answers to the research questions asked at the beginning of the analysis.

1. *Do people seem to be selecting particular types of sites and situations for habitation?* Yes.
2. *Are ceramic and projectile point sites in different types of situations?*

Middle Woodland ceramic types and projectile point sites appear to occur in different types of situations. This is not true of Late Woodland sites, however.

3. *How are these situations different? That is, what are the characteristics of the different situations?* Two types of Middle Woodland ceramic sites are discernable. The first is analogous to that reported for the Havana Tradition in many places throughout Illinois and nearby areas. Additionally, this analysis has discerned an upriver counterpart. These are sites situated at the base of slopes, generally at forest edge, and near a permanent source of water. They are well above the floodplain, in such a position that threat of flooding is virtually non-existent. The sites are on medium textured and probably at least moderately permeable soils. They are generally ideally located in relation to all resource zones, but a catchment area of 3-mile radius seems to include rather small amounts of upland prairie.

At the lower end of the Sangamon River a second ceramic site type is on or near the front edge of a terrace. The sites are generally near closed bodies of water. Their 3-mile radius catchment areas do not include the same diversity or quantity of upland forest and upland prairie resources as the ceramic type I sites.

Projectile point sites are found primarily in the Springfield Section of the Grand Prairie Division (Natural Division 4b). They are within the upland forest, but are generally some distance from the main stream and, accordingly, have little access to floodplain forest or bottomland prairie. They do, however, have excellent access to upland forest and upland prairie. Although these sites are well above flood levels, they are on fine textured, not readily permeable, soils and are subject to standing water during periods of high precipitation.

Two types of Late Woodland sites are defined. They do not correspond to material evidence types of sites as well as do the Middle Woodland sites.

The first type of site is in some ways similar to the first type of Middle Woodland site discussed, but is probably slightly less predictably placed. These sites are usually in the general area of the bottomland-slope transition, in the upland forest. They have access to all major resource zones within three miles. They are near a permanent watersource and generally on a soil of medium coarse texture.

The second type of Late Woodland site is a floodplain or at least bottomland type of occupation, apparently often near the edge of a terrace or near the river or closed body of water. Access to upland vegetation resources is limited. Large amounts of water are included within a 3-mile radius of some sites.

4. *How greatly does spatial variation within the Sangamon drainage affect site location?* Several of the site types discussed occur in all natural divisions, but show variation according to which natural division they are in. This includes Middle Woodland ceramic type I, and both Late Woodland types. Although the sites occur in different clusters, their situations can be shown to vary primarily according to the structure of the natural environment.

The linear structure and presence of the broad terrace at the lower end of the

Sangamon differentiates this portion of the valley from that farther up the river. Relations of Middle Woodland ceramic type I sites to upland resources vary little, if at all, with the portion of the river valley. This is also true of Late Woodland type I sites. The narrowing of the valley upriver would seem to be the major difference between Late Woodland site clusters 1, 2, and 6, and subcluster 4a.

It has been mentioned several times in the course of this study that the diversity of the Sangamon from a setting similar to the archaeologically better known Illinois River Valley, to a prairie setting quite different has been of the great use in examining the gradation of change in settlement over space. Examination of the possibility of structural change in the settlement pattern as a response to the change in structure of the natural environment should lead to a better understanding of prehistoric adaptive processes.

5. *Do Middle and Late Woodland settlement patterns differ?* Apparently they do.

6. *If so, how?* Taking into account the various settlement types defined here, and the distribution of the material evidence types within these settlement types, it is apparent that some sort of structural change has occurred within the settlement pattern.

The Middle Woodland settlement pattern appears to be one of a base camp or village, at bluff-base, supplemented by use, probably seasonal, of camps in the bottomlands, at the confluence of the Sangamon and Illinois rivers. In addition, there is the temporary use of hunting camps, up smaller streams, probably by only portions of the population for short periods of time.

The impression of the Late Woodland settlement pattern is that there is more of a seasonal movement from place to place than during Middle Woodland times. The bluff-base camp or village is still used, but the bottomland occupation is greatly increased in Late Woodland times, and this type of site attains equal prominence with the bluff-base camp. Evidence of hunting activities is present all over, not just in the uplands. The Late Woodland settlement pattern therefore seems to pose an interesting parallel with the settlement pattern of other groups ethnographically known in the Great Lakes and Plains. We know, for example, that the Kickapoo who inhabited the Sangamon Valley in the late eighteenth and early nineteenth centuries practiced a seasonal shift in settlement, practicing horticulture in one place during the summer, and then during the winter, moving out into the river bottoms for hunting. A similar sort of pattern existed among the Plains village groups along the Missouri River (e.g., Hurt 1969).

It must be emphasized that the models and conclusions arrived at in this study are based on a consideration of characteristics of a settlement's *situation* rather than of its *site* alone. The utility of this concept can be demonstrated by comparing evaluations of different types of Middle Woodland sites, for example, on landforms, and in their topographic situation. If the null hypothesis that different types of sites—i.e., ceramic sites and projectile point sites—were not on different landforms is tested, the null hypothesis is not rejected ($\chi^2 = 4.52$, $DF=3$, $p>.2$). Yet, as shown in Chapter V, these two types of sites do differ very greatly in their situation. Consider slope, for example. Twelve of the 63 Middle Woodland sites evaluated in this study are listed as being on the slope. Seven of these 12 are ceramic sites of one type or another, the other five are projectile point sites. The nearly even distribution obscures the fact that most of the ceramic sites are near the base of the slope, while most of the projectile point sites are nearer to the bluff-crest and in far different situations. It further betrays the fact that ceramic sites at the back edge of a terrace are in virtually identical situations to those low on the slopes. The artificial division of landforms into floodplain, terrace, valley slope, and uplands is simply too gross to pick out locational variation within the Middle Woodland settlement pattern and to be predictive of location of different types of sites. Yet it is exactly this gross sort of division that is typically employed in a stratified research design which has as its goal the reconstruction of prehistoric settlement patterns.

In short, the present study argues for an approach to settlement patterns that is consonant with a model of how a human community interacts with its natural environment. A similar approach has already proved itself useful in Old World studies (e.g., Vita-Finzi and Higgs 1970; Higgs and Vita-Finzi 1972; Jarman 1972; Jarman, Vita-Finzi and Higgs 1972) although usually on a more limited scale and with simpler statistical methods than in the present study. Even if further survey were to refute the settlement pattern models put forward in this paper, the study would be considered a success if it served to make New World archaeologists more aware of the utility of the method.

Acknowledgments

Many people have contributed to the success of this study. In particular, I should thank Robert A. Benfer, chairman of my dissertation committee, and William H. Marquardt, Robert F. G. Spier, W. Raymond Wood—all of the Department of Anthropology, University of Missouri, and Jesse H. Wheeler of the Department of Geography, the remainder of my committee; Walter E. Klippel, formerly of the Illinois State Museum, who conceived and directed the Sangamon River Valley research program; all the people who worked in the field and laboratory at the Quaternary Studies Center; and several individuals whose patience and friendship sustained me both morally and intellectually while the dissertation was being prepared: William B. Butler, Ann M. Johnson, Judi Johnson, Walter E. Klippel, Patricia J. O'Brien, the entire staff of the Quaternary Studies Center, and various other graduate students at the University of Missouri.

I must also thank the farmers and landowners of the Sangamon River Valley for access to their land, and especially Mr. and Mrs. Eugene Eilers for permission to test 11Cs^{v}20.

The research in the Sangamon River Valley has been supported by the National Science Foundation (Grant GS–28986), the Illinois State Museum Society, and the Illinois Archaeological Survey Historic Sites Survey program.

University of Missouri
Columbia, Missouri

References

Anderson, Adrian D.
    1971   Review of Iowa River Valley Archaeology. In *Prehistoric Investigations*, edited by Marshall McKusick. Report No. 3. Office of State Archaeologist, pp. 1–23. Iowa City, Iowa.

Arensberg, Conrad M. and Solon T. Kimball
    1965   *Culture and Community*. Harcourt, Brace, and World, New York.

Asch, Nancy B., Richard I. Ford, and David L. Asch
    1972   Paleoethnobotany of the Koster Site: The Archaic Horizons. Illinois Valley Archaeological Program *Research Papers*, Vol. 6 and Illinois State Museum *Reports of Investigations*, No. 24. Illinois State Museum, Springfield.

Baker, Frank C., James B. Griffin, Richard G. Morgan, Georg K. Neumann, and Jay L. B. Taylor
    1941   Contributions to the Archaeology of the Illinois River Valley. *Transactions of the American Philosophical Society*, Vol. XXXII, Pt. 1. Philadelphia.

Beardsley, Richard K. et al.
    1956   Functional and Evolutionary Implications of Community Patterning. In Seminars in Archaeology: 1955, edited by Robert Wauchope. Memoir No. 11, pp. 129–57. Society for American Archaeology.

Bellrose, Frank C.
    1968   Waterfowl Migration Corridors East of the Rocky Mountains in the United States. *Biological Notes*, No. 61. Illinois Natural History Survey, Urbana.

Benfer, Robert A.
    1975   Classification and Sampling. In *Sampling in Archaeology*, edited by James W. Mueller, pp. 227–247. University of Arizona Press.

Bennett, John W.
    1945   *Archaeological Explorations in Jo Daviess County, Illinois*. University of Chicago Press, Chicago.

Bettarel, Robert Louis and Hale G. Smith
    1973   The Moccasin Bluff Site and the Woodland Cultures of Southwestern Michigan. *Anthropological Papers*, No. 49. Museum of Anthropology, University of Michigan. Ann Arbor.

Binford, Lewis R.
    1964   A Consideration of Archaeological Research Design. *American Antiquity* **29** (4): 425–41.

Blalock, Hubert M., Jr.
    1960   *Social Statistics*. McGraw-Hill Book Company, New York.

Bluhm, Elaine
    1951   Ceramic Sequence in Central Basin and Hopewell Sites in Central Illinois. *American Antiquity* **16**(4):324–29.

Borchert, John R.
    1950   The Climate of the Central North American Grassland. *Annals of the Association of American Geographers* **XL**(1):1–39.

Bourdo, Eric A., Jr.
    1956   A Review of the General Land Office Survey and of its Use in Quantitative Studies of Former Forests. *Ecology* **37**(4):754–68.

Braun, E. Lucy
    1950   *Deciduous Forests of Eastern North America.* Hafner, New York.

Brown, James A.
    1964   The Northwestern Extension of the Havana Tradition. In Hopewellian Studies, edited by J. R. Caldwell and R. L. Hall. Illinois State Museum, *Scientific Papers,* Vol. 12, pp. 108–22. Springfield.
    1965   The Prairie Peninsula: An Interaction Area in the Eastern United States. Ph.D. Dissertation, University of Chicago.

Bushnell, David I., Jr.
    1919   Native Villages and Village Sites East of the Mississippi. Bureau of American Ethnology, *Bulletin* 69.
    1922   Villages of the Algonquian, Siouan, and Caddoan Tribes West of the Mississippi. Bureau of American Ethnology, *Bulletin* 77.

Carns, Jack M.
    1973   *Magnitude and Frequency of Floods in Illinois.* Division of Water Resource Management, United States Department of the Interior.

Chang, K. C.
    1962   A Typology of Settlement and Community Patterns in Some Circumpolar Societies. *Arctic Anthropology* **1**(1):28–41.

Claflin, John
    1975   An Archaeological Survey of a Holocene Lake in Central Illinois. Ms. on file, Anthropology Department, Illinois State Museum. Springfield.

Cleland, Charles E.
    1966   The Prehistoric Animal Ecology and Ethnozoology of the Upper Great Lakes Region. *Anthropological Papers* No. 29. Museum of Anthropology, University of Michigan. Ann Arbor.

Clifton, James A.
    1968   Cultural Anthropology: Aspirations and Approaches. In *Introduction to Cultural Anthropology,* edited by James A. Clifton, pp. 2–47. Houghton Mifflin, New York.

Cole, Fay-Cooper and Thorne Deuel
    1937   *Rediscovering Illinois.* University of Chicago Press, Chicago.

Curtis, John T.
    1959   *The Vegetation of Wisconsin: An Ordination of Plant Communities.* University of Wisconsin Press, Madison.

Doxiadis, Constantinos A.
    1970   Ekistics, The Science of Human Settlements. *Science* **170**(3956):393–404.

Dunnell, Robert C.
    1971   *Systematics in Prehistory.* The Free Press, New York.

Enos, Zimri
    1909   Description of Springfield. *Transactions of the Illinois State Historical Society* **14**:190–97.

Eschman, Donald F. and Melvin G. Marcus
    1972   The Geologic and Topographic Setting of Cities. In *Urbanization and*

Evers, Robert A.
   1955   Hill Prairies of Illinois. Illinois Natural History Survey *Bulletin,* Vol. 26, Article 5. Urbana.
Farnsworth, Kenneth B.
   1973   An Archaeological Survey of the Macoupin Valley. Illinois State Museum *Reports of Investigations* No. 26, Springfield.
Faulkner, Charles H.
   1961   *An Archaeological Survey of Marshall County.* Indiana Historical Bureau, Indianapolis.
   1972   The Late Prehistoric Occupation of Northwestern Indiana: A Study of the Upper Mississippi Cultures of the Kankakee Valley. *Prehistory Research Series,* Vol. V, No. 1. Indiana Historical Society, Indianapolis.
Fehrenbacher, J. B., et al.
   1967   Soils of Illinois. *Bulletin* 725. Agricultural Experiment Station, University of Illinois.
Fitting, James E.
   1969   Settlement Analysis in the Great Lakes Region. *Southwestern Journal of Anthropology* **25**(4):360–77.
   1970   *The Archaeology of Michigan.* Natural History Press, Garden City, New York.
Fitting, James E. and Charles E. Cleland
   1969   Late Prehistoric Settlement Patterns in the Upper Great Lakes. *Ethnohistory* **16**(4):289–302.
Flannery, Kent V.
   1968   Archaeological Systems Theory and Early Mesoamerican Prehistory. In *Anthropological Archeology in the Americas,* edited by Betty J. Meggers, pp. 67–87. Anthropological Society of Washington, D.C.
   1976   Empirical Determination of Site Catchments in Oaxaca and Tehuacán. In *The Early Mesoamerican Village,* edited by Kent V. Flannery, pp. 103–17. Academic Press, New York.
Forbes, Stephen A. and Robert E. Richardson
   1920   *The Fishes of Illinois* (2nd edition). State of Illinois, Natural History Survey.
Fowler, Melvin L.
   1952   The Clear Lake Site: Hopewellian Occupation. In Hopewellian Communities in Illinois, edited by Thorne Deuel, pp. 131–74. *Scientific Papers* Vol. V. Illinois State Museum, Springfield.
   1955   Ware Groupings and Decorations of Woodland Ceramics in Illinois. *American Antiquity* **20**(3):213–25.
Freeman, Joan E.
   1969   The Millville Site, A Middle Woodland Village in Grant County, Wisconsin. *The Wisconsin Archeologist* **50**(2):37–88 (N.S.).
Gardner, William M.
   1969   The Havana Cultural Tradition Occupation in the Upper Kaskaskia River Valley, Illinois. Ph.D. Dissertation, University of Illinois. University Microfilms, Ann Arbor.

1973 The Vandalia Complex: A Late Woodland Complex in the Central Kaskaskia River Drainage. In Late Woodland Site Archaeology in Illinois. Illinois Archaeological Survey *Bulletin* No. 9, pp. 214–27. Urbana.

Garner, B. J.
1967 Models of Urban Geography and Settlement Location. In *Models in Geography,* edited by Richard J. Chorley and Peter Haggett, pp. 303–60. Methuen and Co., Ltd.

Gleason, Henry Allen
1907 A Botanical Survey of the Illinois River Valley Sand Region. *Bulletin* of the Illinois State Laboratory of Natural History, Vol. VII, Art. VII, Pt. II, pp. 149–94. Urbana.

Green, Ernestene L.
1973 Location Analysis of Prehistoric Maya Sites in Northern British Honduras. *American Antiquity* **38**(3):279–93.

Gregg, Michael L.
1974 Three Middle Woodland Sites from Henderson County: An Apparent Congruity with Middle Woodland Subsistence-Settlement Systems in the Lower Illinois Valley. *The Wisconsin Archeologist* **55**(3):231–45.

Griffin, James B.
1952 Some Early and Middle Woodland Pottery Types. In Hopewellian Communities in Illinois, edited by Thorne Deuel. Illinois State Museum *Scientific Papers* Vol. V, pp. 93–130. Springfield.

1956 Prehistoric Settlement Patterns in the Northern Mississippi Valley and the Upper Great Lakes. In Prehistoric Settlement Patterns in the New World, edited by Gordon R. Willey. *Viking Fund Publication in Anthropology* No. 23, pp. 63–71. Wenner-Gren Foundation for Anthropological Research, Inc., New York.

Griffin, James B., Richard E. Flanders, and Paul F. Titterington
1970 The Burial Complexes of the Knight and Norton Mounds in Illinois and Michigan. *Memoir* No. 2. Museum of Anthropology, University of Michigan, Ann Arbor.

Griffin, John W. and Donald E. Wray
1945 Bison in Illinois Archaeology. *Transactions of the Illinois State Academy of Science* **38**:21–26.

Grüger, Eberhard
1972 Late Quaternary Vegetation Development in South-Central Illinois. *Quaternary Research* **2**(2):217–31.

Haggett, Peter
1965 *Locational Analysis in Human Geography.* St. Martin's Press, New York.

Hamilton, William J., III and Kenneth E. F. Watt
1970 Refuging. *Annual Review of Ecology and Systematics* **1**:263–86.

Harlow, William M.
1957 *Trees of the Eastern and Central United States and Canada.* Dover, New York.

Harn, Alan D.
    1971   An Archaeological Survey of the American Bottoms. Illinois State Museum *Reports of Investigations* No. 21, Pt. 2. Springfield.

Higgs, Eric S. (ed.)
    1975   *Palaeoeconomy.* Cambridge University Press, Cambridge.

Higgs, E. S. and C. Vita-Finzi
    1972   Prehistoric Economies: A Territorial Approach. In *Papers in Economic Prehistory,* edited by E. S. Higgs, pp. 27–36. Cambridge University Press, Cambridge.

Hoffmeister, Donald F. and Carl O. Mohr
    1972   *Fieldbook of Illinois Mammals.* Dover Publications, Inc., New York.

Hudson, John C. and Phillip M. Fowler
    1972   The Concept of Pattern in Geography. In *Man, Space, and Environment,* edited by Paul Ward English and Robert C. Mayfield, pp. 545–50. Oxford University Press, New York.

Hurley, William M.
    1974   Silver Creek Woodland Sites, Southwestern Wisconsin. *Report* No. 6. Office of State Archaeologist, University of Iowa, Iowa City.

Hurt, Wesley R.
    1969   Seasonal Economic and Settlement Patterns of the Arikara. *Plains Anthropologist* **14**(43):32–37.

Jarman, M. R.
    1972   A Territorial Model for Archaeology: A Behavioral and Geographical Approach. In *Models in Archaeology,* edited by David L. Clarke, pp. 705–33. Methuen, London.

Jarman, M. R., C. Vita-Finzi, and E. S. Higgs
    1972   Site Catchment Analysis in Archaeology. In *Man, Settlement, and Urbanism,* edited by Peter J. Ucko, Ruth Tringham and G. W. Dimbleby, pp. 61–66. Schenkman Publishing Co., Cambridge, Mass.

Johnson, Gregory D.
    1971   How Agricultural Practices Affect Surveying in the Lower Sangamon River Drainage Basin in Illinois. Ms. on file, Anthropology Department, Illinois State Museum, Springfield.

Johnson, Judith B.
    1972   Proto-Euro-American Phytogeography of the Lower Sangamon River Drainage. Ms. on file, Anthropology Department, Illinois State Museum, Springfield.

Jones, Almut G. and David T. Bell
    1974   Vascular Plants of the Sangamon River Basin: Annotated Checklist and Ecological Summary. *Bulletin* 746. Agricultural Experiment Station, University of Illinois, Urbana.

Kaesler, Robert L.
    1970   The Cophenetic Correlation Coefficient in Paleoecology. *Geological Society of America Bulletin* **81**(4):1261–65.

King, Frances B.
    n.d.   Potential Edible Plants of the Sangamon River Drainage. Ms. in preparation, Illinois State Museum, Springfield.

King, Frances B. and Donna C. Roper
- 1976 Floral Remains from two Middle to Early Late Woodland Sites in Central Illinois and their Implications. *The Wisconsin Archeologist* **57**(3):142-51.

Koelz, Stephen Earnest
- 1936 An Ecological Survey of the Sangamon Floodplain and Adjacent Areas, with Special Reference to Vertebrates. M.S. Thesis, University of Illinois, Urbana.

Kruskal, J. B.
- 1964 Multidimensional Scaling by Optimizing Goodness of Fit to a Nonmetric Hypothesis. *Psychometrika* **29**(1):1-27.

Kuttruff, Carl
- 1974 Late Woodland Settlement and Subsistence in the Lower Kaskaskia River, Illinois. Ph.D. Dissertation, Southern Illinois University. University Microfilms, Ann Arbor.

Lee, Richard B.
- 1968 What Hunters Do for a Living, or, How to Make Out on Scarce Resources. In *Man the Hunter*, edited by Richard B. Lee and Irven DeVore, pp. 30-48. Aldine, Chicago.

Leopold, Luna B.
- 1974 *Water: A Primer*. W. H. Freeman, San Francisco.

Leopold, Luna B., M. Gordon Wolman, and John P. Miller
- 1964 *Fluvial Processes in Geomorphology*. W. H. Freeman, San Francisco.

Lewis, R. Barry
- 1975 The Hood Site. *Reports of Investigations* No. 31. Illinois State Museum, Springfield.

Linder, Jean
- 1974 The Jean Rita Site: An Early Woodland Occupation in Monroe County, Illinois. *The Wisconsin Archeologist* **55**(2): 99-162 (N.S.)

Linderman, Frank B.
- 1932 *Pretty Shield: Medicine Woman of the Crows*. University of Nebraska Press, Lincoln.

Logan, Wilfred D.
- 1958 Analysis of Woodland Complexes in Northeastern Iowa. Ph.D. Dissertation, University of Michigan. University Microfilms, Ann Arbor.

McGregor, John C.
- 1952 The Havana Site. In Hopewellian Communities in Illinois, edited by Thorne Deuel, pp. 43-92. *Scientific Papers* Vol. V. Illinois State Museum, Springfield.
- 1957 Prehistoric Village Distribution in the Illinois River Valley. *American Antiquity* **22**(3): 272-79.
- 1958 *The Pool and Irving Villages: A Study of Hopewell Occupation in the Illinois River Valley*. University of Illinois Press, Urbana.
- 1959 The Middle Woodland Period. In Illinois Archaeology, edited by Elaine Bluhm, pp. 21-26. *Bulletin* 1. Illinois Archaeological Survey, Urbana.

Mason, Ronald J.
- 1966 Two Stratified Sites on the Door Peninsula of Wisconsin. *Anthropological Papers* No. 26. University of Michigan, Museum of Anthropology, Ann Arbor.

Miller, James Andrew
- 1973 Quaternary History of the Sangamon River Drainage System, Central

Illinois. *Reports of Investigations* No. 27. Illinois State Museum, Springfield.

Mitchell, S. Augustus
    1837   *Illinois in 1837*. Published by S. Augustus Mitchell and by Grigg and Elliot, Philadelphia.

Mueller, James W.
    1974   The Use of Sampling in Archaeological Survey. *Memoir* No. 28, Society for American Archaeology.

Munson, Patrick J.
    1966   The Sheets Site: A Late Archaic-Early Woodland Occupation in West-Central Illinois. *Michigan Archaeologist* **12**(3): 111–20.
    1971   An Archaeological Survey of the Wood River Terrace. *Reports of Investigations* No. 21, Pt. 1. Illinois State Museum, Springfield.

Munson, Patrick J. and Alan D. Harn
    1966   Surface Collections from Three Sites in the Central Illinois River Valley. *The Wisconsin Archeologist* **47**(3): 150–68 (N.S.).

Munson, Patrick J., Paul W. Parmalee, and Richard A. Yarnell
    1971   Subsistence Ecology of Scovill, A Terminal Middle Woodland Village. *American Antiquity* **36**(4): 410–31.

Page, John L.
    1949   Climate of Illinois. *Bulletin* 532. Agricultural Experiment Station, University of Illinois.

Parmalee, Paul W.
    1967   The Fresh-Water Mussels of Illinois. *Popular Science Series* Vol. VIII. Illinois State Museum, Springfield.

Parmalee, Paul W. and Walter E. Klippel
    1974   Freshwater Mussels as a Prehistoric Food Resource. *American Antiquity* **39**(3): 421–34.

Parmalee, Paul W., Andreas A. Paloumpis, and Nancy Wilson
    1972   Animals Utilized by Woodland Peoples Occupying the Apple Creek Site, Illinois. *Research Papers* Vol. 5, Illinois Valley Archaeological Program, and *Reports of Investigations* No. 23, Illinois State Museum. Springfield.

Perino, Gregory
    1966   A Preliminary Report on the Peisker Site, Part 1—The Early Woodland Occupation. *Central States Archaeological Journal* **13**(2): 47–51.

Plog, Fred and James N. Hill
    1971   Explaining Variability in the Distribution of Sites. In *The Distribution of Prehistoric Population Aggregates*, edited by George J. Gumerman, pp. 7–36. Prescott College Press, Prescott, Arizona.

Rackerby, Frank
    1968   Carlyle Reservoir Archaeology: Final Season. *Southern Illinois Studies, Research Records* Series '68 S1A. Southern Illinois University Museum, Carbondale.
    1973   A Statistical Determination of the Black Sand Occupation at the Macoupin Site, Jersey Co., Illinois. *American Antiquity* **38**(1):96–101.

Rohlf, F. James and David R. Fisher
    1968   Tests for Hierarchical Structure in Random Data Sets. *Systematic Zoology* **17**(1): 407–12.

Rohlf, F. James, John Kishpaugh, and David Kirk
    1972   *NT-SYS—Numerical Taxonomy System of Multivariate Statistical Programs*. State University of New York, Stony Brook.

Roper, Donna C.
 1974 The Distribution of Middle Woodland Sites Within the Environment of the Lower Sangamon River, Illinois. *Reports of Investigations* No. 30. Illinois State Museum, Springfield.
 1975 Archaeological Survey and Settlement Pattern Models in Central Illinois. Ph.D. Dissertation, University of Missouri-Columbia.
 1977 A Key for the Identification of Central Illinois Woodland Ceramics. *The Wisconsin Archeologist* 58(4): 245–55.
 1978 The Airport Site: A Multicomponent Site in the Sangamon River Drainage. *Research Series, Papers in Anthropology* No. 4. Illinois State Museum, Springfield.
 n.d. The Method and Theory of Site Catchment Analysis: A Review. *Advances in Archaeological Method and Theory*, Vol. 2. Ed. Michael B. Schiffer. Academic Press, New York. (in press, ms. 1978).

Runge, E. C. A., L. E. Tyler, and S. G. Carmer
 1969 Soil Type Acreages for Illinois. *Bulletin* 735. Agricultural Experiment Station, University of Illinois, Urbana.

Sanders, William T.
 1956 The Central Mexican Symbiotic Region: A Study in Prehistoric Settlement Patterns. In Prehistoric Settlement Patterns in the New World, edited by Gordon R. Willey. *Viking Fund Publication in Anthropology* No. 23, pp. 115–27. Wenner-Gren Foundation for Anthropological Research, Inc., New York.

Schiffer, Michael B.
 1976 *Behavioral Archeology*. Academic Press, New York.

Schnell, Gail Schroeder
 1974 Hotel Plaza. *Reports of Investigations* No. 29. Illinois State Museum, Springfield.

Schoenbeck, Ethel
 1946 Cord-Decorated Pottery in the Peoria Region. *Transactions of the Illinois State Academy of Science* 39: 33–42.

Schwartz, Charles W. and Elizabeth R. Schwartz
 1959 *The Wild Mammals of Missouri*. University of Missouri Press, Columbia.

Schwegman, John E.
 n.d. The Natural Divisions of Illinois (map). Developed by the Illinois Nature Preserves Commission. Department of Conservation.

Shelford, Victor E.
 1963 *The Ecology of North America*. University of Illinois Press, Urbana.

Shepard, Roger N.
 1972 Introduction to Volume I. In *Multidimensional Scaling: Theory and Applications in the Behavioral Sciences, Vol. I: Theory*, edited by Roger N. Shepard, A. Kimball Romney, and Sara Beth Nerlove, pp. 1–20. Seminar Press, New York.

Smith, Bruce D.
 1974 Middle Mississippi Exploitation of Animal Populations: A Predictive Model. *American Antiquity* 39(2): Pt. 1:274–91.

Smith, Hale G.
 1951 The Crable Site, Fulton County, Illinois: A Late Prehistoric Site in the Central Illinois Valley. *Anthropological Papers* No. 7. Museum of Anthropology, University of Michigan, Ann Arbor.

Smith, Phillip W.
    1961   The Amphibians and Reptiles of Illinois. *Bulletin* Vol. 28, Article 1, Illinois Natural History Survey, Urbana.
    1971   Illinois Streams: A Classification Based on Their Fishes and an Analysis of Factors Responsible for Disappearance of Native Species. *Biological Notes* No. 76, Natural History Survey, Urbana.
Sneath, P. H. A. and R. R. Sokal
    1973   *Numerical Taxonomy.* W. H. Freeman and Company, San Francisco.
Snyder, J. F.
    1883   Indian Remains in Cass County, Illinois. *Annual Report of the Smithsonian Institution for the Year 1881.* Washington D.C.
Soil Survey Staff
    1951   Soil Survey Manual. *Handbook* No. 18. USDA.
Sokal, Robert R. and F. James Rohlf
    1962   The Comparison of Dendrograms by Objective Methods. *Taxon* **XI**(2): 33–40.
Stephens, Denzil
    1975   Excavations at the Stoner and Lowe Sites. *Research Series, Papers in Anthropology* No. 2. Illinois State Museum, Springfield.
Steward, Julian H.,
    1938   Basin-Plateau Aboriginal Sociopolitical Groups. Bureau of American Ethnology *Bulletin,* 120. Smithsonian Institution, Washington, D.C.
Strahler, Arthur N.
    1964   Geology: Pt. II. II. Quantitative Geomorphology of Drainage Basins and Channel Networks. In *Handbook of Applied Hydrology*, edited by Ven Te Chow, pp. 4–39—4–76. McGraw-Hill, New York.
Struever, Stuart
    1965   Middle Woodland Culture History in the Great Lakes Riverine Area. *American Antiquity* **31**(2): Pt. 1:211–23.
    1968a   Problems, Methods and Organization: A Disparity in the Growth of Archaeology. In *Anthropological Archeology in the Americas*, edited by Betty J. Meggers, pp. 131–51. Anthropological Society of Washington.
    1968b   A Re-Examination of Hopewell in Eastern North America. Ph.D. Dissertation, University of Chicago.
    1968c   Woodland Subsistence-Settlement Systems in the Lower Illinois Valley. In *New Perspectives in Archeology*, edited by S. R. and L. R. Binford, pp. 285–312. Aldine, Chicago.
Struever, Stuart and Gail L. Houart
    1972   An Analysis of the Hopewell Interaction Sphere. In Social Exchange and Interaction, edited by Edwin N. Wilmsen, pp. 47–79. *Anthropological Papers* No. 46. Museum of Anthropology, University of Michigan, Ann Arbor.
Suttles, Wayne
    1968   Coping with Abundance: Subsistence on the Northwest Coast. In *Man the Hunter*, edited by Richard B. Lee and Irven DeVore, pp. 56–68. Aldine, Chicago.
Telford, Clarence J.
    1926   Third Report on a Forest Survey of Illinois. *Bulletin* Vol. XVI, Article I, Division of Natural History Survey, State of Illinois, Department of Registration and Education, Urbana.

Thomas, David H.
　1970　Archaeology's Operational Imperative: Great Basin Projectile Points as a Test Case. *Archaeological Survey Annual Report* Vol. 12. Department of Anthropology, University of California, Los Angeles.
Tiffin, Edward
　1815　Surveying Instruction, Issued by Edward Tiffin, Surveyor General Northwest the Ohio, July 16, 1815. Bureau of Land Management, U.S.Department of Interior, Washington, D.C.
Transeau, Edgar Nelson
　1935　The Prairie Peninsula. *Ecology* **16**(3): 423–37.
Turner, Lewis M.
　1934　Grassland in the Floodplain of Illinois Rivers. *American Midland Naturalist* **15**: 770–80.
Vayda, Andrew P.
　1967　Pomo Trade Feasts. In *Tribal and Peasant Economies: Readings in Economic Anthropology*, edited by George Dalton, pp. 494–500. American Museum Source Books in Anthropology.
Veldman, Donald J.
　1967　*FORTRAN Programming for the Behavioral Sciences*. Holt, Rinehart and Winston, New York.
Vita-Finzi, C. and E. S. Higgs
　1970　Prehistoric Economy in the Mount Carmel Area of Palestine: Site Catchment Analysis. *Proceedings of the Prehistoric Society* Vol. XXXVI: 1–37. Cambridge.
Wanless, Harold R.
　1957　Geology and Mineral Resources of the Beardstown, Glasford, Havana, and Vermont Quadrangles. *Bulletin* 82. Illinois State Geological Survey, Urbana.
Watanabe, Hitoshi
　1968　Subsistence and Ecology of Northern Food Gatherers with Special Reference to the Ainu. In *Man the Hunter*, edited by Richard B. Lee and Irven De Vore, pp. 69–82. Aldine, Chicago.
Wedel, Waldo R.
　1957　The Central North American Grassland: Man-Made or Natural? In *Studies in Human Ecology*, edited by Lawrence Krader and Angel Palerm, pp. 39–69. Anthropological Society of Washington.
Weide, David L. and Margaret L. Weide
　1973　Application of Geomorphic Data to Archaeology: A Comment. *American Antiquity* **38**(4): 428–31.
White, Anta M.
　1965　Typology of Some Middle Woodland Projectile Points from Illinois and Michigan. *Papers of the Michigan Academy of Science, Arts and Letters* Vol. L:355–60.
　1968　The Lithic Industries of the Illinois Valley in the Early and Middle Woodland Period. *Anthropological Papers* No. 35. Museum of Anthropology, University of Michigan, Ann Arbor.
Wickersham, James
　1885　Mounds of Sangamon County, Illinois. *Annual Report of the Smithsonian Institution for the Year 1883*, pp. 825–35. Washington, D.C.
Willman, H. B. and John C. Frye
　1970　Pleistocene Stratigraphy of Illinois. *Bulletin* 94. Illinois State Geological Survey, Urbana.

Wilson, John Philip
    1961   An Archaeological Survey of the Upper Central Spoon River Drainage. M.A. Thesis, University of Illinois, Urbana.

Winters, Howard D.
    1967   An Archaeological Survey of the Wabash Valley in Illinois. *Reports of Investigations* No. 10. Illinois State Museum, Springfield.
    1969   The Riverton Culture. *Reports of Investigations* No. 13. Illinois State Museum, Springfield.

Wood, W. Raymond
    1976   Vegetation Reconstruction and Climatic Episodes. *American Antiquity* **41**(2): 206–208.

Wray, Donald E.
    1952   Archaeology of the Illinois Valley: 1950. In *Archaeology of Eastern United States*, edited by James B. Griffin. University of Chicago Press, Chicago.

Wray, Donald E. and Richard S. MacNeish
    1961   The Hopewellian and Weaver Occupations of the Weaver Site, Fulton County, Illinois. In *Scientific Papers* Vol. VII, No. 2. Illinois State Museum, Springfield.

Wright, H. E., Jr.
    1968   History of the Prairie Peninsula. In The Quaternary of Illinois, edited by Robert E. Bergstrom, pp. 78–88. *Special Publication* No. 14. University of Illinois, Urbana.

Wright, R. Glen
    1973   Archaeological Salvage in the Oakley and Friends Creek Reservoir Area, Illinois, 1972. Report to the National Park Service.

Yanovsky, Elias
    1936   Food Plants of the North American Indians. *Miscellaneous Publication* No. 237. USDA.

Zawacki, April Allison and Glen Hausfater
    1969   Early Vegetation of the Lower Illinois Valley. *Reports of Investigations* No. 17, Illinois State Museum, and *Research Papers* Vol. 1, Illinois Valley Archaeological Program. Springfield.